THAT THEY MAY BE ONE

THAT THEY MAY BE ONE

*Catholic Social Teaching on Racism,
Tribalism, and Xenophobia*

DAWN M. NOTHWEHR

ORBIS BOOKS

Maryknoll, New York 10545

Founded in 1970, Orbis Books endeavors to publish works that enlighten the mind, nourish the spirit, and challenge the conscience. The publishing arm of the Maryknoll Fathers and Brothers, Orbis seeks to explore the global dimensions of the Christian faith and mission, to invite dialogue with diverse cultures and religious traditions, and to serve the cause of reconciliation and peace. The books published reflect the opinions of their authors and are not meant to represent the official position of the Maryknoll Society. To obtain more information about Maryknoll and Orbis Books, please visit our Web site at www.maryknoll.org.

Library of Congress Cataloging-in-Publication Data

Nothwehr, Dawn M.
   That they may be one : Catholic social teaching on racism, tribalism, and xenophobia / Dawn M. Nothwehr.
       p.   cm.
   Includes bibliographical references and index.
   ISBN 978-1-57075-793-8
1.   Racism—Religious aspects—Catholic Church.   I. Title.
   BX1795.R33N68   2008
   241.6'75—dc22
                                        2008018824

This book is dedicated to all who work for racial justice

Contents

PART II
CHURCH DOCUMENTS ON RACIAL JUSTICE

Preface

The impetus for this book grew from teaching a seminar on the ethics of power and racism at Catholic Theological Union, Chicago, Illinois. Because my students came from the six continents, I needed texts and resources that addressed racism, tribalism, and xenophobia from both a global focus and a Catholic perspective. I quickly discovered there is precious little in the literature that fits this need. Here I hope to begin to fill this gap, and that a more adequate literature will grow to bring Catholic social thought to bear on the global dimensions of racial justice. The audience for this book includes lay adults, pastoral ministers, undergraduate and graduate theology students, or anyone seeking to explore racial justice from a Christian and global perspective.

The book has two parts. Part I introduces key historical, theological, ethical, and social factors that have influenced the kind and quality of the Church's stance against racism, tribalism, and xenophobia. Part II presents excerpts from forty four Catholic social teaching documents on racial justice, accompanied by an abstract of each, and a brief historical note placing it in its context. A short instruction about how to read a Church document on racial justice precedes the collection of excerpts.

Part I, Chapter One provides a skeletal history of ideas and movements (east and west) that shaped the context in which the Church's Magisterium grappled with acknowledging the evils of racism, tribalism, and xenophobia and acting to confront them. This history of ideas concerning "race" and racisms bears witness to how the People of God and the Church's Magisterium can easily be influenced more by the character of their milieu than by the Holy Spirit and divine revelation.

Part I, Chapter Two exposes the mixed message of the Church's magisterial teaching concerning the serious sin of racism, tribalism, and xenophobia. Over the course of its history, at times the Church was blinded to its complicity in any wrongdoing when treating peoples as "Other" and in ways that were actually or effectively inhumane.

However, especially after Vatican II, as the Church opened to more sufficient methods of social analysis and the methods of theologies of liberation, as well as to the requisites of the social teachings of the Church, more satisfactory definitions and resolutions began to be promulgated. Providentially, the Church continues to recover from its complicity in racial injustices and it calls believers back to greater fidelity and justice.

Part I, Chapter Three brings together the most frequently cited doctrinal, theological, and ethical warrants for racial justice among all peoples of the earth. Those warrants are explored in light of their relevance for challenging the sins of racism, tribalism and xenophobia.

Whether the source of unjust discrimination against people is based on skin pigmentation, tribal origins, or culturally rooted hatred, sinful racialized relationships take on one or more of several identifiable patterns. In the fourth chapter of Part I, such patterns are raised to high relief by reviewing (global perspective) the nine forms of racism set forth by the Pontifical Commission for Justice and Peace, and (U.S. perspective) the four forms of racism proffered by Francis Cardinal George. Together, these two sets define the global patterns or forms of racisms. I also address insights from the social sciences and three major theories accounting for prejudice and discrimination.

Finally, Part I, Chapter Five raises some important areas that will continue to challenge the Church in the future. No attempt is made here to present an exhaustive list or a complete analysis of each area.

Part II presents the excerpts from diverse Church documents. Admittedly, this collection of social teaching documents is uneven in that they represent various levels of official authoritative Church teaching. This bears witness, first, to the reality that only rarely has the Church explicitly addressed racism. Secondly, it is the very nature of racism that while following an overarching pattern, it is manifested in particular ways that are dependent on a specific context. The complex mix of any set of personal, social, political, economic, religious, or cultural factors of racism, tribalism or xenophobia defy any easy "one size fits all" analysis or resolutions.

Racial injustices, because they cut so deeply and so quickly to the heart of what constitutes human dignity, often require a strong immediate response from the Church at the local level that can swiftly rob racist thought and actions of any possible guise of moral legitimacy. Thus the moral significance of any one official statement by the Church, such as a press release in the midst of a racialized crisis, may be more effective and carry more practical weight than an elaborate pastoral letter or an encyclical. Certainly all forms of teaching are needed, but only rarely has it happened that there is a set of formal social teachings focused on racial justice at all magisterial levels and that is accessible to the local Church.

The criteria for selecting the documents presented in Part II were to include documents that illustrate the numerous levels at which teaching on racism takes place, show how various forms of racism are addressed, represent major regions of the world, and are accessible to an English speaking audience.

Several terms require definition. The term *racialization* indicates a *process* of attributing racial differences to groups (not as a *problematic* that seeks to explain those differences). "Race" set off in quotation marks emphasizes that it is a construct and ideology, not a morally just basis for discrimination. Since racism takes many forms, "racisms" is used to indicate that reality. "Other," either in the singular or plural, communicates the objectification of people who justly deserve reverence and respect based on their God-given dignity. "Church" is capitalized to indicate the institutional Roman Catholic Church (both its leadership and its membership), since our discussion is ultimately focused on that specific body and its social teaching on racisms.

Finally, I am grateful for the support of my colleagues at Catholic Theological Union, especially Stephen Bevans who encouraged me to write this text. Also, I am thankful for the Faculty Development Grant that allowed me to travel abroad to do research for this work. I am also indebted to CTU students—Leandro Fossa, CS, Toshio Sato, CM and friends—Gisela Grundges-Andraos and Maria Lucia Uscategui who confirmed the accuracy of my reading or translated various Portuguese, Japanese, German, or Spanish documents.

I pray that in some small way this text will serve to bring about greater racial justice in our global community and that we can come a bit closer to fulfilling the profound desire of Jesus "That they may be one..." (John 17:22).

A Word on Formatting and Documentation within the Documents

The second part of this volume is comprised of excerpts from documents issued in a variety of formats and styles from authoritative Roman Catholic sources from around the world, including papal, Roman congregations, episcopal conferences, and other official sources. Each issuing body has its own formatting conventions. In this volume, however, we present all documents in a common format to avoid the typographical hodge-podge that would result if we attempted to reproduce the many different formats and styles.

A characteristic of official Roman Catholic documents is the way in which one issuing authority (an episcopal conference such as the U.S. Conference of Catholic Bishops, for instance) cites other documents issued by itself or by other authorities (Vatican Council II, for instance). For the most part, this internal documentation is omitted in this volume. We recommend that readers refer to the original document for these cross references, which are both distracting in an introductory book of this sort and a rich source of suggestions for further reading and help in understanding a given text in its full context.

PART I

BACKGROUND ON RACISM AND DISCRIMINATION

1

Construction and Definition of "Race" and Racism

Powerful Ideas That Challenge the Church

Introduction: The Idea of "Race"[1]

Human beings are "hard-wired" to distinguish differences,[2] and thus, there is a perennial need for people to give the differences distinguished among fellow humans significance, to interpret their meaning, and then, to act accordingly.[3] However, "race" is a relatively new idea and one that has changed over time—depending on the historical, geographical, scientific, technological, or academic settings. Scientists widely agree that there is no scientific basis for setting any absolute boundaries that determine the inferiority or supremacy of any one group of humans over another.[4] Scholars concur that prior to the thirteenth century B.C.E., "race" simply signified distinctions of difference.[5] However, especially from the medieval period, through the Age of Discovery, to the Enlightenment, "race" took on increasingly more connotations of a deterministic classification of humans in hierarchies of superiority. Here we focus on developments in Europe, China, and Japan simply because of the extensive impact of these regions on the entire world. Taken together, these sets of ideas provide the basic framework for the major constructs of "race" and racisms around the globe and across time.

In the early sixteenth century, people began to use the term *race* (from *racial stock*, a term used when breeding *animals*) to describe traits of human beings, a fatal step toward deterministic interpretations of difference.[6] The list of distinguishing characteristics for different "races" varied and grew, but it usually included factors such as skin color, eye color, types of hair, customs, language, and religious beliefs. Those attributes were used to determine whether a group of people was "civilized" or qualitatively equal to those making the judgment. Thus, when we speak of "race" we are dealing with a "social construct"[7] that takes many forms.

In the seventeenth century, "civilized" Europeans questioned whether other people (not "civilized") of particular "races" could "progress" or "advance." Debates about human monogenesis or polygenesis[8] also surfaced. Following the biblical creation stories, the majority of scholars supported the notion of monogenesis. That humans could interbreed meant that human differences are *within the same species* and do not mark different species. Also influential was Baron Montesquieu, who in 1784 held that environmental and historical factors accounted for human differences. Thus, it was possible to accommodate differences through education.

Sadly, Swedish naturalist Carolus Linnaeus' 1758 *Systema Naturae* changed the course. He included humans as a species of "primates," and then divided the "primates" into different groupings of creatures based on physical structures, emotional temperament, and intellect, ranging from mythical monsters to *"Homo afer."* Subspecies were distinguished by skin color, hair color, eye color, behavioral propensities, and biological traits.

From the eighteenth century to the present, three prototypic and particularly ethically egregious systems for interpreting the meaning of human differences stunted human life around the world: (1) U.S. chattel slavery, (2) South African Apartheid, and (3) Nazi Aryan white supremacy. These three systems crossed a line by *legally establishing racism in the structures of the entire societies.*[9]

From "Race" to Racism, Tribalism, and Xenophobia in the Twenty-First Century

In the twenty-first century, postcolonial, post-Holocaust, and post-9/11, globalized world, the distinction and value of differences between and among human persons bears great moral weight. Though U.S. chattel slavery has long been outlawed, it still affects all U.S. systems.[10] The shadows of the Holocaust were seen in the world's neglect and carnage of Darfur.[11] Throughout Africa, colonialism's legacy of devastation is manifested in favoritism, exclusion, and corruption in all aspects of society and government. And, more than five years after September 11, 2001, it was viewed as a threat that six imams prayed their evening prayers at the gate of an airport prior to the plane's 5:15 P.M. departure.[12] Indeed "race" and racisms are still with us!

The most adequate definition of racism for the twenty-first century is given by Albert Memmi in his volume *Racism*:

[A] generalizing definition and valuation of differences, whether real or imaginary to the advantage of the one defining or deploying them [*accusateur*], and to the detriment of the one subjugated to the act of definition [*victime*], whose purpose is to justify (social or physical) hostility and assault [*aggression*].[13]

In light of this definition, three forms of racism require greater attention, namely, color-coded racism, tribalism, and xenophobia.

Color-Coded Racism

Color-coded racism is most viperous in that it presents the criteria for the inferiority of the "other" in biological and phenotypical terms such as skin color, bodily shape, cranial structure, Negroid, Caucasoid, or Mongoloid. Through a process of racialization, one group (the white majority, for instance) targets the "other" as inferior, formulating a mythical or ideological construct to support and provide rationale or justification for legal, social, political, and unjust discrimination and oppression.[14] The particular characteristics defining inferiority or superiority are indelibly stamped into the very body of the "other" and, thus, cannot be changed through any form of assimilation into the "superior" way of being or culture.

Tribalism or Ethnocentricity

Tribalism is a negative term that names a form of racialized relations between ethnic groups. A tribe is "a social organization or division comprising several local villages, bands, or lineages or other groups sharing a common ancestry, language, culture, and name."[15] A general sense of belonging that comes through membership in a tribe or some group is necessary for human well-being. But *tribalism* is the attitude and practice of harboring such a strong feeling of loyalty or bonds to one's tribe that one excludes or even demonizes those "others" who do not belong to that group. This exclusion is manifested in engaging or failing to engage with the "other" in obtaining the necessities of life, education, employment, just and fair governance, healthy political and economic relations, membership in social and religious groups, or equitable opportunities for rising to positions of authority or leadership.

Tribalism or ethnocentrism is a universal human tendency rooted in the reality that people are most comfortable with those familiar to and like themselves. However, people prosper and thrive best in a way of life that allows *all* groups to sustain themselves within a stable social, political, and economic order. The legacy of colonialism is the deep disruption of such systems among those colonized.

Significantly, colonizers needed to justify their overtaking the property and persons of those they conquered. Justification required demonizing tribal peoples, exaggerating any conflicts among them. The most common technique used to gain control (of often powerful groups) was that of "divide and conquer." Colonizers' most egregious practices were to arm one tribe, set that group up against their neighbors, and then employ them to "catch" their "enemy" and sell them to the slave traders. Their eliminating one group or favoring another over against the "others" was a genocidal activity.

The effects of this damage live on in the postcolonial world in many ways. The most devastating effect that has plagued newly independent nations (in the former Yugoslavia, for example) is divisions remaining among peoples that threaten formation of any positive cohesive national unity. Tribalism and ethnocentrism infect all aspects of life with corruption, graft, incompetence, and injustices, resulting in a general sense of distrust and disenfranchisement among all citizens. Such an unstable political situation when combined with dire economic poverty has frequently been volatile—even to the point of genocide (for example, 1994 Rwanda and Burundi).

Xenophobia

Literally, *xenophobia* means "fear of the stranger" (from the Greek— *xenos* = stranger or foreigner; phobos = fear). A fitting definition is given by E. Cashmore:

> A somewhat vague psychological concept describing a person's disposition to fear (or abhor) other persons or groups perceived as outsiders. Xenophobia may have a rational basis to it, such as when it refers to a worker whose job is threatened by the intrusion of migrants whom he labels as outsiders and therefore fears. It may also take an irrational form, for example when someone fears Sikhs because he or she believes they carry knives for use as potential weapons. But to call a person xenophobic does not necessarily say anything about the rationality of that condition. Nor does it entail examining the underlying causes of their disposition.[16]

Xenophobia is so lethal because (rational or not) it is easily manipulated and fueled toward mass hysteria that can fling even the most level-headed and altruistic persons into aggressive oppression of the "other."[17] Evidence for this development is in emerging political parties: the French Front National, the Dutch Centrumdemocraten and Centrum Partij, the Austrian Freiheitlichen, the German Republikaner and Deutsche Volksunion, the Belgian Vlaams Blok, and the Front National.[18]

In recent history (1974–2000), according to MacMaster's analysis, three interrelated phenomena have combined to feed xenophobia and xenophobic behavior:

> [T]he skillful elaboration and diffusion of a "New Racism" that offered a powerful ideological revision of traditional biological racism; the concurrent emergence and electoral challenge of xenophobic "National-Populist" parties that made use of the new current of thinking on cultural racism and national identity; and lastly, the tendency of the "New Right" conservative parties, as well as socialist and all mainstream parties, to play to the same gallery, particularly

through the construction of "Fortress Europe" and the scapegoating of refugees.[19]

The "New Racism" plays on latent xenophobia by lauding the importance and the natural necessity of cultural difference. A typical statement of the proponents of this position is this: "I'm not xenophobic, nor does the fact that I like the French and France best mean that I hate foreigners or hate other countries."[20] Here the vocabulary of "culture" is the code word for the language of "race." Antiracists' efforts toward affirming the values of cultural diversity and creating "multicultural societies" are manipulated to exaggerate and emphasize the impending loss of a comfortable, predictable, homogeneous society. These manipulations are supported theoretically using Italian Marxist philosopher Antonio Gramsci's claim that the state depends on material force, economic relations, but also on a cultural hegemony enforced by controlling people's world view through managing ideas, language, and their discourse, and thus creating meaning.[21] The "New Racism" supporters also rely on sociobiology, reasoning that certain ways of doing things are right because they are natural, and if they are natural they must be true.[22] Such reasoning argues that people live in particular countries just like fish thrive in certain habitats or wolves live in packs.

Further support is garnered by claiming that the ruling hegemonic majority is a "victim" of the disruptive invasion of the "other" and the support given those invaders by the "race relations industry."[23] This victimization is proclaimed and popularized using cartoons showing ordinary citizens being battered by "the loony leftists," "fanatic liberals," or "radical teachers." The media is flooded with the new vocabulary that recasts racism in populist "common sense" terms that plays to those who experience themselves disenfranchised by the governing "elites" who control the society.[24]

The xenophobic national populists were able to gain ground in electoral and parliamentary systems by focusing on this strategy.[25] They gave an "acceptable face" to their biases and strategies as the "reasonable right thing to do" to protect national identity and culture. They offered strong, simply stated solutions to two basic fears held by the hegemonic majority: (1) the loss of power and control due to the influx of vast numbers of immigrants and refugees of various colors, religions, and cultures from all over the globe into Europe and North America, and (2) anxiety about the threat these movements posed for keeping the wealth secure. These solutions were to be accomplished via mainstream political involvement.

Ambiguities among the mainstream political parties in Europe and North America made it easier for xenophobic ideas and actions to take hold. The complexities of the new issues brought about by globalization, immigrants, and refugees caught the mainline politicians without a vocabulary and a plan to address these issues in a popular commonsensical manner.[26] Thus, conventional politicians found themselves in a defensive posture that required compromises and self-preserving strategies to "get tough on immigration." Numerous harsh draconian measures were passed on both sides of the Atlantic to limit immigration and fortify national identities.[27] Many formal declarations about combating racism were brilliantly paraded, but they were weak, rarely enforced, and effectively utterly symbolic.

The Complicity of the Church and the Idea of "Race"

The Catholic Church's record concerning the ethics of power and racism, tribalism, and xenophobia is at best mixed.[28] The actions of Church leaders ranged from the biblical prophetic to the near demonic when they and lay Christians yielded to the pressures of their contexts and lost sight of the deepest convictions of respect, equality in Christ, justice, and charity.[29] Just as today, the degree of compliance by Catholics with magisterial teaching varied widely. As Timothy E. O'Connell has shown, it is the stories believers tell rather than their knowledge of doctrines that express their appropriation of the Christian faith in their personal lives, and are most influential for their moral actions.[30]

Thus, it is vital that the Church and its ministers not merely impart doctrinal and dogmatic condemnations of racial injustices of the past but *also* proactively engage the faithful in experiential learning toward preventing racism's sinful violence, now and in the future.[31] The challenge for present-day Catholics and all people of goodwill is to learn from the past and honor the victims by not repeating the oppression. While never denying the horrific complicity of the Catholic Church in oppression, slavery, or genocide, significantly and ultimately the official Church held a line in favor of its ideals on at least two counts.

First, the Church constantly returned to its fundamental position that each human person is created in the image and likeness of God and that each person bears an inviolable dignity that must be respected *at all cost*. How this foundational principle was interpreted in relation to those understood to be "other" frequently had more to do with the current cultural and scientific understanding of the human person than theological tenets. Greek dualism allowed the possibility of tolerating slavery, providing there was a harmonious spirit of charity between masters and slaves.[32]

Secondly, the Church held that in Christ, all persons were redeemed and redeemable. Doctrinally, the Incarnation and the Cross placed no one beyond the bounds of salvation. Thus, early Christians, influenced by their contexts and cultures[33] drew distinctions of difference, but did not practice a kind of racism or ethnic exclusion rooted in systematic segregation or elimination of those considered "other."[34] For example, Greeks allowed that barbarians could be civilized; Romans believed all slaves could be emancipated; and Africans could be converted as was the biblical Ethiopian (Acts 6:26–39). Divergence from these liberating interpretations of human difference has roots in a long history of ideas and contextualized experiences. It is to those concerns we now turn.

The Construction of "Race" and Racism in Europe and North America: A Sample of Western Thought

Greek Influences

One critical idea that shaped Christian thought is the "Greek black aesthetic."[35] Robert E. Hood notes that African images are found in Greek art as early as the thirteenth century B.C.E. and that Greece colonized northern Africa in the seventh century B.C.E. During this time frame, Greeks contrasted the physical appearance of the Africans they encountered with their own and explained the differences in a variety of ways. But what "stuck" in people's minds were explanations of difference that purported the existence of mythical animal-like creatures with "thick lips, broad noses, and wooly hair"[36] and who engaged in lustful erotic acts and had insatiable appetites for sex. Most importantly, disparaging the positive connotations of blackness was useful in justifying Greek dominance over peoples in Southeast Asia and Egypt.[37]

By the fifth century B.C.E., Greek ethnocentrism emerged and one of its major spokespersons was Euripides (c. 485–406) who claimed that all foreigners were slaves and servile by nature.[38] However, Herodotus (480 B.C.E.) praised the military might of the Ethiopians.[39]

Plato (427–347 B.C.E.) in his *Republic* noted the human "approaches the world and others as an object resulting from the need to control that which is different."[40] However, he also is well known for his dualistic philosophical system. As Hopkins notes, "Dichotomies give rise to hierarchies that give rise to normative valuations."[41] Plato set the stage for Aristotle (384–322 B.C.E.) whose *Politica, De generatione animalium, and Physiognomics* deepened the distinction of white, blue-eyed, straight-haired, northern Scythians as superior to black, wooly-haired, Ethiopian southerners.[42] Significantly, Aristotle held there were some peoples who were thus "natural slaves" while others were natural masters,[43] and Ptolemy (87–150 C.E.) created a scale of the shades of blackness found among Africans and, along with other Greek scholars, coined words for various skin tones.[44]

Roman Influences

The Romans similarly held that, that which was most familiar, was superior,[45] and the Latin poets claimed that white signified divinity, while black indicated bad luck and dread. Generally, Roman culture attributed unusual sexual prowess to African males, even accusing them of seducing Roman women. Virgil (c. 70–19 B.C.E.) and Cicero (106–143 C.E.) asserted

Roman aesthetics over those of African peoples, thus justifying Rome's colonization of northern Africa by force.[46]

Early Christians: "Of the World"

Early Christians took on the cultural ethos of Greece and Rome such that in the first six centuries of Christianity "Egypt," "Ethiopia," and "blackness" were equated rhetorically with being unorthodox, heretical, sexually lustful, demonic, evil, licentious, temptresses, or ugly.[47] Black was also the color "for all non-Christians without favorable features."[48]

Also festering within the Christian community was the notion that "the Jews" were responsible for the death of Jesus. As Léon Poliakov suggests, based on Matthew 27:25, "it was essential the Jews be criminally guilty people."[49] Significantly, beginning with Augustine of Hippo (354–430 C.E.), the Church officially held that conversion was possible for *all*—including Jews—and the sin of those involved in the trial and crucifixion of Jesus was not indelible or insurmountable.[50] Deplorably, however, elsewhere Augustine (and others) is virulent against Jews.[51]

European Middle Ages: 400–1400 C.E.

Throughout the European Middle Ages (400–1400 C.E.), anti-Jewish bias gained momentum. "Anti-Judaism became anti-Semitism whenever it turned into consuming hatred that made getting rid of Jews preferable to trying to convert them, and anti-Semitism became racism when the belief took hold that Jews were intrinsically and organically evil rather than merely having false beliefs and wrong dispositions."[52]

Generally, in the twelfth and thirteenth centuries C.E., Jews competed against Christian guilds in the newly evolved mercantile system. That Jews lent money for interest was viewed by Christians as usury. It was the perceived "spiritual" threat Jews posed that motivated Christians to oppress and even massacre them in the First Crusade (1096). Yet, officially Church leaders protected Jews from the zealous crusading mobs, employed them for their finance talent, and preferred to baptize and not to kill them. Compared to the militarily and politically dangerous Muslims, the Jews were harmless.[53]

Nonetheless, Jews were increasingly demonized. Amid the angst of the rise of market economics and the growth of the power of the state, threats to Christian orthodoxy abounded.[54] Ultimately, the Black Death[55] locked Jews in as scapegoats for the anti-Semites. Indeed, anti-Semitism served to solidify those who needed their identity and beliefs reinforced. Ironically as a "scavenger ideology" racism "adopted a Christian garb while implicitly repudiating its offer of salvation to all humanity, including Jews."[56]

While the Jews were identified as scapegoats, Hopkins outlines three root formative factors of negative perceptions of blackness in medieval times.[57] First, there were the Muslim victories over the Christians and the colonization of the Holy Land by the dark-complected Muslims between the seventh and twelfth centuries C.E. Second, the Moors' victory over the large sections of Europe confirmed that they were "emissaries from Satan" because only "evil" and "demonic" people would perpetrate such acts.[58] And thirdly, the European slave trade began in 1441 in Portugal.[59]

As Catholicism spread its influence, indigenous peoples were also dominated in Europe (Slavs and the Irish), Asia, Africa, and the Americas. As Robert Bartlett writes,

> On all the newly settled, conquered or converted peripheries, one can find the subjugation of native populations to legal disabilities, the attempt to enforce residential segregation, with natives expelled into the "Irish towns" of colonial Ireland, and the attempts to proscribe certain cultural forms of native society. Ghettoization and racial discrimination marked the latter centuries of the Middle Ages.[60]

Europe was "a persecuting society," but there was yet no codified and systematized ideology that would justify such oppressive practices.[61]

The Age of Discovery—Fourteenth and Fifteenth Centuries

Iberia is one Christian region that illustrates how negative black images became associated with servitude. Christians learned from the Muslims to associate blackness with servitude.[62] There is also evidence that Muslims were first to associate the "Curse of Ham" with the subservience of Sub-Saharan Africans.[63] Iberians had slaves of various hues, but the blacks were given the most menial tasks. In fact, fifteenth-century Iberian Christians viewed blacks as "hewers of wood and carriers of water" rather than as exemplars of Christian virtue.[64]

Before the Portuguese arrived, slave trade within Africa was well established.[65] Ownership of slaves for Africans (not property) was symbolic of wealth, and laws were in place to recognize that. Thus, prisoners of war were exchanged, and it became unseemly to enslave a fellow Christian. Europeans thought because "the Africans were not Christians," their enslavement could conceivably be justified. Indeed, some thought that enslavement could be a kind of "missionary project" because slaves would be exposed to Christians and then converted. Sadly, the striking contrast of black-complected slaves in a free white world made those darker-complected psychologically "other," inviting brutality toward them, "justified" in the name of salvation.

Fifteenth- and Sixteenth-Century Spain

The case of the Jewish *conversos* in fifteenth- and sixteenth-century Spain also exemplifies the move from persecution to codified racism. Early medieval Spain was a diverse society of Jews, Muslims, and Christians. But as the conflicts with the Moors intensified, by 1391 *pogroms* for Jews were put in place in Castile and Aragon, giving them the choice of "conversion or death." Discriminatory laws set in place in 1412 resulted in the expulsion of Spanish Jews. Yet large numbers actually converted to Christianity. It is estimated that by 1492 there were more than a half million newly converted Jews. This presented a "problem for assimilation" of people who were nominally Christian, yet culturally distinct. Rampant suspicion about the commitment of the *conversos* led to the Inquisition. The Inquisitors "proceeded from the assumption that Jewish ancestry *per se* justified the suspicion of converts' 'judaizing.' "[66] Even though from the first generation forward, most Jewish converts were faithful practicing Catholics, according to *impieza de sangre* (purity of blood), persons of Jewish ancestry were presumed doctrinal heretics, with an enmity toward Christians!

That violence done to former Jews was more racially than religiously motivated is exemplified by the Archbishop of Toledo. In 1547 he applied the blood laws to all Church entities of his archdiocese, requiring certificates of pure blood for membership in religious orders or ecclesiastical or secular organizations. And, significantly, only those of "pure blood" could go to the Americas as missionaries or *conquistadores*.[67] As Léon Poliakov states, "Jews were evil by nature and not only because of their beliefs ... sectarian hatred ... became racial hatred."[68]

Following the *Reconquista* of 1492, the *impieza de sangre* laws were applied to the *Moriscos* (Muslims forcibly converted to Christianity) in Spain. Being primarily peasants and artisans, their further assimilation was difficult, and they remained culturally distinct. Following a rebellion against the proscription of the Muslim religion in 1568, and from 1609 to 1614, the entire Muslim population (about a third of million) was driven out of Spain.

As Spain entered the Americas, Christopher Columbus brought two traditions with him concerning the indigenous peoples: the medieval lore that subhuman "monstrous creatures" lay in wait in strange lands; and the primal innocent pagan in need of the protection and care of the Christian world. Those who treated him well were deemed "simple children of nature" and those who greeted him with resistance were "cannibals" to be met with force or killed.[69]

The Great Debate: Las Casas versus Sepúlveda

The defining moment concerning the humanity of Native Americans came in 1550 when Las Casas won over Sepúlveda at Valladolid. In the debate, Aristotelian philosopher Juan Ginés de Sepúlveda applied Aristotle's notion of "natural slavery" to all Native Americans: "In wisdom, skill, virtue, and humanity these people are inferior to Spaniards as children are to adults, women are to men, and monkeys are to men."[70] Dominican Bishop of Chiapas, Mexico, Bartolomé de Las Casas countered by defending the humanity of the natives as equal human beings on the basis of their way of life, their innocence, gentleness, and generosity, and in terms of their readiness for conversion to Catholicism. While Las Casas won the debate, and no official enslavement was allowed, the Spanish system of *encomienda*, the right of a Spaniard to conscript the labor of an Indian community, was allowed. It was all but slavery—and at times worse.[71]

According to Fredrickson the enslavement of blacks and Native Americans must be considered in relation to the missionary enterprise. Christians believed that the difference in Africans' skin color was due to the hot sunny climate in which they lived and thus, they could be converted through their contact with their Christian masters. When Indians with lighter skin tones were discovered in similar climatic conditions to the regions of Africa, many deemed the "curse of Ham" the only viable explanation for the difference.

Interestingly, though Spain and Portugal were racist societies, their colonies were less so in relation to the indigenous peoples. Because Spanish women did not migrate to the New World in large numbers, blood laws were forgotten and relatively soon there was intermixture of peoples. The numerous *castas* devolved into three: white, *mestizo*, and Indian that "lacked the rigidity of true racial divisions."[72]

Sixteenth- and Seventeenth-Century Developments: A Segue between Religious Tolerance and Naturalistic Racism

During the fifteenth and sixteenth centuries *Hispanidad*, national identity and universal religious commitment were synonymous. To not be Christian and Spanish was to be less than a full human being. "Blood" made one prone to religious heresy of unbelief. Interestingly, "innocent 'savages' who embraced Spanish civilization and Catholicism did not carry impure blood."[73] Discrimination was based on culture, particularly among Spanish Jews and the Moors who kept their identity and ancient pride.[74] The official Catholic Church position was that Africans who were baptized were not to be enslaved.[75] Even the Dutch Calvinist Synod of Dort in 1618 "forbade the sale of Christian slaves and declared that they ought to enjoy equal liberty with other Christians. But despite this language, it did not actually require their manumission."[76] Indeed, there continued to be a need to justify holding "others" especially fellow Christians in bondage and the "curse of Ham" was the justification of choice in the popular mind.

The Curse of Ham

The earliest use of the curse of Ham to explain black slavery was by the Portuguese upon discovering Guinea in the mid-fifteenth century. Interestingly, they confused Ham with Cain (Gen 9). The first English use of the curse of Ham was in George Best's 1578 account of Martin Frobisher's search for the Northwest Passage. Best attempted to quell fears that skin color could change with climate and to encourage exploration of new lands. Best held that skin color could not change because, due to the curse of Ham, it was "fixed for all time by divine decree" and those who were subjects of the curse were to perpetually be slaves.[77] Thus, the popular position became that, because the curse had entered the blood, it could not be lifted—even by baptism. The official Church and numerous intellectuals, using the tools of sixteenth- and seventeenth-century biblical exegesis, refuted the claim showing that "the curse fell on Canaan specifically, not on his brother Cush, who ... was the actual progenitor of the African race."[78] None the less, the mythic curse of Ham lingered in the popular mind through the U.S. proslavery movement in the 1850s. Without a strong, consistent, well-coordinated and systematic attack on slavery there was growth in the stigmatization of blacks, in spite of even the efforts of Roman Catholic Popes. The continued growth toward modern racism can be accounted for by citing developments in philosophy, anthropology, and missiology. It is to this we now turn.[79]

Key Developments in Seventeenth- and Eighteenth-Century Europe: Setting the Conditions for the Possibility of Modern Racism

Two main forms of racism evolved in modern times in the West. Color-coded white supremacy holds the ideological position that light-complected (white) peoples are inherently superior in every way.[80] Essentialist anti-Semitism claims that by divine intent there are inferior human beings and the traits of that inferiority are passed on through the bloodline of a people. The official Catholic Church and many intellectuals challenged these positions yet justification of such ideologies remained. Christian tenets that all humans bear the Divine Image and that all are redeemed through the blood of Christ barred such beliefs. If racism were to triumph, these tenets had to be made impotent. We now address these developments.

Philosophical Developments

Several philosophers of the European Enlightenment and early modernity set the primary ideological framework for the eventual development of systemic racism in the modern period: Francois Marie Arouet, known as Voltaire (1694–1778), Charles-Louis Montesquieu (1689–1755), David Hume (1711–1776), Immanuel Kant (1724–1804), John Locke (1632–1704), and Georg Hegel (1770–1831).

In Kant's *Observations on the Feeling of the Beautiful and Sublime* (1764), he claimed the "Negroes" have no feeling. He stated, "So fundamental is the difference between these two races of men, and it appears to be as great in regard to mental capacities as to color."[81] David Hume presented the precursor for this argument in his 1748 and 1754 essay, "On National Characters." Hume, a polygenesist, claimed that of the five species of "man," Negroes are naturally inferior because they have no arts or manufacturing abilities. He compared Negroes to a parrot who "speaks a few words plainly."[82]

Philosopher John Locke was also a white supremacist who advocated polygenesis. Important in the development of modern racism was his political and commercial influence. As the secretary of the powerful Carolina Proprietors of South Carolina, he played a major part in writing the constitution and the instructions to the colonial governor of the infant Virginia colony. With his aid, in the late seventeenth-century Virginia passed a law stating that baptism did not give slaves their freedom.[83]

In his *The Spirit of the Laws* (1784), the French Baron Charles-Louis Montesquieu argued for personal and political slavery for Africans and Asians. He claimed "hot climates produce races possessed with 'bodily pleasures and sloth' and that cold climates yielded races of high intelligence."[84] He and fellow Frenchman Voltaire thought that God would not have given dark people a soul and thus, he questioned their humanity. In his 1734 *Traité de Métaphysique*, Voltaire opposed the Church's position on monogenesis.[85]

Hopkins correctly concludes that these philosophers brought together a lethal set of ideas,[86] giving Greek notions of aesthetics ontological value and placing it at the top of a hierarchy of aesthetic value. They also drew on Aristotle (*Politics*), who asserted that Greeks possessed the right balance of brains, courage, skill, and will power to maintain a superior civilization as opposed to Northern European, Africans, and Asians, who lacked this equilibrium.[87] Thus, those at the top rightly can rule over or enslave the others. In short, these philosophers joined aesthetics, identity, and power as a force to keep white Europeans absolutely supreme over the "nonwhite" peoples of the world.

Georg Wilhelm Friedrich Hegel gave an additional layer of credibility to this construct. As Hopkins suggests, he "combined the 'transcendental speculative with the racialized historical' to situate once again the white spirit/ intellect at the peak of human creation, thought, and activity."[88] Hegel thought that as each group of people interacts with others, the development of spirit and reason advances forward from "primitive social encounters to superlative civilization."[89] In his schema of interactions, Orientals, Greeks and Romans, and German Christians are included, but Africans are "outside of human history."[90]

Anthropological Developments

Anthropologists also developed theories and ideas from the white, male, European perspective that—when joined with the major philosophies of the day—bolstered the conditions for the possibility of the absolutist racism of the modern period. The eighteenth-century general consensus was that racial differences resulted from variances in climate and environment. Though there was one human species, there was a hierarchy with white people at the top and blacks at the bottom.

In 1684, French physician François Bernier first used facial and bodily standards of measure to form a racial hierarchy and moved the criteria for defining the human from space and place to biology.[91] Yet, biblical narratives asserting the creation of a single human race still predominated. However, in the 1730s, Swedish botanist Carolus Linnaeus set forth the framework for future discussions on race by arguing that there were several biological human races.[92]

Georges Louis Leclerc, Comte de Buffon, a French naturalist, mathematician and biologist, claimed that differences in the one human race were from food, manners, and climate. But, the white biological race was the norm. In the 1770s, Johann Friedrich Blumenbach, professor of medicine at the University of Göttingen, held that there is one human race, but that there is legitimate aesthetic differentiation. In fact, "Caucasian" names "the most beautiful race of all time, based on measures of color, hair, face, and skull."[93]

Theories of polygenesis lived on. The English physician John Atkins held that "black savages and civilized whites emerged from divergent primal parents."[94] Peter Camper, a Dutch naturalist and medical expert, analyzed human skulls, and using the Greek facial angle as the standard, placed whites at the top and blacks at the very bottom of the polygenetic racial hierarchy.[95] Beyond this, the German physician Franz Joseph Hall's study indicated human head shapes determined human character and concluded there was a rigid divide between blacks and whites.[96]

Joseph Arthur, Comte de Gobineau, French ethnologist and racial theorist, claimed in his *Essays on the Inequality of Races 1853–1855*,[97] that there was an historical struggle among the races and the whites triumphed over blacks. Indeed the strength of civilization depends on the "forcefulness of that dominant race." And, he argued, because the yellow and black races did not create anything significant, the world belongs to the whites.

Taken together, these early anthropological data presumed and promoted a "teleological view of history," "a continuity of the human and the animal world" that highlighted "the evolutionary basis of racial categorization as natural," and "mental abilities related to physical characteristics" as "further evidence that humanity resulted not from culture but from nature."[98] By the 1850s scientific polygenesis and biblical pre-Adamism were accepted as cogent explanations for white supremacy in all dimensions of what is definitively human. Following upon publication of Charles Darwin's *Origin of Species* in 1859, some thinkers combined his ideas with earlier hierarchies to create "Social Darwinism." Then in 1869, Francis Galton, "the father of eugenics," in *Hereditary Genius* claimed to have "'definitively' correlated group skin color (heredity) with brilliance (genius)."[99] Perhaps most devastating was U.S. ethnologist Henry Lewis Morgan's *Systems of Consanguinity and Affinity of the Human Family* (1870).[100] He held that there are seven stages of development from human savagery to civilization. Only European and American societies were fully civilized, based on their advanced writing abilities and accomplishments. Thus, it became possible for science, white supremacy, and law to join, creating a racist society in the United States and elsewhere. Hopkins summarizes,

> Constitutional law drew from the objective science of racial anthropology. And both philosophy and anthropology assisted and, thereby, engendered the broader worldview of inevitable manifest destiny: monopoly, capitalist democracy; rational manners, and advanced religion—hence commerce, civilization, and Christianity as God's gift to the darker skinned peoples of the world. Globally, black was seen as evil (a religious aesthetic) the opposite of white (in human identity), and naturally subservient (not deserving power). Consequently, the white races of Europe and especially North America bore the burden of lifting up the lesser races throughout the earth. In a sense, God had ordained it that way. White supremacy's manifest destiny was the Great Commission of Jesus Christ.[101]

Missiological Developments

With all of this in mind, it is easy to recognize the "grounding" for the "errors" of past approaches to mission. In tracing these errors, the intent here is to condemn such practices that robbed (and continue to rob) numerous peoples of their God-given dignity. However, our more important task is to inform ourselves, and to learn from past injustices so as to not repeat them.

Hopkins cites Cameroonian theologian Jean-Marc Ela's five elements that combined to allow racism to pollute the Christian mission activity from the fifteenth century forward. European Christians possessed power of empire and privilege: The colonial governments were from "Christian" nations (crown); the colonies were established forcibly by invasions or as trophies of war (cannon); the burgeoning capitalist economic systems of Europe and North America were fed by labor and resources from colonized lands (commerce); power and privilege enabled white Europeans to impose their "superior culture" and way of life on those conquered (civilization); and the symbols, narratives, and rituals of Christianity were imposed to ensure that the colonization was indeed the will of God (cross). This project required the participation and compliance of the whole of Western societies, including the Church. Effective patterns for imposing power were established, and then repeated in various sites across the globe. The pattern eventually included removing indigenous peoples from their religious traditions and cultures and building schools and medical facilities to "civilize" them into the European culture. Hopkins quotes a telling passage from David Livingston: "If we call the actual amount of conversions the direct result of missions, and the wide diffusion of better [Western culture] principles the indirect, the latter are of infinitely more importance than the former."[102]

Hopkins illustrates that in West Africa, slave traders, commercial companies, and the government of Portugal all had clergy on their payrolls.[103]

After the partition of Africa in 1884, missionaries served as a link between the colonial administrations and the indigenous peoples, and prepared them to serve the colonizers as clerks or interpreters.[104] Throughout Africa, the humanity of indigenous blacks was constantly questioned and native cultures disparaged. [105]

Some Christian Churches justified a white supremacist position well into the twentieth century; Dutch Protestants of South Africa from 1652 on, a case in point. In 1806, the British took the country from the Dutch *Afrikaners*. The Anglican Church subsequently endorsed white supremacy. The Dutch Reformed *Afrikaners* and other missionaries provided housing for their black servants, but kept separate churches for blacks. These practices gave moral sanction to Apartheid.[106]

The Spanish brought a feudal system to Latin America and a hierarchy that placed God at the top, then the king, the landlord, with indigenous peoples at the bottom. The mentality of the conquistador ruled the day.[107] As Hopkins observes, "[T]he dominant scenario was missionary submission to the crown's authority. Indeed the Spanish king nominated bishops and enforced papal proclamations in the new world. The Roman Catholic Church compromised its independence with dual submission—one to the government and the other to a small group of colonial land owners."[108]

Especially egregious was the Church's policy of *branqueamento* used in Brazil (1530–1850)—that held that "the human ideal is being white" and that "being white and being human are completely equated."[109] This policy resulted in internalized self-hatred (internalized racism). According to Silvia Regina De Lima Silva, the first path of the policy was the promotion of a theology of transmigration; whereby blacks were taught that they had to pass through several levels of purification from the "curse of Ham" in order to gain salvation.[110] Their first step on that path was becoming enslaved in the New World where Christian masters would expose them to the Gospel. The second path was the promotion of a theology of retribution, where slaves gained virtue through enduring hard labor and suffering imposed by their masters. The latter justified whippings and other forms of torture.

In the Caribbean, Martin Fernandez de Enciso, a Spanish religious leader, arrogantly proclaimed in 1513 that the region was Yahweh's Promised Land and that the indigenous peoples were to give it up or be killed.[111] In Jamaica, Roman Catholic figures profited from their compliance with conquistadores obsessed with mining gold. And in Cuba the Jeronimite Order of Monks forced the Amerindians to mine gold.

In 1768 James Cook was commissioned by the British crown to take Australia from the Aboriginal peoples. And in 1788, English settlers came to settle the land, calling it *"terra nullis"*—"empty land." Then, in the name of evangelization Christians kidnapped children and chained Aboriginals to mission compounds. Others terrorized indigenous women as part of a population pacification program.[112] In Hawaii, as elsewhere, James Cook and his crew brought domination, alcohol, and gonorrhea to the natives when they arrived in 1778. By the 1820s, the United States gained control of the sandalwood industry and by the 1840s the Hawaiian population had fallen by nearly 90 percent to less than 100,000.[113] According to Suliana Siwtabau, missionaries destroyed the communal culture of the indigenous peoples of Fiji. That shift led to rapid exploitation of resources, devastation of the environment, and a spiritual decline characterized by accumulation and hoarding.[114]

In the case of India, between 1500 and 700 B.C.E. Aryan aggressors dominated the indigenous populations of the region and created a caste system. The Dalit (literally "the broken") were set as the "outcastes"—beyond society. Or, as V. Davasahayam puts it, "the stigma of untouchability due to their 'polluting' professions such as leather works, skinning, moving carcasses, carrying night soil on their heads, and so on," leaves them without land and poverty stricken.[115] Sadly, Christian missionaries, such as seventeenth-century Jesuit Roberto de Nobili, who dressed like a Brahman, failed to successfully defeat the caste system. Still today, Christian Dalits remain "triply discriminated against"—socially outcastes, ineligible for government aid, and poorly treated by clergy, bishops, and fellow Christians.[116]

The Construction of "Race" and Racism in China and Japan: A Sample of Eastern Thought

"Race" is not only a Western idea.[117] Thinkers indigenous to the East made select appropriations of outside thought such as that of nineteenth-century theorist Arthur Gobineau's notions of "purity and pollution" and blended them with ideas of the divine origin of the imperial line, and more.

"Race" is at least equally influential, complex, and contextually meaningful in the East as it is in the West. Sun Yatsen (1866–1925), the principal proponent of Chinese *minzu* (linage of the people; nationality, race) stated in his *Three Principles of the People,*

> The greatest force is common blood. The Chinese people belong to the yellow race because they come from the blood stock of the yellow race. The blood of ancestors is transmitted by heredity down through the race, making blood kinship a powerful force.[118]

East or West, the common thread found in formulations of racism is, "[T]hey all primarily group human populations on the basis of some biological signifier be it skin color, body height, hair texture or head shape."[119] Absolute and immutable boundaries separate one group from the "other," and assert that one group has some kind of power over the "other" (even to the point of justified genocide).

Eastern thought emphasizes harmony and hegemony. This has had a significant impact on the maturity of the notions of "race" and "racism" in the developmental history of these ideas. The Confucian hierarchical categories were ready structures that could be morphed, shaped, and conflated with a variety of other categories (such as folk myths) to yield the desired mix; to serve or explicitly oppose the state. The overarching characteristics of "race" and racism in China and Japan were thus primarily influenced by the desired image of the "pure and authentic" lineage and blood relationship. Eastern racism therefore stressed "inclusion" or "exclusion" for the purpose of fulfilling the ideal hegemony. On one hand, race was the only category that could include both the Emperor and the peasant. On the other hand, the need to remain a pure race, required the exclusion of the "others" who were considered "impure" such as blacks, Jews, Japanese (by Chinese), or Chinese (by Japanese). The discourse that accompanied these exclusions and inclusions varied. We now turn to examine the contributions of China and Japan to the way "race" is understood in the East.

"Race" in China: An Historical Overview of the Development of an Idea

The first scientific work to reference the idea of the "yellow race" was François Bernier's *Étrennes addressées à Madame de la Sabiliére pour l'anne 1688*. He noted that the color yellow was one of the five colors of purity of China and represented the grandeur of the Emperor. This was accompanied by the legendary account of the Emperor of the Middle Kingdom and his descendents who lived by the Yellow River.[120]

After the fall of the Ming dynasty and the invasion of China by the Manchus, Wang Fuzhi (1619–1692) wrote the 1656 *Yellow Book* (*Huang-shu*) in which he contrasted the imperial color, yellow, to "mixed" colors. He held China as the "yellow center" (*huongzhong*). Nobles were made of yellow mud, while ignobles were made of vulgar rope.

In China's reform period of the 1890s, the reformers constructed their racial identity utilizing New Text Confucianism, statecraft scholarship (*zhuzi xue*), and concepts from Mahayana Buddhism.[121] Hang Zunxian (1848–1905), for example, promoted the yellow race as a positive symbol to unite and mobilize the reformers.

Earlier in the Quing Era (1644–1911) competition for resources, need for control of the towns, an erosion of social order, and lineage feuds marked by military conflict led to a consolidation of the cult of patrilineal descent. At the court level, there was an erosion of cultural identity and an increased stress on ideologies of descent.

As Dikötter explains, during the Qianlong Period (1736–1795), there was a turn to rigid traditional descent lines (*zu*) Han, Manchu, Mongol, and Tibetan with three social levels of popular culture, gentry society, and court politics.

In the last decade of the nineteenth century, reformers worked toward a deep renewal of China, transforming its institutions and challenging its orthodox ideologies. They promoted independent sources for legitimating knowledge, and viewed the notion of "race" in scientific categories. Throughout the reform, popular culture and elite cultures stressed patrilineal descent.[122]

The two main figures of the reform that shaped the thought on "race" were Liang Qichao (1873–1929) and Kang Youwei (1858–1927). They selectively appropriated foreign concepts and manipulated evolutionary theories to bolster the theory of pure origin. They reconfigured folk ideas of patrilineal descent such that it became common knowledge that all the inhabitants of China were the descendents of the Yellow Emperor. The concepts of "lineage" (*zu*) and "race" (*zu*) were restated as (*huanghong*) "yellow race" and "lineage of the Yellow emperor." They played on the people's fear of their possible extinction as the result of contamination by other groups—whites, browns, blacks, or reds.

Liang Qichao redesigned the traditional Chinese social hierarchies into a new racial taxonomy: noble/low (*guizhong/jianzhong*); superior/inferior (*youzhong/liezhong*); historical/ahistorical (*youlishi/dezhongzu*).[123] Additionally Tang Caichang (1867–1900) restated the notions of "common people" (*liangmin*)/"mean people" (*jianmin*) as "fine races" (*liangzhong*)/"mean races" (*jianzhong*). He also composed a poem that tells it all:

> Yellow and white are wise, red and black are stupid;
> yellow and white are rulers, red and black are slaves;
> yellow and white are united, red and black are scattered.[124]

But some revolutionaries sought to return to the prior situation where the Han were the preeminent people of China. They used the "Yellow Emperor" as a starting point for the exclusion of the Manchu and they sought to infuse kinship terms with racial references into the commonsense vocabulary of all Chinese people. Chen Tianhua (1875–1905) accomplished that task. As Dikötter summarizes, "Culture, nation, and race had become coterminous in the symbolic universe of China's revolutionaries."[125]

By the fall of the Qing Empire in 1911, the promotion of racial definitions was widespread. This was possible first, because new and powerful elites emerged and economic trade expanded into a global economy and that brought more contact with outsiders. Also, there was a shift away from traditional Confucian values and cosmology to embryology, genetics, anthropology, craniology, and raciology. This shift was possible because of the availability of private printing presses and popular efforts.

Dikötter shows that several persons played prominent roles in the development of the Chinese new self-understanding.[126] Chen Yucang (1889–1947), the director of the Medical College of Tongji University, held that cranial weight was the singular indicator of the degree of civilization a person had attained. Liang Boqiang published his study of the *Chinese Race* in 1926, claiming that the "index of blood agglutination" was the indicator of purity. Lin Yutang (1895–1976) held that the absence of body hair indicated membership in the "Chinese Race." Yi Jaiyue promoted the pseu-doscience of eugenics among medical professionals, in school biology text-books, in popular literature, and in official marriage guides. The shift to a racialized self-understanding was possible because of a "convergence of pop-ular culture, state sponsored discourses of race, the scientization of folk models, and reconfiguration of more stable notions of descent, lineage, and genealogy."[127]

The regime of Deng Xiaoping (1904–1997) used racialized identity to promote Chinese national unity from the1970s until the 1990s. State pro-moted campaigns warned that "polluted outsiders" caused sexually trans-mitted diseases, HIV/AIDS, and syphilis. On November 25, 1988, the Stand-ing Committee of the People's Congress of Gansu Province passed a law forbidding "mentally retarded people" from having children.[128] In Novem-ber 1993, a research project was initiated to isolate "Chinese genes." In June 1995, sterilization was mandated for people with hereditary disorders, as well as those with mental illness or infectious diseases, in order to prevent in-ferior births (eugenics).[129]

The promotion of Peking Man as the ancestor of the mongoloid race was revitalized and renewed efforts to lay claim to the origins of the "miss-ing link" between apes and humans were made. This was all part of a wider effort to instill a renewed national pride and identity of China as the origi-nal and most authentic and pure human community of the Yellow Emperor while excluding "others" deemed immutably inferior.[130]

"Race" in Japan: An Historical Overview of the Development of an Idea

The Japanese term *minzoku* is usually used synonymously for race, *ethnie*, and nation.[131] Indeed, in the 1968 edition of the Japanese *Encyclopedia of the Social Sciences*, race (*jinshu*) is defined in terms of skin color, physical stature, hair texture, cranial form, nose shape and blood type; and ethnicity (*minzoku*) is not characterized by "fixed physical characteristics."[132] But ac-cording to Michael Weiner, the term *minzoku* is used in varied ways, and in the popular mind, it denotes both cultural and physiological determinants.

Historically, in the Tokugawa period (1603–1867) the Japanese viewed themselves as separate from other nations and they had xenophobic laws against Christian missionaries. But these conditions did not exist for racial reasons. Rather, claims the others were *yabanjin* (barbarians) were sup-ported with political and cultural rationale.[133]

The beginning of Japanese use of racialized terms came after the Meiji Restoration of 1868. Numerous attempts were made to define Japanese na-tional consciousness as a historic primordial community, linked directly to an ancient past; to the notion that the Japanese were an extended family linked together in relationship through a blood line to the Emperor who was the nation's semidivine father.[134] The Shinto religion was renewed and the people were required to again pay homage, be loyal, and obey the Emperor as the *minzoku no ōsa* (head of the people). As they interacted with other nations they were influenced in their construction of a racialized national identity. The shifts that took place resulted from incorporation of Western ideas and the appropriation and manipulation of indigenous myths by "academics, educators, journalists, politicians, and government officials."[135]

At the end of the nineteenth century, reacting to an extensive "westernization" of the nation, the Japanese endeavored to establish specific criteria for "Japaneseness."[136] Social Darwinism fit this need to provide a legitimate way to that goal. Shiga Shigetaka popularized the term *minzoku* in the late 1880s, as well as terms such as *kokusui* (national essence) and *kokuminshugi* (civic nationalism). Kuga Katsunan's interpretation of *minzoku* stressed the unique history, geography, and culture of the nation. Hozumi Yatsuka identified the notion of *kokutai* (national polity) with the Imperial line and ancestor worship, appealing to common ancestry and shared culture for all Japanese. In 1905, Kato Hiroyuki published an analysis of the strife between Russia and Japan for hegemony in East Asia and asserted the superiority of the Japanese on the basis of "a homogeneous polity that had been thoroughly integrated within the emperor system."[137] By 1910, the state-supported notion of *kazoku kokka* (family state) had gained valance in all areas of Japanese society. Several important developments led to this hegemonic racialized national consciousness.

Yanagawa Kenzaburo's account of a mission to the United States by Japanese scholars in 1860 reveals his apparent uncritical absorption of the racial prejudice of their U.S. host in that he reports: "inherent stupidity and inferiority of blacks."[138] Similarly, in 1878 Kume Kunitake published a two-volume account of scholars' encounters with the Iwakura in 1871–1873 titled, *Tokumei zenken taishi Beiō kairen jikki* (*A True Account of the Tour in America and Europe of the Special Embassy*).[139] In this and other works he accounted for the decline of Spain in terms of the Spanish racial inferiority. He used the term *shu* to compare the physical traits of the North American Indian and the *sennin* (lowly people) of Japan, "a category which during the Tokugawa period incorporated the *Eta* and *Hinin* outcaste groups."[140]

Concepts of Social Darwinism are used in 1883 by Takahashi Yoshio, in *Nihon jinshu kairyōron* (*Improvement of the Japanese Race*), advocating for intermarriage with Westerners in order to improve the inferior physical and intellectual capacities of the Japanese. Kato Hiroyuki's 1887 article, *Nihon jinshu kairō no ben* (*A Justification for the Improvement of the Japanese Race*) supported the same ideas.

Much of the government support for the *kazoku kokka* (family state) came through the work in Social Darwinism at the Tokyo Imperial University: the 1877 zoology lectures by Edward Morse, and the wide use of the 1879 Japanese edition of Thomas Huxley's *Lectures on the Origin of*

Species.[141] Also Morse's Tokyo lectures were published in 1881, and Herbert Spencer's evolutionary theory was available by 1884. All of this combined to give scientific support to the creation of a hierarchy of race and a means for national survival.

Japanese intellectuals also eagerly adopted eugenics and serology. Studies by Firihata Tanemoto and Furukawa Takeji claiming links between blood type and social character of the Ainu of Hokkaidō and the aboriginals of Taiwan were widely disseminated in major criminology and racial hygiene journals.[142]

Theories of geographical and climate determinism were also widely published in school textbooks. The most popular work was that of Thomas Buckle, *History of Civilisation in England*.[143] Fukuzawa Yukichi's 1869 *Sekai kunizukushi* (*World Geography*) set countries in evolutionary hierarchical groupings ranging from barbarians, to semicivilized, to civilized. Still, even after the Imperial Rescript on Education in 1890, the pseudoscientific disciplines of eugenics, serology, and Social Darwinism thrived. The result was an acceptance of the view of the world's population comprising three races as theorized by Arthur de Gobineau. While the Japanese, Koreans, and Chinese were all of the same "racial stock," "... this did not, however, preclude the existence of a further definition, which, in equally deterministic terms, distinguished members of the Yamato *minzoku* from Chinese or Koreans."[144] Together this all set the stage for the justification of colonization as well as for social and economic inequalities within Japan.[145]

These notions of "race" affected the exclusion of the urban and rural poor, as well as the other nations, based on their physical and cultural traits deemed to set them apart.[146] The *shakai* (lower class society) were not only poor, but they were judged to be innately lacking in moral capacities. Urban slum dwellers of the Meiji period (1868–1912) and in Osaka in 1897 (ancestors of today's *Burakumin*) were seen as living beyond civilization like descendents from "remote foreign races." In his *Minami koizumi mura*, Mayama Seika stated that he could not accept that "the blood flowing in those miserable peasants also flows in my body."[147] These attitudes were similar to those "negative images of commoner and peasant held by the samurai elites of the Tokugawa period and ... the lower orders in ... late nineteenth- and early twentieth-century Europe and North America."[148]

Hokkaidō was colonized (1869–1889) and the indigenous Ainu were described as being primitive and racially impure. Comparable assertions were made of Koreans and Taiwanese that the lack of industrial development was sure evidence of inferiority and the Japanese would uplift those colonized. Ainu scholar Kōno Tsunekichi in 1918 reasoned that the responsibility for the colonization of Hokkaidō was given to Japan "because 'no other superior race was in contact with the *Ezo*.'"[149] Also, Fukuda Tokuzo claimed "that the transformation of Korea from pre-industrial to a modern capitalist society could only be accomplished through Japanese intervention."[150]

Among the more dark implications of all this was the suggestion that "some peoples were unfit to survive in the struggle for existence."[151] In 1918, Hiraoka Sadataro wrote concerning the Ainu defining them as,

> Unadapted members of humanity . . . who have nothing to contribute to its well-being . . . [and] the introduction of Ainu blood into that of the Japanese will violate the movement to preserve our *kokusui* (national essence).[152]

Thus, the Japanese were "justified" in simply fulfilling their duty imposed by racial superiority and cultural maturity. In addition, the Confucian hierarchical concept of *taigi mibun* (proper place) served to reinforce the necessity that colonized peoples submit to the political oppression and labor exploitation imposed by the Japanese. Their only option was full assimilation into the Japanese culture, and even then, there was no guarantee that they would ever gain full rights as Japanese citizens.

In 1901, Hozumi Nobushige argued in his *Ancestor Worship and Japanese Law* that there had always been three key determinants of the Japanese peoples—Imperial family, regional clan, and the family unit.[153] And by the 1920s, there was a trend toward linking blood, nation, and culture firmly and immutably together.[154] In 1930, Ihei Setsuzo wrote that the uniqueness of the Japanese was the *ketzuokushugi*—the ideology of family blood.[155]

Further, in the 1930 edition of the Japanese *Encyclopedia of the Social Sciences,* "*minzoku* is defined as having three essential components: common blood, a shared culture, and collective consciousness."[156] According to Weiner, in 1938, Takakusu Junjiro held that there is "a dominant Yamato or stem 'race'" and that race had assimilated all others. He used the term "culture of Japanese blood" and claimed this had been preserved through "the virtuous rule of succeeding emperors."[157] By 1940, Kada Tetsuji, published *Jinshu, minzoku, senso*, concluding, "We cannot consider *minzoku* without taking into account its relation to blood." Kada held that *minzoku* originates in the particular *jinshuteki* (racial) and *seishinteki* (spiritual) qualities of the people and he lists the specific properties of a *minzoku* as common blood, culture, language, customs, and religion.[158]

Nearly seventy years later, not much has changed concerning the Japanese perception of themselves as a homogeneous people. As recent as 1986, Anwar M. Berkat, Director of the World Council of Churches Programme to Combat Racism, said this concerning people such as the Buraku and the Korean residents of Japan: "Their condition and maltreatment have often been hidden or ignored due to the assumed homogeneity of Japanese society."[159] And as late as 2001, Richard Werly reported in *The UNESCO Courier* that "some bourgeois Japanese families make illegal checks on the ancestors of their children's future spouses 'to avoid polluting the family.'"[160]

Conclusion: From the Past toward the Future

At the beginning of this chapter, I said that humans are "hard-wired" to notice difference. The moral and ethical significance of this reality is made known in the several seconds that follow the realization of what difference one perceived. Unfortunately, many today believe that the scientific defeat of the biological basis for "race" and the outlawing of unjust discriminatory practices is sufficient to control what happens after perceiving difference. Indeed, there are few places in the world today that officially and openly promote racism, tribalism, or xenophobia as an honorable and desirable policy. Or, alternatively, others assert humans can do little to settle the problem of race.

Racism, tribalism, or xenophobia is not easily defeated in part because racism is the dark side of the Enlightenment appeal to universalism. As Etienne Balibar suggests, the power of racism is its power to define the "frontiers of an ideal humanity."[161] To define what is *ideal*, one needs also to determine what is *not ideal*, and what is indeed not tolerable. As Balibar puts it, "Universalism and racism are indeed (determinate) contraries, and this is why each of them has the other inside itself—or is bound to affect the other from the inside."[162] The notions of the "universal human" were developed in tandem with the growth of the nation-state and the "ideal" was defined by the most powerful holding themselves as the norm. As we have seen, the racialization of the majority of the world's population cannot be divorced from the requirements of the imperialist expansion—East or West. Hannah Arendt suggests that ultimately the colonial project was a way to gain access to humanity.[163] Colonizers' holding the "motherland" as the exemplar and creating a bureaucracy through which the colonized might become "emancipated," in reality rendered such emancipation impossible to accomplish because race-based terms set by the colonizers prevented that. Usually, the only thing the colonized gained by attempting a healthy self-defined emancipation was that their "inferiority" as a colonized person was "proven;" and in the mind of the colonizer the subject was seen as "rebellious and uncivilized."

There is a destructive side to "progress" that was recognized after the Holocaust by Adorno and Horkheimer in which they acknowledged that by repressing the dark side of "progress" we fail to address it, and therefore open the possibility of allowing it to rule us.[164]

As Alana Lentin suggests, a countermeasure, when considering the possibility of "race" is to constantly question:

> "[W]ho you are in a certain social world, *why* there are some compulsory places in this world to which you must adapt yourself, imposing upon yourself a certain *univocal* identity." … Racism provides the answer to the dilemma of a universalism that seeks to homogenize us

when, in fact we feel different and strive toward uniqueness. Or as Balibar... puts it, racism has successfully been instituted as a mode of thought, "because we are *different*, and, tautologically because difference is the universal essence of what we are—not singular, individual difference, but collective differences, made of analogies and, ultimately, of similarities. The core of this mode of thought might very well be this common logic: differences among men are differences among sets of similar individuals (which for this reason can be 'identified')."[165]

The community here has and does find its home in nationalism and that pressed to its logical conclusions comes full circle to violence for some and privilege for others. Recent situations of genocide show us the extremes to which this logic can lead. Yet, it is also widely recognized that the thoroughgoing nature of such oppression required the complicity of entire societies to be carried out. Similarly, less egregious manifestations of racism have social, political, and economic dimensions that need to be addressed, if indeed they are—at least, to be held in check or—at best, eliminated. Sadly, there is evidence that there has been a replacement of a "statist" approach to antiracism by a "culturalist" approach.[166]

Globally, the "UNESCO 1968 Statement on Race and Racial Prejudice" set a trend for language of racism becoming apolitical. This bolstered an illusion that racism is "taken care of." Significantly, that document failed to address the implications of racial theory in recent history and it did not attend to colonialism's racism as a deliberate act of expansionist states.[167] The "sin" in dealing with human difference shifted from biological racism to cultural ethnocentrism. Also, the 1968 document gave no method to replace the Western paradigm as the universal standard for measuring human progress, nor did it provide any practical guidance for separate cultural groups occupying the same geographical space. As we saw, given that vacuum, Right Wing organizations concerned with "the difference of cultural entities" found more palatable ways to frame their racist ideas.[168]

As we have seen, policies of the state can be set to include or exclude groups of people. Often today antiracism purports to uphold values such as democracy, human rights, freedom, fraternity, or equality. However, for many these principles that undergird the modern state are in fact the "hypocritical anchorings of the state in principles that belie the selective nature of their application."[169] There is ample evidence that while more recently, intellectuals have been concerned with issues of "cultural identity" or "globalization," poor housing, poor health care, inadequate access to education, high unemployment, low incomes, racial profiling, and the interrelationship of immigration and criminality persists, if indeed it is not on the increase.[170] Close examination of the social welfare history of the nations of the world show that the policies are often applied with biases toward internal populations as well as to immigrant "others." As Barnor Hesse states,

> Somehow the end of the twentieth century has constructed a position in which the history that produces racism has been satiated, such that we can no longer speak of a history producing racism. In order to begin to talk about racism, we cannot anchor that historical discussion at all ... So we get to a position of what I call political relativism, which is that people are simply in different racialized positions, and the politics arises simply from being in a different position.[171]

The phenomenon of globalization certainly has an impact on how we need to understand racism, but in the end stark local reality of racism at the level of the city or the neighborhood must never be reified into abstract categories of "minority ethnicity," or "immigrant groups." The real needs of real human beings in the concrete demand that present-day manifestations of racism must be named as such and that the similarities to past deliberate decisions be made clear, lest we repeat yet one more time the atrocities of the past.

Over the centuries, Catholic social teaching has addressed racism, though often not adequately. In the post-Vatican II era, the Church teaches that racism involves more than personal prejudices, but also social structures and institutions. It is to the development of that teaching that we now turn.

2

Foundations for a Diagnostic Dilemma

Magisterial Ambiguity on Human Difference,
Human Servitude, and Colonization

Introduction

Albert Memmi holds that racism is fundamentally a structure and a set of social relations, and not only an idea or feeling of prejudice toward an "other."[1] Thus, racism is

> a generalizing definition and valuation of differences, whether real or imaginary to the advantage of the one defining or deploying them [*accusateur*], and to the detriment of the one subjugated to the act of definition [*victime*], whose purpose is to justify (social or physical) hostility and assault [*aggression*].[2]

The archetype of this oppression is colonialism in which the "other" is disparaged, and that disparagement is justified by racism. According to Memmi, colonialism's

> aggression against a weaker society requires the disparagement of the other to justify itself, to legitimize having appropriated others' land and homes, and having benefited from truncating others' lives and social dignity. Racism is indispensable to the colonist mentality, to make its domination appear reasonable to itself.[3]

Memmi distinguishes four moments that, when occurring together, constitute an absolute and timeless occasion of oppression called racism.[4] Racism is first an instance in which one recognizes that a "difference" exists between

29

persons or among groups. Secondly, a negative value judgment is imposed on those persons who bear or manifest certain characteristics and who are different, and a positive valuation is given to the correlative characteristics borne by the one(s) providing the judgment. Thirdly, the difference and its value are generalized to an entire group, which is then depreciated. And finally, the negative value imposed on the group becomes the justification and legitimatization for hostility and aggression.

Memmi has shown that racism has no real content, and therefore, it can change at the will of the oppressor. Indeed, it is not the *nature* or the *kind* of difference that matters, only that a *negative* difference is perceived to exist. "What counts is the form, the self-approbation that emerges from the assumptions and disguises inherent in any negative valuation of the other group."[5] It is illogical that racism can be *only* a *personal* matter because to make a generalization requires the presence or consideration of a group; thus, racism is a *social* mater. Racism as a social system relies on its ability to define the "other." The act of definition requires the exercise of the power of one *group* over another. The fact of definition sets up a dependency of the dominant on the "other" for their own social identity and on the hostility engendered by that dependence. Only legitimization of the dominance as a relationship provides any semblance of content.

Colonization: An Archetype of Racism

In the West, the phenomenon of colonization (the archetype of racism[6]) took on a particularly malicious character in the Age of Discovery in the form of colonies of settlement and colonies of exploitation. The former resulted when citizens from another country (the colonizers) migrated to a place and eventually took full control of the new region. These places came to be occupied and dominated not only by foreign peoples, but also by strange crops and animals. The local culture was overtaken and dominated by the interlopers. The settlers excluded the native populations from their society or (often) killed many of them in violent confrontations or by exposure to disease. The United States, Canada, and Australia are examples of colonies of settlement.

Colonies of exploitation did not attract large numbers of European settlers. Rather some went to strange places as explorers, planters, administrators, merchants, or military officers. The dominance of the colonizers was established by gaining political control—by force if necessary—but they did not normally kill or exclude entire native societies, nor intentionally destroy their cultures. The colonies of exploitation had an economy based on the local products and utilized the labor of the local inhabitants, working on either their own land or plantations established by the colonizers for the production of cash crops. Indonesia, Malaya in Southeast Asia, Nigeria, and Ghana are examples of colonies of exploitation. Though, in many ways this latter form of colonization was perhaps a bit more benign, the shift of power and self-determination away from local inhabitants was real, enduring, and no less personally devastating. The inhabitants were no longer self-determined, and the products of their labor were not theirs—rather, they benefited primarily those who exploited them. A powerful and penetrating effect of exploitative colonization was that norms shifted to the standards of the colonizers, and indigenous peoples were led to doubt the value of their own norms and gradually abandoned them, robbing their descendents of the wealth of their cultural birthright.

While it can be argued that many colonizers were "well-intended," the racist nature of their actions still stands in light of Memmi's definition. Colonizers considered culture and development a process in which they were further along than Africans, in particular, but also other non-Europeans. Ideally, this was not about economics, race, or superiority, but rather about "parenting."[7] Often, the intent was to bring the light of culture and progress to a "benighted" world, to develop the "underdeveloped," or to take responsibility for the progress of "civilization." But there are many problems with these good intentions when viewed from the perspective of those inhabitants who were the objects of this "enlightenment," "civilization," "development," or "parenting." It is difficult to miss the paradox of the frequent need on the part of colonizers to establish "civilization" through military force. Similarly questionable is the coveting of physical territory, the exploitation of human labor through racialized oppressive slavery, and the grab for wealth. As Young puts it, "Savagery had to be created in the nineteenth century as an antithesis to the values of European civilization."[8] Without a doubt, Europeans suffered from a superiority complex. The belief that Africans had degenerated from the original Adamic form is an inherent claim to superiority. The Christian religion and the Bible were perverted to support such claims. Cultural elitism claimed the culture of Western Europe was the only worthy culture.[9] The most devastating of all, however, was that racism came along as the wedded spouse of colonization. Again as Young argues, colonizers had to justify themselves by calling themselves superior to indigenous peoples, otherwise their benign reasons of progress and salvation were unnecessary, arbitrary, and unable to hide actual economic reasons.[10] The "modernization" project from the fifteenth century forward, took form from religiously inspired views of the barbarity and inferiority of indigenous peoples of Africa, Asia, and the Americas that legitimated invasion, exploitation, slavery, and genocide.

In his classic work *Slavery and the Catholic Church*,[11] John Francis Maxwell attempted to trace the veracity of the perception that the Catholic Church was at best a latecomer to the effort to eradicate racism and at worst an agent contributing to the justification of that reality. He chose to examine how the Church dealt with the institution of slavery, since at many levels enslavement serves as a vivid indicator of how human difference, human dignity, respect, and freedom are actually valued. His work traced some of the key movements, the complex mix of theological and ecclesial influences, and the varied interpretations of biblical material that stand as an important starting point for our discussion of the Church's mixed record in addressing the evils of racism in its various forms. Maxwell correctly saw the Church's teaching on slavery as a telling illustration of how conflicting social, political, economic, theological, and ecclesial pressures combined with strong pressing influences from legal and philosophical contexts of early Christian communities and shaped the Church's understanding and praxis concerning the freedom and dignity of all human persons, and how those conceptions held sway well into modern times.[12] Especially in the Age of Discovery when Europeans "discovered" Africa, Asia, and the Americas, it was the Church's fundamental understanding of the human person that was the axis that determined how any one dimension of the person was allowed to define the human person as such. While skin color was rarely explicitly named as the sole factor distinguishing a people as prospective slaves, other factors effectively isolated particular groups of people as subjects of oppression. Several reasons explain why Catholic Church teaching concerning the moral legitimacy of the institution of slavery was not always as clear as it might have been.[13]

First, the principle of the continuity of doctrine served to blind magisterial leaders to dimensions of current events requiring development or a revised articulation of a particular teaching. Second, four hundred years of ecclesial censorship of the literature of the Enlightenment (*Index Librorum Prohibitorum*—"List of Prohibited Books") left little room to benefit from important insights of eighteenth-century humanism that later positively influenced Christian anthropology and moral theology. Third, Roman civil law concerning legal titles of slave ownership, framing and setting conditions for various kinds of servitude, was reintroduced.[14] Fourth, vagueness abounded concerning the extent to which original sin and personal sin affected human freedom and unfree suffering and what is, thus, morally lawful or unlawful for human nature. Fifth, there was a split between what was rightfully a private matter of individual choice and a socially ethical matter of public concern. This ambiguity effectively lent force to the creation and maintenance of social structures that sustained institutional racialized slavery. The slave-master relationship was understood in terms of individual intentions and motives, and a private confessor could deal with violations. Sixth, the institution of slavery set innumerable persons outside the bounds of society often with no legal standing but simply as a nullity, and what we now consider structural evil, went unaccounted for. Seventh, the Magisterium failed to recognize the full impact of shifts in the context and practices of slavery; conditions for the biblical Philemon were vastly distinct from U.S. chattel slaves, for example.[15]

Finally, no body, such as the International Theological Commission (initiated in 1969 after Vatican Council II), could provide collegial counsel and critique to the popes. As we shall see, the popes themselves were often at the center of political and economic entanglements that led to some deplorable judgments, resulting in tolerance of oppressive radicalized enslavement of peoples in every nation in the Christian milieu.

For antiracists, it seems quite counterintuitive that the Bible is actually quite mixed on the question of race as such.[16] However, if we recall the historical and contextual span the biblical corpus covers, this seems more reasonable. But, definitely, the Bible is not silent on these matters or void of directives concerning racial justice.

Slavery in the Hebrew Testament: Model or Mandate?

Slavery was common and an accepted institution in the Ancient Near East, Ancient Mediterranean, and Northern Africa. Biblical texts recount the enslavement of Israel by Egypt, Assyria, and Babylon at distinct moments in history. Yet, the institution of slavery in Israel was unique in that it provided some modicum of humaneness within potentially brutal conditions.

Israelites could enslave a fellow national for one of four reasons: as a penalty for crime (Ex 22:3); as a means of repaying a debt (Lev 25:39; Ex 21:2–4; Prov 22:7; Am 2:6 and 8:6); as a means of ransoming an Israelite from a foreigner (Lev 25:41–55); or a father could sell his daughter on the condition that the master married her or gave her freedom (Ex 21:7–11).

Persons enslaved because of a debt were freed after six years (Deut 15:12–15, 18) or less according to the Jubilee Year (Lev 25:10, 40–41). People could choose to become permanent slaves (Ex 21:5–6; Deut 15:16–17). Masters emancipating a slave were to be generous, providing for the person upon release. Yet, not surprisingly, there were abuses to these regulations (II Kgs 4:1; Neh 5:1–8; Jer 34:8–22).

The policies for enslaving foreigners were also outlined. Foreign slaves served in perpetuity (Lev 25:46) and children of slaves remained enslaved (Gen 27:12–13; Ex 23:12; Lev 22:11). Foreign slaves could be bought and sold (Lev 25:44–46) or acquired as prisoners of war (Num 31:26) or as booty of a conquest (Deut 22:11). Women who were prizes of conquest, if selected as wives, were not necessarily enslaved (Deut 21:10–14).

Runaway slaves were not to be returned to their master (Deut 23:15–16). Serious punishment awaited a master who murdered or seduced a slave (Ex 23:20–21; Lev 19:20–22). A slave injured by their master was to be set free (Ex 21:26–27). Israelite slaves retained their religious duties (Ex 12:44; Lev 22:11; Deut 11:12); they could acquire property as sons and heirs (Prov 17:2) or marry the master's daughter (I Chron 2:35). They also had the right to a day of rest (Ex 22:10; 23:12; Deut 5:14). Slaves could even take up legal action against their master (Job 31:13–15).

In the Hebrew Scriptures, there are at least two major categories of law concerning slavery.[17] The first type—what Alt called "statute law"—is intended to be a positive or negative command, and it is given in the second person singular. Alt's second type of law—"case law"—provides examples of civil or criminal cases and concludes with a decision or penalty. It is expressed as a conditional clause, and is not intended as a divine command. Thus, because the three major biblical texts (Ex 21:1–11; Lev 25:39–55; and Deut 21:10–14) slavery proponents utilized over the centuries are expressed as "case law," it is not justifiable to claim that slavery was revealed by God as morally legitimate.

According to Carolyn Osiek, in the first century C.E., slavery functioned in the Roman Empire as a social and economic system. Roman agricultural, industrial, and penal type slavery placed enslaved persons outside of recourse to the law, making them property at the disposal of the masters who held absolute power over them.[18] In light of Roman law, no slaves had religious rights or the possibility of emancipation or manumission. Therefore, slaves could be treated viciously with impunity (though it would be economically counterproductive for the owner). Ironically, classical Roman jurists were quite clear that freedom is a natural human right.[19] Yet, the question remained whether the slave was in fact truly human. Eventually, several provisions in Roman law held the master liable for harming a slave (likely for economic reasons) and placed some limits on the absolute power of the master over the slave.[20]

The Institution of Slavery in the Second Testament

Understanding the institution of slavery in the Second Testament requires attention to the work of St. Paul.[21] There are two distinct but related themes present in the Pauline corpus. First, there is Paul's "dogmatic theology," in which he teaches that all of the baptized are equally and fully heir of the same Father and coheirs with Christ (Gal 3:26–28; Col 3:11; or I Cor 12:13).[22] Then, there is Paul's "moral theology," in which he requires the slave and the master to live out of their equality in Christ, their mutual duties in light of the Roman household codes (Eph 6:5–9; I Tim 6:1–2; Titus 2:9–10). Slavery is an "unavoidable evil," but it is qualified by mutual Christian charity. But Christians should not volunteer to be slaves and should accept freedom if it is offered (I Cor 7:20–24).

Two other phenomena are critical for biblical exegesis concerning slavery. First, there is what Cain Felder calls

> the phenomenon of "sacralisation" by which we mean the transposing of an ideological concept into a tenet of religious faith in order to serve the vested interest of a particular ethnic group. Second, is the process of "secularisation" or the diluting of a rich religious concept under the weight of secular pressures (social or political).[23]

Felder uses the "Table of Nations" (Gen 10) and the genealogy I Chronicles 1:1–2:1ff to illustrate "sacralisation." His critical study shows that by subtly giving more attention to the descendents of Shem, the author of Chronicles effectively edits the Gen 10 listing and this effectively shows Israel as having preference over all other peoples. "Here, the ethnic particularity evolves with a certain divine validation and inevitably the dangers of rank racism lie just beneath the surface."[24]

Further, Felder illustrates how "sacralization" phenomenon skewed inter-pretations of "The Curse of Ham" (Gen 9:20–27). The numerous inconsis-tencies were set aside over the centuries. "In one instance, the Canaanites 'deserve' subjugation; in another instance, the Hamites 'deserve' to be hew-ers of wood and drawers of water."[25] The "sacralization" of this ambiguous and frequently racialized text is evident as early as the Midrashim of the fifth century C.E. and the Babylonian Talmud (sixth century C.E.), through the seventeenth-century use of the text to justify enslavement of Africans, and into the present-day *Dake's Annotated Reference Bible* that provides a highly racialized commentary.[26]

Felder's "sacralisation" process also distorted Israel's claims to particular-ity as the "Chosen People." Its laws, covenant, and the promise of land as link-ing ethnic particularity and "chosenness" develops through the Deuterono-mistic history.[27] But the Second Testament clearly disconnects being "chosen" and ethnic particularity. [28] For Paul the crux of inclusion is being "in" and "with" Christ. Indeed, in I Peter 2:9 the use of the term *race* is clearly metaphorical. Felder summarizes,

> Thus, by the end of the first century and throughout the New Testa-ment period which extends into the second century the elect in Christ-ian literature becomes virtually synonymous with the Church and more particularly those true believers within the confines of the Church in the world, without any explicit ethnic or racial restrictions.[29]

The second phenomenon, "secularization" is illustrated by showing the diminishment of the significance of Jerusalem in preference for Athens and Rome, notably in Mark, Luke, and Luke-Acts. The limits of the known world for the early Christians designated the boundaries of Spain and the known Roman Empire. In Mark, the confession of the Roman centurion brings the Gospel to a climax. Luke positively stresses the role of the centurion; in Acts 6, he is ambiguous concerning whether the Ethiopian official was a Gentile (black) or a Jew.

However, Felder notes that Hellenistic Christians believed that a Nubian was the first Gentile convert. Therefore, it is significant that Luke's editori-alizing results in a de-emphasis of a Nubian (African) in favor of an Italian (European) enabling Europeans to claim that Acts 6 demonstrates some di-vine preference for Europeans.[30] A hostile political environment in the last third of the first century may have played a subtle role in Luke's assuming a Roman-centered world, and he effectively marginalized a darker race.

The Positive Value of "Race" and Ethnicity: Interpretation of Gal 3:28

While early Christians did not utilize physiological differences as justifi-cation for oppressive treatment, enslavement, or genocide, there is also evi-dence that distinctions *were* made.[31]

One important case is Paul's use of ethnic terms in Gal 3:28. As Denise Kimber Buell and Caroline Johnson Hodge show, many exegetes hold that here Paul shows that the Christian identity is above bodily characteristics that account for race or ethnicity. [32] According to Buell and Hodge, such an approach allows Christians to side step their own racist interpretive frameworks and to fail to see how early Christians did rely on distinct understandings of the "other."[33]

Hodge and Buell take their lead from Diana Hayes' statement that the early Christian community was "not only Jewish, but also Greek, Roman, and African."[34] Therefore, rather than set ethnicity aside entirely, Paul writes from his social location as a Judean. He understands the Gentiles to be "others" but not necessarily immediately fully excluded and unredeemable.[35] Paul brings together the best of his understanding of religious practices and loyalty, ethnic identity and moral standing, and he constructs a way for all peoples to become "adopted" into the family of the chosen people of Israel. The key is that Jews *and* Gentiles need to be of a common kinship with Christ. So as Paul sees it, if Gentiles freely elect to be baptized into Christ, they can become "sons of God." The kinship is thus established on the basis of shared *spirit*, rather than shared *blood*. Gentiles now share in spirit, the common ancestor with Christ and all Jews—Abraham. They are a kind of sibling with Christ the Son in their status as "adopted" sons.

This does not necessarily require the Gentiles to give up their ethnic identity. Buell and Hodge turn to Judith Nagata's model of "multiple identities" to show how this is possible.[36] Just as Paul is Judean and "in Christ" so too it is possible for the "others" to maintain their ethnic identity and be Christian. Clearly, Paul envisions the relationships in the Christian community as "ethnically complex *and* asymmetrical."[37] In Paul's hands, the reality of ethnicity is maintained, yet it is flexible and malleable so that the overall effect is that the "others" are included without losing their core ethnic identity. In this light, all peoples must be profoundly respectful of one another and include one another as kin, yet the dynamics of real differences also require an accounting.

Thus, we can see that the proper interpretation of sacred scripture requires careful exegetical work to not impose meanings on the texts that are not there. We now turn to a review of the varied teaching concerning slavery, beginning with the first century.

Teaching of the Fathers of the Church through the Twelfth Century

From the first to the twelfth century, at least eight distinct approaches were taken to slaves, enslavement, and the institution of slavery.[38] From time to time, theologians and bishops addressed all three of these dimensions alone or in different combinations and to varying degrees. Space here does not allow a thorough discussion of all of the pertinent texts of this period that shaped the Church's moral position on slavery. Instead, the following charts illustrate eight of the major Christian positions of this period along with some of the key sources, figures, and councils that defined them.

The continued ambiguity of the Church's teaching on moral issues concerning slavery resulted from the promulgation of various versions of two main contradictory positions on slavery taught from biblical time to through the twelfth century. On one hand, some theologians, popes, and councils, based on a literal reading of scripture, particularly the Pauline household codes, held that slaves must remain subject to their masters, though masters must treat their slaves well. On the other hand, the equality of all Christians as children of the same Father and as sisters and brothers in Christ was stressed as grounds for abolishing slavery. Similar divergences in thought and teaching persisted through the scholastic period.

Eight Basic Teachings on Slavery

ONE: Slavery can be tolerated if slaves and masters live under the same conditions and/or under non-Christian rule		
TEXT	AUTHOR	
Doctrina 100 C.E.		God views all people as having equal worth
Didache 4: 10–11 150 C.E.		Slaves accept their station in life and view their masters as a presence of God[39]
	Council of Gangra 390 C.E.[40]	Advised slaves to serve their masters with good will and not withdraw from service
Monastic Rule, 75, c. 1 and c. 2	Basil of Caesarea 329–379 C.E.	Philemon 10:12 Duty of slaves to their masters Run-away slaves to be returned to their masters Only exception—if the master oppression broke the moral law
"Homily on Philemon" 400 C.E.	John Chrysostom	It was fitting for slaves to remain enslaved
"Second Homily on Philemon"	John Chrysostom 386–398 C.E.	True brotherly relationship of the master and slave is reserved for heaven, that is, slaves cannot be set free now
	Augustine 400 C.E.	Exhorted slaves to fulfill their duty to serve and not to think about manumission
	Archbishop Radulphus of Rheims, France early twelfth century	Cited I Peter 18 and Canon 3 of the Council of Gangra and renounced the communes created by slaves who had rebelled and left their masters

TWO: All masters and slaves share the same human nature and are subject to the same laws of life and death		
TEXT	**AUTHOR**	
	Cyprian of Carthage 250 C.E.	Citing Job 31:13–15 claims that all masters and slaves share the same human nature and are subject to the same laws of life and death
"Fourth Homily on Ecclesiastes"	Gregory of Nyssa 385 C.E.	Argues that the institution of slavery is immoral
"Pastoral Rule"	Pope Gregory I 590 C.E.	Slaves must behave humbly and not despise their masters Masters need to remember that they are by nature equal to their slaves and they themselves are slaves of God
"Instructions for the Laity"	Bishop Jonas of Orleans 830 C.E.	Masters and slaves possess the same human nature equally though differences in culture and skin color do exist
	Pope Alexander III 1174 C.E.	Urged that all people are created by God to be equal by nature, and not slaves

THREE: Slavery was viewed as the consequences of original sin		
TEXT	**AUTHOR**	
"Sermon on Love for the Poor," 14	Gregory Nazianzen 380 C.E.	Although humans were created to be free, and as the recipients of God's wealth, subsequent original sin led to slavery and poverty
On Genesis n. 4; *Homilies on Ephesians*; *Homily on Lazarus*	John Chrysostom 400 C.E.	Asserted that avarice, envy, and insatiable greed are at the root of servitude, and it is the child of original sin
Quaestiones in Heptateuchum	Augustine of Hippo 419 C.E.	Slavery is the result of sin as in the case of Ham (Gen 9) or of adversity as in the case of Joseph (Gen 37–45)
City of God, 19:4, 15, 16	Augustine of Hippo 425 C.E.	Slavery can be justly imposed on sinners for their own benefit and those children born from enslaved mothers could justly be enslaved, as well

FOUR: The master's duty was to fulfill God's will and be a caretaker—due to sin God ordained a hierarchy of merit and rulership		
TEXT	**AUTHOR**	
On Providence VII	Theodoret of Cyrus 436 C.E.	Claimed that slavery of children born of mothers can be ascribed to the will of divine providence It was the duty of the master to fulfill God's will and take on the burden of being a caretaker
	Pope Gregory I	All people were equal, but because of sin God has ordained a hierarchy of merit and rulership for the fulfillment of justice; some people are born to rule, others to serve
Sententiae, L. III, c. 47	Isadore of Seville eighth century	Slaves are those who have a strong urge to do wrong and need an equally strong master to restrain them; it is better to be a submissive slave than to be a proud free person

FIVE: Slavery can be beneficial for vicious or stupid people		
TEXT	**AUTHOR**	
Liber de Spiritu Sancto C. 20, n. 51	Basil of Caesarea 374 C.E.	Slavery can benefit persons who are sinners and whose stupidity demands direction from others[41]
City of God, 50.19	Augustine of Hippo	Slavery is a result of iniquity, however slaves can benefit from the direction of upright masters

SIX: Slavery could be imposed as a penalty		
TEXT	**AUTHOR**	
Canon 32	Fourth Council of Toledo 633 C.E.	Slavery was imposed on women who were involved with promiscuous clerics
Canon 10	Ninth Council of Toledo 655 C.E.	The offspring of promiscuous clerics were permanently enslaved to service of the Church
Canons 2 and 4	Council of Pavia 1012 C.E.	The children born to even free women (as well as female slaves) who were involved with promiscuous clerics were punished by enslavement to the Church
Canon 12	Pope Urban III Synod of Melfi 1089 C.E.	Gave secular princes the power to enslave the wives of clerics as a means of enforcing clerical celibacy Enslavement of those convicted of abducting a woman by force[42]

SEVEN: Christian slaves and masters are both children of the same Heavenly Father and brothers and sisters in Christ		
TEXT	**AUTHOR**	
Institutionum Divinarum, L.V, C. 15 and 16	Lactantius 315 C.E.	
	Pope Julius mid-fourth century	Made this claim when addressing marriage and divorce among slaves and free persons
Commentary on Gal 3:28 and I Cor 7: 21–22	Ambrose of Milan 386 C.E.	Held that it is faith, not status as slave or free persons that merits real aristocracy
Homily 40 on I Cor 15: 29–34	John Chrysostom 400 C.E.	Asserted that because there is no slave or free in Christ, Christian masters should train their slaves to be self-sufficient and set them free
Commentary on Col 3: 9–11	St. Agobard of Lyon ninth century	Slaves are subject to masters in their bodily existence, but their spiritual life is subject only to God

Scholastic Influences on Slavery: Roman Law, Aquinas, Bonaventure, and Scotus

As we saw, Aristotle taught that some persons were "natural slaves." The rediscovery of Aristotle in medieval Europe renewed his influence on moral judgments through the Age of Discovery and beyond. Aristotelian thought joined with the revival of Roman Law in the medieval universities to influence theology. Roman Law had a variety of provisos concerning slavery. In war, the enemy captives could be enslaved. By the twelfth century, this meant primarily the enslavement of Muslims who were captured by Christians. Slavery was also a form of capital punishment and the enslaved were slaves for life. A debtor could be enslaved. Parents could sell their newborn child under certain conditions if they were impoverished. A person over the age of twenty could sell him- or herself into slavery and share in the price. Most commonly, regardless of the status of the father, a child born of a slave mother would also become a slave. Because of the wide-ranging influence of the Roman Empire, these practices held sway well through the seventeenth century.

Thomas Aquinas (1227–1274)

The Angelic Doctor held that the original, "first intent" of the Divine was that all people live in innocence but influenced by Aristotle he also claimed

EIGHT: Christian masters should emancipate their slaves		
TEXT	**AUTHOR**	
"Third Prayer for Easter"	Gregory of Nyssa fourth century	Easter was the season to free slaves and release debts according to Church custom
"Sermo XXI,"	Augustine of Hippo	Described a Church ceremony of manumission
Quaestiones in Heptateuchum L. II, n. 77	Augustine of Hippo 419 C.E.	States that the Law of Moses granting freedom of slaves is not a model for Christians; to the contrary, Christian slaves are to be subject to their masters
	Council of Agde 506 C.E.	Bishops could not sell the Church's slaves; the slaves emancipated by the bishop were to be given land, vines, and buildings and were not to be enslaved by the successor of the emancipating bishop
Canon 8	Council of Jena in Gaul 517 C.E.	Held that monks were not to free their slaves because it was not just that monks work while the slaves were idle
Canon 7	Council of Orleans 511 C.E.	When a bishop died, the slaves he had freed could not leave the service of the Church however, even though the deceased bishop had paid the Church compensation for the property given them from his own resources
Canon 67	Fourth Council of Toledo 633 C.E.	Reversed the fourth Council of Orleans and held that a bishop must compensate the Church for the slaves he freed. If he did not do so, his successor bishop could re-enslave them
Canon 10	Council of Chelsea Saxon England 816 C.E.	At a bishop's death, his English slaves were to be freed, and each abbot or bishop who attended his funeral was to free three slaves and give each three *solidi*
A book addressed to Emperor Louis the Pious	Benedictine Abbot Smaragdus of Saint Mihiel 830 C.E.	Argues for the abolition of slavery based on the reality that all people are equally sinners, but also equally empowered to forgive and be forgiven[43]
Testament, n. 4	Theodore the Studite 826 C.E.	Monks must not have slaves for any purpose, and the ownership of slaves was the prerogative of lay people
	Council of Armagh 1117 C.E.	The Irish bishops ordered all slaves should be freed in all of England and Ireland

that, due to original sin, the "second intent" of the Divine was to allow that there are some natural slaves.[44] Because of their sins, some people cannot work for their own benefit, but must be punished.[45] He recognized there is a symbiotic relationship between master and slave that is mutually beneficial.[46] Yet Thomas also supported the institution of slavery as a penalty as a matter of positive law.[47] Though illogical to the mind of the present day, Aquinas ultimately accepted the morality of the enslavement of children born of enslaved mothers, in spite of their innocence of any personal sin.[48]

Bonaventure of Bagnoregio (1217–1274)

In this same period, Bonaventure also held that slavery is a penalty for sin. Making an argument similar to Aquinas, he also supported the possibility of legal title to enslavement of the children born of enslaved mothers. In his view, enslavement of some by others is part of the greater Divine plan that there are various states among Christians—kings, princes, masters, and slaves.[49]

John Duns Scotus (1265–1308)

As one would expect, the Subtle Doctor was more discerning about the teaching of Aristotle as well as the provisions of Roman Law. Scotus saw slavery as against nature, and thus, there are only two conditions under which slavery could be morally tolerable—self-enslavement and as a punishment by the state. He clearly rejected chattel slavery as well as enslavement of prisoners of war because people are not property. Thus, in the teaching of these medieval masters, we are again left with a mixed and ambiguous message about slavery, and by implication, how people and their freedom are valued.

Religious Racism

This moral ambiguity on slavery at the end of the fourteenth century added force to an already lethal combination of racialized interpretations of Christian thought which deeply marked the development of racism through the Age of Discovery. It also opened the way for this application of the fifteenth-century Spanish notion of *limpieza de sangre* in the New World.

Recall that *limpieza de sangre* emerged during the Spanish Inquisition to prevent "new Christians" (Muslims and Jews) from becoming highly influential in Spain. According to Maria Elena Martinez, this "pure blood" standard was conveniently applied in the Americas as a means of identifying and categorizing peoples.[50]

Those people categorized were children of Spaniards (*Criollos*) and an indigenous person or an African (*mestizos*). Though the application of the laws was illegal against Christians, they along with the Inquisition's idolatry statues *were* used. It was argued that since Africans and indigenous peoples were forcibly baptized in massive numbers, these peoples had never *truly* accepted Christ and the authority of the popes.

So the Church's moral ambiguity effectively legitimated increased "scientific," philosophical, and anthropological efforts to define humans encountered in newly "discovered" lands. Indeed, Christians were faced with ever more complex and often contradictory ideas concerning the treatment of the "other."[51]

It is important, however, to acknowledge that through the cacophony of voices, a pattern of papal teaching can be uncovered. Yet it is far from the case that the promulgation of papal teaching lessened the moral ambiguity that existed concerning racialized slavery. As we will note, the deep involvement of the papacy in the political and economic matters of the day frequently drew a deep and thick fog over what might have otherwise been sound and powerful moral denouncements of slavery and the unadulterated racism that it embodied. It is to this line of teaching that we now turn.

The Popes on Slavery: 1435–1890

A Cautionary Note: The Political Climate and the Power of the Papacy in This Age

We must recognize the reality that in this period the popes engaged in large-scale economic and political exchanges in Europe and around the world.[52] The Roman pontiffs, as the ultimate authority in Christendom, established international laws and solidified relationships among nations. National leaders and powerful people sought the popes' legitimatization of their actions and explorations.

Two of the major political and economic forces of the time were the "Catholic nations" of Portugal and Spain, and their sovereigns sought papal approval. Lest we misunderstand the impact of the papal moral denunciation of racist slavery, we must also keep in mind how papal activities created the broader climate in which their pronouncements were established, and consider in light of that, how any one teaching might be received.

In *The Popes and Slavery*, Joel S. Panzer recounts a brief history of magisterial pronouncements on the immorality of slavery.[53] As we highlight the themes and the documents discussed there, it will become amply clear that moral teaching is not necessarily adhered to by the faithful, especially when there are vast inconsistencies in the teaching, the teachers are of questionable character, or when obviously political and economic enterprises and favoritism are involved.[54]

Nonetheless, significantly, it is clear that the kind of slavery condemned by the popes is, in all cases, servitude that is characterized by "a distinctive racial element" and enforced out of human greed and a desire for cheap human labor.[55] The magisterial documents make a distinction between two types of servile encumbrance. First is the notion of *servitus* that refers to "just title" encumbrance and is translated by Panzer as "servitude."[56] A second notion is *servitus* that does not rest on "just title" encumbrance and is translated by Panzer as "slavery." In the documents the institution of slavery is referred to as *servituti subicere* (to subject to slavery) or *in servitutem redigere* (to reduce to slavery). These latter two forms indicated situations in which the state of servitude was in clear violation of human dignity. Certainly, the indignities of racism were visceral elements in the processes and strategies of "reducing" peoples to slavery.[57]

The First Hundred Years (1435–1536)

Panzer's study first examines the period from 1435–1536, which saw the promulgation of four papal bulls—*Sicut Dudum*, January 13, 1435, by Pope Eugene IV and by Alexander VI: *Eximiae Devotionis*, May 4, 1493; *Inter Caetera*, May 4, 1493; and *Ineffabilis et Summi Patris*, June 1, 1497. He notes that Pope Eugene IV, though a pious man, engaged in the fray of politics. Indeed, he was "forced to flee a revolution in Rome due to his suppression of the vindictive Colonna family" and he settled in Florence from 1434–1443.[58] *Sicut Dudum* was a papal bull addressed to Bishop Ferdinand in Rubicon on the island of Lanzarote, and it condemned the enslavement of the Guaches and others of the Canary Islands. It was the practice to enslave the baptized inhabitants and then to take them to Europe. Significantly, the penalty this bull imposed for not halting this practice, as well as failing to free those already enslaved within fifteen days, was excommunication *ipso facto*! The same penalty was attached to any future enslavement activity. The condemnation of unjust racist slavery could not be stated more powerfully.[59]

Panzer then reviews Alexander VI's *Eximiae Devotionis* of May 4, 1493, *Inter Caetera* of May 4, 1493; and *Ineffabilis et Summi Patris* of June 1, 1497. But Panzer fails to treat several developments that most certainly would have colored the reception by the faithful of the three papal bulls. In 1452, Pope Nicholas V, with the promulgation of the bull, *Dum diversa*, granted King Alfonso of Portugal "general and indefinite powers to search out and conquer all pagans," enslave them, and appropriate their lands and their goods.[60] His favoritism toward the Portuguese is again visible in the 1455 bull *Romanus pontifex* that extended the bull of 1452 and granted Portugal the exclusive right to "a vast southerly region" ripe for missionary pursuit of converts.[61] In turn, Pope Calixtus III issued a bull in 1456 that explicitly confirmed *Romanus pontifex* and made Portugal spiritually responsible for all the lands it acquired. This bull, *Inter Caetera*, specified the Azores, Cape Verde Islands, Madeira Islands and colonies on Africa's coast and the Spice Islands, in particular.

Similar favoritism is found in the act of Sixtus IV and his promulgation of *Aeterni Regis* in 1481. That bull confirmed *Romanus pontifex* (1455) and

Inter Caetera (1456) and affirmed Portugal's right Guinea, West Africa. Primarily political, this document favored Portugal over France and Spain, and encouraged Castile to abide by the Treaty of Alcaçovas.[62] This papal meddling assured Portugal free and easy access to trade routes and missions in Guinea and the Atlantic.

When Alexander VI became pope, as a member of the Spanish Borgia family his loyalties lay with the kings of that realm. Alexander held bishoprics and abbeys and was the second wealthiest cardinal at age twenty-six![63] As pope he continued to engage in bribery, cronyism, and promiscuity. Significantly, he continued to finance expeditions to the New World during his reign.

Not surprisingly, Alexander VI took Portugal's privileges and grants for Spain via the papal bull *Eximiae Devotionis* on May 4, 1493. Then, in *Inter Caetera* of May 4, 1493, he entrusted Ferdinand and Isabella of Spain with bringing the faith to the lands discovered by Columbus, granting them dominion over all the lands existing 300 miles to the west of the Azores. According to the Treaty of Tordesillas of June 7, 1494, the bull *Inter Caetera* of May 4, 1493, was modified so that Portugal retained the right to the territories it had already gained for the faith. The papal intent is made clear in the letter to Emmanuel, king of Portugal, *Ineffabilis et Summi Patris* (June 1, 1497) that "he is giving to Spain and Portugal the rights to bring Christianity to these lands *on the presumption that the peoples of these lands freely choose the kings of Spain and Portugal as their sovereigns.*"[64] Alexander intended that indigenous peoples be free to choose Christianity and their rulers, and he repeats the phrase, "have wished to be subject to you" in two successive paragraphs.[65] Indeed, similar phrases are used in subsequent documents. Yet, the very fact that this objective freedom is stressed so strongly also indicated that such freedom of choice was not the ongoing practice, and that a change was urgently needed.

The Second Hundred Years (1597–1638)

A key debate concerned whether the conquered peoples were actually fully human. Were these people "slaves by nature" as Aristotle had posed or were they fully human and of the same nature as their conquerors? In 1512, Spain issued the Laws of Burgos, which held that the Indians were fully capable of becoming Christians, and elaborated programs for their conversion.[66] Unfortunately, conversion to Christianity soon became the cause and the occasion for the enslavement of native peoples, claiming that the indigenous peoples were better off (more easily converted) when controlled by Christian masters. Fortunately, at the request of Dominican missionaries and the likes of Bartolomé de Las Casas, Pope Paul III intervened by issuing the papal decree, *Sublimis Deus* on June 2, 1537.[67] The document was a universal statement and a teaching against slavery. Significantly, Paul III followed this decree with two additional documents, issuing severe penalties for not obeying the decree, and spelling out the sacramental significance of the reality that Indians were truly fully human.

Sublimis Deus clearly taught that the call to receive the faith and salvation is universal. The single qualification for receiving the faith is the possession of a human nature. It held that those who enslaved fellow humans lacked faith. This clearly confronted those who claimed the necessity of enslavement as the best way toward conversion. Indeed, the second major assertion of *Sublimis Deus* was that the complete and full freedom of all peoples must be acknowledged and it was imperative that the Indians' liberty and property be restored. Clearly, conversion, not domination was intended.

Paul III issued *Altitudo Divini Consilii* on June 1, 1537. He addressed the Bishops of the Indies concerning the preparation of the Indians for reception of the sacraments. With reference to *Sublimis Deus*, he insisted the Indians be prepared according to the ordinary norms of the Church. In addition, to counter the fears of the Indians who worried that to become Christian would be to give up their property, Paul III issued *Motus Proprio Cupientes Judaeos* on March 21, 1542. There he forbids such manipulation and theft.

On April 18, 1591, Gregory XIV issued the bull *Cum Sicuti* in response to the hostile situation in the Philippines, where the Spaniards had used force to subdue the indigenous peoples and deprive them of their goods. He insisted that the natives should be compensated, their goods and property be restored by the Spaniards, and he set up a process to facilitate this action. The document also supported King Philip II's antislavery decree that banned taking of slaves "whether by just or unjust war" and claimed that "What is in harmony with reason and justice" should prevail.[68]

The Third Hundred Years (1639–1740)

By this time, a papal antislavery tradition existed and popes quite consistently referenced their predecessors' teaching. Yet, these same popes were often plagued with challenges to character and credibility, as well as powerful social, political and economic forces that propagated racism and slavery.[69]

Pope Urban VIII was known for his nepotism and extravagant spending. He centralized the papacy and he all but ignored his advisors. However, on April 22, 1639, he issued *Commissum Nobis* upon the request of the procurator of the Province of Paraguay and to lend support to the 1626 Royal Edict of King Philip IV opposing enslavement of Indians. He referred to Paul III's *Sublimis Deus* and *Pastorale Officium* of May 29, 1537, and claimed to be "following in the footsteps of Paul III."[70]

During the pontificate of Innocent XI the *Response of the Congregation of the Holy Office*, No. 230, of March 20, 1686, was given. This involved the possibility and conditions of African slavery. Some claimed that since

Africans were Muslims (not Christians) war could be waged on them with impunity, and they could be enslaved. The *Response* concluded that the capture of black people for enslavement is condemned. Since "they have harmed no one" they cannot be considered enemies of Christianity or be enslaved as a punishment for waging war. Further, trade in black slaves was condemned, and slave marketing could not be justified by the current trading practices. Beyond that, anyone seeking to purchase a slave must investigate the title that binds the person in question. If the person is held by an unjust title, the slave must not be purchased. Finally, all black people and other residents must be freed and restored to their prior state and with proper compensation.

The Last Hundred and Fifty Years (1741–1890)

Benedict XIV issued *Immensa Pastorum* on December 20, 1741, to the bishops of Brazil and all regions under Portuguese King John. The pope cited his predecessors' denunciations of slavery and enslavement and the attached penalty of excommunication—especially those of Paul III and Urban VIII. He instructed the bishops to provide both material and spiritual aid to the Indians and he enumerated those religious orders that had particular responsibility to help. Indeed, every Christian was required to participate in this provision, and those who failed were to incur *ipso facto* excommunication *latae sententiae*, that could be lifted only by the pope. Punishable actions included reducing Indians to slavery, separating their families, stealing their property and goods, or doing anything to deprive them of their liberty. Also included was giving counsel, aid, or favor to anyone acting to harm the Indians in any way.

Following his predecessors, Gregory XVI promulgated *In Supremo* on December 3, 1839. He instructed Christians to turn from enslaving blacks and other peoples. He renounced all who enslaved their fellow humans for "sordid gain," and he expressed intent to protect Indians from the "excessive greed" of Christian traders.[71] Gregory XVI also prohibited anyone from defending the trade of blacks or publicly or privately publishing opinions contrary to his teaching. He used language that condemned both institutions—the slave trade and slavery.[72]

During Pius IX's papacy, the Sacred Congregation of the Holy Office, in *Intstruction 1293*, responded to questions by William Massaia, Vicar Apostolic of the Galla tribe in Ethiopia. Slaves and slave holding was thoroughly integrated into the society and culture of the people such that life there was impossible without being compliant with slavery. Citing "just title" servitude, the Holy Office ruled that such servitude was permissible if the person offered herself or himself for service. The document carefully specified what characterized the just title arrangement; which slaves could be bought and sold. Slaves must be treated humanely, and they were not to be sold to abusive masters. Marriage rights were to be honored, and Christian slaves were to be in the care of Christian masters. Slaves unjustly encumbered were encouraged to flee, while those justly enslaved were to stay (unless the master solicited their participation in sin).

On May 5, 1888, Leo XIII promulgated *In Plurimis* in which he encouraged the Brazilian bishops to support Brazil's ban on slavery. The Brazilian Emperor Dom Pedro II abolished slavery in 1850. In 1871, children of slaves were declared free, and by 1888, all legal slavery had ended.[73] After recounting early Church history and its efforts to prevent slavery in Africa, Asia, and America, he noted these labors had now achieved some satisfaction.

Leo XIII moved beyond current papal antislavery tradition when in his *Catholicae Ecclesiae* promulgated May 20, 1890, he grounded human equality, not only in redemption and vocation, but also in its origins.[74] There, he also charged the founder of the Society of Missionaries in Africa (The White Fathers) to bring Europe to agree to end "this gloomy plague of slavery in Africa."[75] Leo XIII also thanked European leaders for their cooperation at the 1890 conference in Brussels toward ending slavery. Finally, he established a papal collection to be taken up on Epiphany to help rid the world of the "yoke of human slavery."[76]

Facing the Diagnostic Dilemma

In 1988, the Pontifical Justice and Peace Commission issued its statement, *The Church and Racism: Toward a More Fraternal Society*. It defines racism as "rooted in the reality of sin ... awareness of biologically determined superiority of one's own race or ethnic group with respect to others, developed above all from the practice of colonization and slavery at the dawn of the modern era."[77] The Commission then distinguished nine forms of racism (nos. 8–16). This document signaled a tremendous advancement in the Church's willingness and capacity not only to denounce sinful practices, but also to utilize social analysis and to act concretely to effect social, political, and economic change (nos. 24–32). Still the emphasis is clearly on the conversion of heart: "Racial prejudice, which denies the equal dignity of all members of the human family and blasphemes the Creator, can only be eradicated by going to its roots, where it is formed; in the human heart" (no. 24).

Thirteen years later (2001) the Pontifical Council for Justice and Peace issued its *Contribution to World Conference against Racism, Racial Discrimination, Xenophobia, and Related Intolerance*. This document, while it affirmed the 1988 statement, went further to tackle the need for reconciliation for past injustices. Additionally, it focused on the need for teaching the values of human dignity, solidarity, and the common good in a variety of ways. Significantly, it supported concrete affirmative action (just opportunity) to mitigate past injustices and the denial of opportunity to peoples across the globe. The Church also recognized the changing shape of racial injustice due to globalization and the unprecedented numbers of migrants and refugees in the world at the start of the new millennium.

Most significant about recent moral teachings on racism is that their very existence robs racism of any moral legitimacy. But more fundamentally, while requiring a spiritual base, they maintain that much can and must be done to also create a just structural arrangement within which integral conversion can happen. Several individual bishops across the globe have issued pastorals in recent years that even set out "in house" policy changes to model such structural changes. Individual bishops also began to deal directly with issues of "white privilege" for the first time. More magisterial action like this is necessary if racism is to be fought and overcome in our globalized world.[78]

For as Albert Memmi and many others hold, critical to understanding racism in its many forms is to see the integration of the biographical, the historical, the personal, and the analytical. Memmi defines racism in two senses. In the "narrow" sense, racism is the focus of biological difference or specific traits that are given to devised paradigms called "races." Biology (or the criterion given for the discriminating category) acts as a pretext or an alibi. The function of racism is "both the rationalization and the emblem for a system of social oppression."[79] Memmi elaborates:

> [R]acism subsumes and reveals all the elements of dominance and subjugation, aggression and fear, injustice and the defense of privilege, the apologetics of domination with its self-justifications, the disparaging myths and the images of the dominated, and finally the social nullification of the victim people for the benefit of the persecutors and executioners—all of this is contained in it.[80]

Racism in the "broad" sense is self-valuation through the devaluation of the other, and the justification of verbal or physical assault or abuse. Racism in the "broad" sense is more prevalent than it is in the "narrow" sense. As Memmi explains,

> It would seem reasonable to consider biological racism, which is a relatively recent phenomenon, as a special case of the other, whose practices are more widespread and much older.[81]

Memmi and others also warn of the danger of an illusional insistence that the reality is that there is actually *no difference* among peoples. [82] He cautions that some psychoanalytic theories "affirm that racism is built on *heterophobia*, a fear of difference, of those who are different, that is a fear of the unknown. But [the psychoanalysts] ask 'what is this "unknown"?' And they respond: it is our own unconscious, which is frightening because it is strange, and which we then project on the other."[83]

Clearly, this and all other purely theoretical approaches avoid dealing with the concrete realities of human differences that do (at least initially) spark discomfort because they are unknown to us. Heterophobia, fear of difference, and xenophobia, fear of strangers, are each rooted in particular concrete experiences and contexts. Any "cure" for such fears needs to be dealt with in equally concrete and experiential ways. One deeply embedded myth, strongly reinforced by Western education, colonial and slave mentalities, is that it is bad to be different.[84] This stance fully undergirds neo-liberal "color-blind" approaches to resolving racism in the United States and the xenophobic violence involving immigrants in Europe and elsewhere.[85] It would thus be a huge mistake on the part of any antiracist effort, particularly by the Church, to stress the universal without also acknowledging the particularity of differences that exist among all peoples. The real task for the Church is not only to assist people in developing their intellectual capacity, character, and spirituality, but also to teach them the skills and strategies necessary to draw on "difference" as the occasion for empowerment of *all* and celebration of the presence of God's grace in all people, rather than as the basis for fearful exclusion or even violence.

Following Memmi then, it is vital that the Church take care to heed the wisdom of one who has uncovered what he calls "the discriminatory didactic" of the spiraling dynamics of racism: fear, followed by aggression, followed by more fear and aggression. Racists are fearful people. Underneath all racism, according to Memmi, racial affirmation is an instrument for negative self-definition that compensates for the feelings of personal vulnerability that accompany fear. Indeed, racism in the "narrow" sense is easily defeated on its own weak logic. But racism in the "broad" sense requires the ability to generalize and in order to generalize according to the skewed logic (illogic) required by racism, one needs support from a society and its structures. Memmi forewarns, "The relative structural coherence of racism in the narrow sense, even in its obsessive aggressiveness and self-interest, is confirmed precisely by the existence of racism in the broad sense."[86]

Thus, it cannot be stressed strongly enough, that if the Church is to be effective in combating racism, and establishing racial justice, it must remain vigilant and deal with structural sin *as well as* personal sin; it must challenge oppressive social, economic, political, and sexual structures that frame the very world in which it would have "conversion of heart" take place. The Church must not only proclaim doctrines and theological or moral principles, but also engage in training and forming moral agents who can critically analyze concrete realities in light of the Gospel and view differences as gifts and as positive opportunities. As Bryan Massingale stated in his classic analysis of U.S. episcopal teaching on racism between 1990 and 2000, how racism is defined, analyzed, and diagnosed will also determine the judgment concerning what action is required to overcome it.[87] Shamefully, his judgment is correct that out of some twenty teaching documents on racism promulgated in the ten-year period (1990–2000), only four adequately defined racism and addressed action to sufficiently challenge that sin and injustice in any effective way. Definitions of racism ranged from Cardinal Bevilacqua's claim that racism is "a sin against fraternal charity," to the Illinois bishop's more comprehensive definition that also holds "It involves not only prejudice but also the use of social, political, economic, and historical power to keep one race privileged. Racism is personal, institutional, cultural, and internal."[88] It is that latter understanding of racism that Massingale deems more adequate and most likely to lead to effective ministry and moral living to counter all forms of racism.

In the next section of this book we examine some of the more adequate teaching documents on racial justice from the present-day Magisterium. But first, we will examine some of the doctrinal themes that are most frequently raised as the grounds for racial justice.

3

Some Key Doctrinal, Theological, and Ethical Warrants for Racial Justice

Introduction

James H. Cone constantly alleges that white Christian theologians are not saying enough about racism and white supremacy:

> I think their silence stems partly from a distorted understanding of what the Gospel means in a racially broken world. White theologians have not succeeded in making an empathetic bond with the pains and hurts of people of color. If theologians perceived their own sons and daughters and parents as being discriminated against, they would not only write passionately against it, they would make their rejection of injustice an essential part of their reflection on the Gospel.[1]

Chicago Tribune columnist Clarence Page received this from a reader concerning an incident in New York where police fired 50 rounds at a car of an unarmed African American man, Sean Bell, killing him: [2]

> "Black-on-black" crime (especially murder) is such a huge and rampant reality in this country, but God forbid a policeman might make a mistake and hurt or kill a black thug, and they're ready to loot and riot at the drop of the hat. The question is, can you make sense of this African-American hypocrisy?[3]

In response, Page wrote,

> I am often asked why so many black Americans still support Jackson or Rev. Al Sharpton, even though their tactics seem mostly to be stuck in the 1960s. I find my answer in wire stories like this recent dispatch from New York City: "The morning 23-year-old Sean Bell was shot to death by police, his grieving relatives did something that has become almost

routine in such cases: They called Rev. Al Sharpton. Within hours, the longtime civil rights activist had consoled relatives, held two news conferences and begun organizing a community rally for the next day."

Now, just ask yourself: If police shot your son to death before his wedding and wounded two friends after firing 50 shots into their car and there was no gun found in their car, whom would you call?

Our civil societies and our Christian communities are still racist and out of touch with what ethical action toward racially just societies require. It seems that Cone is repeatedly proven correct in instances such as the Sean Bell case. If powerful Christians and Christian theologians—most are still white males—were really *passionate* about ending racism and racist violence, instead of Black Panthers marching in response to Sean Bell's killing,[4] Catholic bishops, every Christian denominational head, major theologians, and droves of Christians would have taken some sort of public action on behalf of the family *and* the (no doubt bewildered or guilty) police, demanding a thorough inquiry with effective and complete follow through and accountability. Nothing close to this took place! Arguably (at least in this incident) Cone is right—Christians and theologians were too busy being comfortable and safe to risk what would "make them unpopular."[5]

Who would know that Christians and Christian theologians have anything significant to say *in the concrete* about racism, tribalism, and xenophobia short of genocide and terrorist bombings?[6] Is not racial justice equally a "prolife" issue?[7] Notably, Cardinal Joseph Bernardin included racism as one of the issues in the famous "seamless garment" of the Consistent Ethic of Life.[8] As Cone and innumerable others proclaim, Christians have been lulled into believing that their meager participation in the civil rights movement of the 1960s resolved it all. Clearly, this is not the case!

True, it is still considered impolite and imprudent, if not immoral, to publicly express racialized sentiments or to admit that one considers the "other" is absolutely and irrefutably inferior to oneself and therefore one is entitled to privileges over the "other." Yet, it is also true that many can be easily aroused to violent racist acts if only presented with the images, such as 9/11 and the U.S. flag; a Jew and an Arab; a Kikuyu and a Maisai; a Chinese, and a Japanese and a Korean; the cross and an aum; or perhaps the Bible and the Koran. These contrasting images symbolize major racist exclusion of the "other" in our time.

In the complex globalized, ecologically threatened world of the first decade of the second millennium in the West, the heteronomy and the dominance of the West is waning, if not already gone. The growth and development of the triangle of the East and South formed by Africa, India, China, and the nations north of Australia pose not only vast religious and cultural differences to peoples of the West and North, but a disturbing economic threat, as well.[9] From the perspective of Europe, there is the utter "invasion" of "the children of the empire" of the past now coming "home to the motherland"; after all, they were taught for generations that the ideal, superior, and "civilized" cultures and the finest places to live were in Europe.[10] And, in the Eastern European nations ethnic divisions have returned and criminal economic monopolies prevent ordinary people from earning a living, and so they seek their fortune in (increasingly unfriendly) nations of Western Europe, that are already struggling with issues precipitated by new diversity.[11] In Africa, nations that gained independence in the last half of the twentieth century still struggle to balance and form national identities that can cohabitate with ethnic and tribal loyalties without devolving into tribalism and violence.[12] As history has shown, the mix of economic insecurity, memories of past negative experiences with the "other," and perceived irreconcilable difference forms the recipe for racialized fear, disrespect, physical violence, or even genocide.

Given this picture, what can Christianity, particularly Roman Catholicism, offer such a world to help resolve the realities of racism, tribalism, and xenophobia? Certainly, the Church's checkered racist past looms large behind any response to this question. Even today, a cursive review of the indices of major Catholic reference books yields the absence of the terms *race* or *racism*, seeming to demonstrate the low priority of these issues in the practice of the Church.[13] Yet, the Church can incorporate lessons from the past into renewed efforts to live authentically out of its rich doctrinal and ethical tradition.[14] But the Church cannot stop there. It is far past "high time" for renewed engagement on these issues, if the Church's voice is to remain credible in the world that is increasingly diverse.[15] A prophetic effort of biblical proportions needs to be taken up by all Christians against racism, tribalism, and xenophobia as the Church's revitalized mission and ministry.

The Church must seek out "best practices" that engage its prophetic and liberating tradition from the grassroots and globally and in a timely manner to bring about *racial justice* (not mere polite conversation or tolerance). Such efforts require profound authenticity and integrity, fidelity to daily encounters with the sacraments, spiritual disciplines and practices, and open transparent participation in the wider community of faith and in the civic community. This is a tall order. The challenge is to recover the rich Christian Classics[16] and retrieve the treasure trove of theory and praxis that has been allowed to lie dormant. Christianity possesses the "theopolitical dynamite"[17] to split away the debris of our complacency and fear of complexity and to free the Gospel treasures, ultimately liberating itself and all humanity. The Pontifical Council for Justice and Peace admonished,

> A change of heart cannot occur without strengthening spiritual convictions regarding respect for other races and ethnic groups. The Church, on its part, contributes to forming consciences by clearly presenting the entire Christian doctrine on this subject.[18]

Given the limits of this book, I can address only some of the theological resources that must be brought to bear on the various forms of racial injustice in the present day. I will highlight resources from the Franciscan theological tradition, a source long overshadowed by Thomism, but which is finding renewed cogency and relevance in our time. Since liturgical celebrations are the prime time when most Catholics gather in large numbers on a regular basis, I will suggest some themes to enhance pedagogical effectiveness of the liturgy in support of transformative action toward greater racial justice.

Race–Racism: The Compendium of the Social Doctrine of the Catholic Church

The Pontifical Council for Justice and Peace issued its compendium in 2005. In this resource, we find the most essential, abbreviated explanations of the Church's social teaching. Amazingly, the index of this book has only four entries listed under the heading "race-racism," and no heading for "tribalism," "xenophobia."[19] The first index entry yields no. 144, found in Chapter Three—"The Human Person and Human Rights" in Part II of that chapter titled "The Human Person as *Imago Dei*," and it is the first paragraph of subsection D. "The Equal Dignity of All People."[20] There in the first paragraph we read this: "The Incarnation of the Son of God shows the equality of all peoples with regard to their dignity." This central claim is preceded by biblical citations—Acts 10:34; cf. Rom 2:11; Gal 2:6; Eph 6:9; and a citation of no. 1934 of the *Catechism of the Catholic Church*.[21] The second paragraph cites no. 29 of *Gaudium et Spes* and stresses,

> Since something of the glory of God shines on the face of every person, the dignity of every person before God is the basis of the dignity of man before other men. Moreover, this is the ultimate foundation of the radical equality and brotherhood among all people, regardless of their race, nation, sex, origin, culture, or class.[22]

The second reference to "Race–Racism" is no. 431, a set of paragraphs situated in Chapter Nine—"The International Community" in section I of that chapter titled, "Biblical Aspects," and it is subsection B. "Jesus Christ, prototype and foundation of the new humanity." Here Jesus is acclaimed as the model and foundation of the new humanity. Following II Cor 4:4, it is held that in Jesus, who is the "likeness of God" that man finds fulfillment. The love of God made manifest in Christ's death on the cross has broken down the barriers of enmity (cf. Eph 2:12–18) "and for those who have a new life in Christ racial and cultural barriers are no longer causes of division (cf. Rom 10:12; Gal 3:26–28; Col 3:11)."

There the Holy Spirit is identified as the one who informs the Church of "the divine plan of unity that invokes the entire human race (cf. Acts 17:26; Eph 1:8–16)." The day of Pentecost, the Christian hallmark of unity amid diversity—when all present heard the same salvific message in their own language (Acts 2:6)—was the starting point of the Church's mission to restore the unity that was lost at Babel (Gen 11:1–9). Then, citing *Lumen Gentium* no. 1, it is asserted that "the human family is called to rediscover its unity and recognize the richness of its differences, in order to attain 'full unity in Christ.'"

The strongest condemnation of "Race–Racism" is in no. 433, found in section II of Chapter Nine, "The Foundational Rules of the International Community." Here it is asserted that the human person is central and "the natural inclination of persons and peoples to establish relationships among themselves are fundamental elements for building a true international community." The aim of such a community must be the common good, as it is understood and articulated in the *Catechism of the Catholic Church* no. 1911.[23] Materialistic and nationalistic ideologies "that contradict the values of the person integrally considered" are to blame for the lack of the existence of the common good in the present world. Then it is asserted, "In particular, any theory or form whatsoever of racism or racial discrimination is morally unacceptable." Here no less than five major conciliar and magisterial documents are cited to illustrate the strength of this tenet in the Church's moral tradition.[24]

Finally, no. 557 is found in section II. "Social Doctrine and the Commitment of the Lay Faithful," under subsection E. "Service in the various sectors of social life," of Chapter Twelve, "Social Doctrine and Ecclesial Action." This paragraph is part of the instruction concerning 2. "Service in culture." It states that the social analytical action of the lay faithful needs to move in several directions. Citing *Gaudium et Spes* no. 59, it asserts that first each person is guaranteed their rights "to a human and civil culture in harmony with the dignity of the human person, without distinction of race, sex, nation, religion or social circumstance." Then there is a list of what is required to support such dignity: "[T]he right of families and persons to free and open schools; free access to social communication that is free from all monopolies and ideological control; freedom of research; sharing thoughts, debate, and discussion." Here poverty and cultural deprivation are linked and the full recognition of cultural rights is acknowledged. The commitment to education and formation of the person is held as "the first concern of Christian social action."

Arguably if practiced these directives could bring the world a long way toward limiting—if not defeating—all forms of racial injustice.[25] But realistically, most Catholic faithful will not or do not have access to either the *Catechism* or the *Compendium*. Thus it is the task of all ministers to make these teachings more concrete and accessible to the faithful in the ordinary life of the Church, and to all people of goodwill. Therefore, it is imperative to passionately and explicitly raise to high relief the themes that reoccur in daily living and that the liturgical cycle requires and illuminates, making racial justice concrete. We will proffer such themes in what follows here. However, we first recall the dynamics at the heart of racism.

Racism and the Roman Catholic Doctrinal, Theological, and Moral Tradition

Facing Racism for What It Is

Following Albert Memmi, racism is the unjustifiable and intentionally permanent exclusion and discrimination against people exclusively based on criteria such as identity, culture, religion, gender, class, or physical constitution. Also racism is a system designed to intentionally or effectively achieve this unjust exclusion. This exclusion is not necessarily dependent on the presence of prejudice or good or bad motives. (Racism is both *de facto* and *de jure*.) In both its systemic and personal forms, it is a power used to subordinate and exclude for the sake of economic, social, political, religious, or ecclesial dominance. The 1988 Statement of the Pontifical Justice and Peace Commission, *The Church and Racism*, names nine types of racism: Exclusion and aggression (no. 8); institutional (no. 9); victimization and genocide of Aboriginal peoples (no. 10); religious and ethnic (no. 11); ethnocentrism (no. 12); social (no. 13); spontaneous racism toward foreigners (no. 14); anti-Semitism (no. 15); and artificial procreation and genetic manipulation (no. 16). With these in mind, we now explore several doctrinal, theological, and ethical themes and make explicit their relevance to a Christian understanding of "race" and racism.

Trinity: The Basis for Reality, Relationships, and Reverence for "Others"

What is there about the God whom Christians worship and seek to emulate that censures racism in all its forms? The God of the New Testament is a relational triune God—Father, Son, and Holy Spirit.[26] The three are so united in love that they are one, just as a three-way light bulb sheds a single light or like the flow from three jets of a fountain forms the thrust of a single upward burst of water. From the early days of Christianity, believers recognized the relations of the persons of the Trinity as a model for community life. The love between the persons formed a communion of radically related persons whose life is expressed "inward" toward one another, and "outward" to the human family, the earth, and all of creation.

Franciscan theologian John Duns Scotus (1265–1308) explained this relationship in a particularly helpful fashion. Scotus' entire understanding of reality is informed by his relational apprehension of the doctrine of the Trinity.[27] Particularly rich is his distinction between the activity of the Trinity *ad intra* and *ad extra*. The life of the Trinity *ad intra* is the internal aspect of Trinitarian life in which God functions necessarily in relation only to the other persons of the Trinity. The life of the Trinity *ad extra* is that aspect whereby the Trinity expresses its divine will, freely choosing creation and the Incarnation, for example. Scotus asserts that the essence of God involves both aspects of Trinitarian life, however. Of the two dimensions, the incommunicable (internal) dimension is seen as the logical *suppositum*,[28] which is necessary for the *ad extra* relationship.

In Scotus' view, the basis for the relationship among the three persons reveals an important aspect of God's essence. Scotus finds each of the persons and the relationship of communion of the three persons essential to the divine life.[29] By insisting on the integrity of each person of the Trinity in the absolute sense, he designates the basis upon which he can later assert that God's essence is also communion. There can be no relationship without at least two terms joined in interaction.[30] For our purposes, what is important about this relationship is that *each* of the persons of the Trinity, though distinct, having particular characteristics, understands each other as having equal worth. In today's terms, we call this relationship mutuality.[31]

Scotus' discussion of the Trinity is significant for understanding mutuality as fundamental to nonracialized or common human relationship for several reasons: First, Scotus' affirmation of both the individual personhood of each member of the Trinity as a *suppositum* of divine relations makes it possible for the Trinity to also stand as a paradigm for human relations. Second, the individuality Scotus claims for each person of the Trinity provides the metaphysical basis for mutuality; the persons of the Trinity are constituted *as persons* through the relationship (*ad intra*) of mutuality. Insofar as the Trinity as a communion of persons models the goal for human community, the Trinity models the relationship of mutuality as the goal of all human activity.[32]

Dr. Martin Luther King, Jr., expressed what this means for relationship among the diverse peoples of the human family:

> In a real sense, life is interrelated. All men are caught in an inescapable network of mutuality, tied in a single garment of destiny. Whatever affects one directly affects all indirectly. I can never be what I ought to be until you are what you ought to be, and you can never be what you ought to be until I am what I ought to be. This is the inter-related structure of reality.[33]

Regardless of our human differences, just as the distinct persons of the Trinity are of equal worth, so too are those humans who are created in the divine image and likeness of equal dignity and worth. And further, just as those persons of the Trinity are not who they are without the relationships of the other two persons, so too are humans, who reflect the divine identity, formed and brought to the fullness of their being through the relationships they engage, or fail to develop. This can take place for good or for ill; if we hold some humans as absolute inferior "others" we will certainly not only fail God, but ourselves and the whole of humankind, as well. Such a failure is idolatrous, in that we place our valuation of the "other" above that of the Triune, utterly relational God, who created, redeemed, and sustains all equally with just love.

Creation and the Imago Dei

Francis of Assisi, the patron saint of peacemaking and ecology, held that humans have an inviolable dignity because God created each person through love and for love. In Gen 1:26 each human being bears God's very image and likeness. This means that humans are whole persons, and distinct from the other creatures that were created "each after their own kind" (Gen 1:24). Each person is unique, yet joined to all "others" in a common human-ness. Humans retain this image of God in spite of the fact that each person is born into a world where each is affected by more sin than he or she actu-ally commits, and even though each personally sins. Overwhelmingly, God's generous love abounds and each person, in the face of sin, is still and contin-ually called to the very heart of God. Humans also have the responsibility of being cocreators and coredeemers with God, using their gifts and talents for the common good of all creation, but especially the poor. Humans must then treat all others with reverence and respect out of deference to the divine image each one bears. All people bear this divine image equally, so this rules out all forms of racism, sexism, and the like.

Bonaventure of Bagnoregio (1217–1277) understood humans as the *similitude* of God, the crown of creation. Created in the image and likeness of God, humans bear the greatest similarity to God. They are body-spirit creatures that know and are known to God both innately and experientially. Human bodies are good and integral to our human self-understanding. There is no place for dualism in Bonaventure's notion of the human per-son; and social and natural sciences have demonstrated how intricately all aspects of the human person affect one another. When this interrelation-ship within the human person is neglected, in interpersonal relationships or in the structures of societies, the quality of life is diminished. In fact dualis-tic ideas concerning the human body are at the root of many serious social, political, and human rights issues of racism and ethnic superiority.[34] In light of the *Imago Dei*, dualistic claims of "superiority" or "inferiority" smack of a false consciousness, a false reality, and sinfulness.

The fundamental error of racism is to deny the full humanity, intelligence, and equality of the "other"—differently skinned, cultured, religious—and thereby justify the limits placed on them.[35] *Gaudium et Spes* no. 27 and no. 29 most clearly and succinctly argue that the fundamental essential equality and dignity of all humans is grounded in their same nature and origin. All are redeemed by Christ and thus share in the same divine calling and destiny. This fundamental equality must be passionately acknowledged and acted upon by Christians and all people of goodwill.

The strong Catholic philosophical tradition also stresses that human persons are rational beings, who have the right to exercise their free will according to their conscience, and in a manner that demonstrates responsible participation in processes of self-actualization, social development, and the common good. However, the human person is complex and while each person is a person in community, each individual needs to be known and understood in her or his particularity as an historical subject, a relational being, an embodied subject, and a being who is fundamentally equal to all other human beings, yet who is uniquely original.[36] All forms of racism quash and destroy all of these dimensions of human vitality.

Incarnation

The humility of the Incarnation enabled Francis to see that because God became human in Jesus Christ, *all* of humanity was deified (*deificet*)—graced by God and empowered to becoming God-like.[37] For Francis, Jesus was the model human being, who set the standard and marked the way for all to journey toward the fullness of life with God. The human imagination could grasp the possibility of a life with God by observing Jesus' union with his *Abba*. Clearly, Jesus was like us, and we humans could see that there was also something about us that could be like Jesus. Just as an artist knows his or her work most intimately, so too, God knew how to best communicate boundless love to humanity.

Thus, it was in the stable at Bethlehem, that things concretely human began to communicate the profound love of God for us. It was the physical, embodied discomfort of an infant in a manger that profoundly marked Francis. In the manger, we see the generous love of God made concrete, but important for our purposes, the marvelous capacity of humanity—even an unsophisticated baby—to communicate that love. Thus, Francis understood humanity as good and uniquely beloved of God, bearing the divine image and likeness and an inviolable dignity from the moment of creation. This image of God is found in *all* humans.[38]

It is this very dignity that is so profoundly violated especially through racism based on skin color or other phenotypical features. One's physical body is not separable from one's identity. To demean or demonize any dimension of the physical body is to detract from the personal dignity of a human person. This is why color-coded racism, physical abuse, or the physical enslavement of persons is so egregious, particularly when combined with myths of sexual depravity and violence.[39]

The Church and Its Mission

Lumen Gentium no. 1 states: "The Church in Christ, is in the nature of a sacrament, a sign and instrument, that is, of communion with God and of unity among all people." The Church's central understanding regarding the significance of history and ordinary human experience as the medium of God's salvation and revelation is compromised and violated by the sin of racism, tribalism, and xenophobia.[40] *All* baptized people are called to act as mediators of God's love and liberality. That can become reality only in the daily activity of the faithful when God's liberating power and universal sacrament of salvation shines through them to reveal to others the characteristics of their identity as people of God. Such activity is always life giving, and does not detract in any way from the fundamental respect and dignity due every human person.

Racism is by definition "not merely one sin among many, it is a radical evil that divides the human family and denies the new creation of a redeemed world."[41] Theologically, racism in all of its forms is idolatry in that it replaces the absolute centrality and superiority of God with the absolute centrality and superiority of a given racialized criteria as the focal value of life. Racism is also a repugnant heresy because it would deny that the gifts of the Holy Spirit are given to all the baptized, who are each called to witness to their oneness in Christ (Gal 3:28). Beyond that, it is a sign of the demonic because it kills by blocking reconciliation, liberation, and the flourishing of the human family.

The Church as Family

One of the strongest images of the unity of the Church and its mission to bring about unity is that of the "Family of God."[42] Recently, the Churches of Africa focused on this image and theologians have recovered its deep tradition in the Church.[43] The main narrative framework of this image includes creation and the fall and the offer of salvation. The two Covenants that form the skeleton of salvation history are at the heart of the development of the three-part narrative. Salvation history is also the story of the Church because it deals with the communities of believers and their rise, decline, and renewal through all of history. While there is no systematic treatise on the Church as such, persuasive efforts have been made toward articulating the components of what this might look like.[44]

Maurice Schepers holds that the development of the Church is both human and divine, the fruit of the presence of the Word in history, Jesus Christ. Thus, through ministerial and lay structures ("family structures") the maturing of the Church takes place. That process included both growth and decline in both individual members but also in the Church as an institution. Thus, the axiom, "*sancta simul et semper purificanda*" is fitting and, as we shall see, reflects the reality of any family in history.[45]

The notion of the Church as family contains a cohesive set of ideas that describe the Church and it can be articulated systematically. Throughout history, the family existed in some form and it provided a matrix for all genuine advancement. The anchor for the model of the Church as family is Jesus the Primal Ancestor (Acts 2:36). There is the forward dimension of the memory of those family members who have died and gone before us (the Communion of Saints) as well as those who are yet to come (unborn children).

The twofold relationship between the Church and Christ and the Church and the Saints and Martyrs (Rev 19:5–10) sustains the Church in history. As *Lumen Gentium* proclaims, at the center of the Church is Christ who adopts us as children (no. 3) and who draws all things to himself (no. 48). Here we have what Schepers calls "the generational or 'vertical' aspect of the Church as God's Family."[46]

Another dimension of the Church is seen in the activity of Jesus. In one instance he declared, "My mother and my brothers are those who hear the word of God and keep it."(Lk 8:21; Mk 3:34; Mt 12:49; cf. Mt 15:24). Here we have a dynamic development that is pertinent to not only the African context, but in the globalized world. While the family unit is the foundational unit of society, it cannot remain healthy without building relationships beyond itself. As Pope John Paul II warned of this when presenting this image to the Church of Africa, loyalties to those who are like us are indeed natural and nurturing; but they can also smother us and keep us from fulfilling our God-given calling, while also preventing others from living life to its fullest.[47]

Within the Church there are tensions between individuals, groups, institutional loyalties, and cultural preferences.[48] Extreme manifestations of any one dimension result in unhealthy situations. Thus, the Church as the Family of God needs to be balanced by the Pauline image of the Church as the Body of Christ. Schepers creatively restates I Cor 12:

> The [family] is not one member but many. Even were one [family member] to say, "I don't belong here, for I am not a [parent]," he/she continues to be a part of the [family] … There are many members but one [family]. The [Father] cannot say to the [Mother], "I do not need you," nor a [brother to a sister], "I do not need you."[49]

Maintaining a *positive and creative* tension between nurturing found through belonging and the assertion found in individuation is necessary. The family is in a position to instill and nurture the moral imagination and sensitivities, as well as the spiritual and intellectual practices to enable new generations of Christians to discern this balance and live accordingly. This image counters tribalism and ethnocentrism that plagues Africa and elsewhere.[50]

The Church as Unity with Diversity

Two important biblical discussions of diversity are found in the story of Babel (Gen 11:1–9) and the account of Pentecost (Acts 2). An important lesson that surfaces through the contrast of these two texts is that life amid the God-given human diversity needs to be Spirit-centered, or it will collapse into idolatry of self-indulgence of all sorts that taken to its logical end, results in death and destruction. By contrast, the presence of the Spirit brings understanding and unity.[51] Any efforts, whether by individual Christians or by Church organizations working against racisms, must be anchored in spiritual practices and prayer that grounds them in God. This is particularly true for those with power and privilege who seek to exchange their trust in those securities for the deeper nurturing that comes through living out the love and justice of God.

The House Divided

"A house divided against itself cannot stand" (Mk 13:35). Indeed, it is Christ who has broken down the dividing wall of hostility between peoples (Eph 2:15).[52] Yet, in many instances, Church leadership cannot recognize or resolve the racial and ethnic divisions that plague the Church and society because they are deeply imbedded and complicit in them.[53] In the North Atlantic nations particularly, while the overt systems of racism have been outlawed, Christians are often caught up in subtler forms of racisms. Still, the stress on persons of color in daily life in a system controlled by the white majority readily includes physical and psychological maladies like identity confusion, alienation, and even self-destructive behavior.

Ched Myers made four strategic suggestions for Christians striving to break down barriers rooted in various forms of racism in the present day.[54] First, is to not reduce racism to merely an individual attitude; social structures also need transformation. Second, is to refrain from universalizing racial problems by reducing racism to acts of only "a few bad apples." Such thinking ignores the reality that not everyone named as a racialized "other" plays on a level field. Third, the resignation that suggests that others "suffer through the present" and look forward to the future heavenly perfection, denies the deliberate and conscious construction of major sources of racialized oppression, and smacks of idolatry, denying the presence and power of God to act through us in history. The need for "affirmative action" or the conscious creation of "just opportunity" programs to correct past injustices of racialized oppression still exists. When hard data on wages, employment, housing, or any other category concerning people classified as "other" is compared with that of the defining majority, wide discrepancies still abound.

Because all forms of racism are rooted in fears and upheld by structures giving security to dominant populations, Myers' insight is particularly useful:

> when a bearing wall has to go, and our fears of collapse paralyse us, let us recall that "the stone that the builders rejected has become the cornerstone" of a new structure (Mk 12:10), in which those of every tribe and tongue and people and nation are welcomed as equals (Rev 5:9; 7:9).[55]

Christian Social Ethics: Biblical Love, Justice, and Mutuality

Racism is a matter of the ethics of power (as well as justice and love).[56] On one hand, it is necessary for the "oppressors" to take up a healthy inner sense of power and self-worth in relation to others. At the same time they need to let go of any sense of self-worth or power that is parasitic and dependent on the oppression or disempowerment of the "other" to thrive.[57] Such a shift requires changes on many fronts and involves moral formation in both cognitive (intellect and reason) and affective (emotional and experiential) forms.[58] It also requires engaging in the dialectic of coercion and persuasion and of consent and command to effect a change of heart as well as a change of habit. Any sound strategy for combating racism must address individuals, groups, and structures. Such strategies can be viewed as "faith seeking realization" that flow from our "faith seeking understanding."[59]

All forms of racism involve matters of justice. Simply put, justice is that which renders to each what is due to them. In light of distributive justice, racism denies the necessities of a life of dignity that is given to all from the origins of creation. In terms of social justice, racisms discount the many gifts of diverse peoples that are needed for the common good, and that must be expressed for the holistic fulfillment of each person. Racism renders commutative justice moot because it breaks down all trust and respect between one and the "other," and no agreement to fulfill obligations is reliable.

Ultimately, racism is an issue of human rights that buttresses the true flourishing of humanity. Moreover, justice (distributive) at times requires *unequal* treatment to assuage morally relevant differences. Thus, strategies of "affirmative action" or "just opportunity" require the diligent attention of the Christian community. This notion is deeply rooted in the tradition of the preferential option for the poor that permeates the Hebrew Testament, in particular. This reality is fully recognized in the Pontifical Council for Justice and Peace 2001 document *Contribution to World Conference against Racism, Racial Discrimination, Xenophobia and Related Intolerance.*[60]

Affirmative action is aimed at providing just opportunities for persons who have traditionally been underrepresented in essential (often life-threatening) ways in society, and it is a function of distributive justice.[61] While various agents are charged with fulfilling distributive justice, the government is a primary agent required to ensure the common good.

The confusion of justice with equality distorts the legitimacy of affirmative action. Equality does not always ensure justice. A tyrant may be equally oppressive to all of his subjects, but he is not just. Indeed, equality is valuable only insofar as it serves what it is set against. Equal rights serve justice when they effectively oppose such things as arbitrariness, prejudice, structural monopolies, or unmerited privileges. Freedom is often misappropriated and allowed to take priority over enforcement of restrictive regulations, but justice is not served when freedom becomes license to serve one's every whim. History shows that to leave the distribution of some dimensions of the essentials of life to "the forces of the market" or to volunteerism fails simply because problems are too complex and the common-sense public morality is too primitive.[62]

Incentives to create just opportunity to serve the common good are numerous. Long ago, Herbert Marcuse stated, "A society is sick if its fundamental institutions and relationships [structures] are so designed that they do not permit the employment of the available material and the development of human experience."[63] The time, talent, and treasure given over to racialized oppression by those who would keep "others" in "their place" as well as efforts to dislodge persons from these unjust situations is lost, and can never be recovered or set toward creative and positive ends that can serve the whole of humankind. Further, excluded peoples, when they can bear their oppression no longer, have exploded into violence and aggression against those who have held them back. These costs are indeed high and affect *entire* societies, not only the victims of racism. The guilt on the part of the powerful privileged who acted to exclude "others" is healthy, for it signals moral imbalance and the need for individual and collective action toward inclusion of the "other." What is legal is not always moral; and following the Catholic moral tradition, what is "just by nature" and in coherence with Divine Law is the standard that must abide.[64]

Distributive justice, the foundation for affirmative action, is deeply rooted in the biblical preferential option for the poor, and the moral maxims developed in the Catholic moral tradition set the stage for four major criteria for preferential affirmative action, opening opportunities for those traditionally underrepresented in vital areas of life and society: (1) No alternatives to enforced preference are available. (2) The prejudice against the group must reach the level of depersonalization. (3) The bias against the group is not private or narrowly localized, but it is entrenched in the culture and distributive systems of the society (its laws, myths, institutions, etc.). (4) The members of the victim group must be visible as such and thus lack an avenue of escape from their disempowered status.[65]

Maguire refutes the most frequently raised objections against affirmative action.[66] The charge of "reverse discrimination" is illogical and is terribly misleading in light of the four criteria that frame who is eligible for preference. Is it ever possible to "niggerize" a white male in North American society? Is it possible to make him dark-skinned, speak in an African American idiom, and constantly experience unjust discrimination in employment and housing on that basis alone? The accusation that "preferential redistribution leads to backlash" also offers a weak argument. Indeed, all governments have policies that give all sorts of preferences to individuals and groups such as veterans, children, elderly, and persons of certain income levels—yet, rarely are objections raised against policies that make special allowances for these. The most controversial objection remains the question, "How do you set quotas?" To this, Maguire responds, "Inflexible quotas do not meet the flexibility of reality. They are not defensible. The guiding principle for flexible quotas or goals is the breakup of monopolies by bringing in ascertainable numbers of available persons from the previously excluded group."[67]

The relationship between biblical love and justice is an intimate one. In the Hebrew Scriptures, God is identified as both "love" and "justice." God is a "God of justice" (Is 30:18) whose heart is set on justice (Jer 9:24). God "loves justice" (Ps 99:4). It is the foundation of God's holiness (Is 5:16). God is holy, because God is just! And love and justice are not separable in the mind of God. The just God "secures justice for widows and orphans, and loves the alien who lives among you, giving them food and clothing" and compels the moral corollary, "You too must love the alien" (Deut 10:17–19). The practice of *sedaqah* (justice) requires living out the *hesed* (steadfast love) of God. And further, "The supreme delicacy of charity is to recognize *the right* of the person being given to."[68] In light of this, racial justice is simply but profoundly an unqualified inalienable right and an absolutely necessary obligation for all humanity.

Xenophobia and the Hebrew Testament Mandate to Love the Stranger

The biblical mandate to love the stranger is particularly pertinent in light of the xenophobia of the twenty-first century.[69] In the Book of the Covenant (Ex 22:20–23:33) two clear statements of the mandate are found: "You shall not oppress a stranger; you know the heart of the stranger, for you were strangers in the land of Egypt" (Ex 23:9) and "You shall not wrong a stranger or oppress him, for you (yourselves) were strangers in the land of Egypt" (Ex 22:20). These two texts need to be linked to the whole of the Torah, and they frame all of the social commands. At the center of these requirements is the authority of God and divine compassion.

Significantly, Israel is compelled to recall their experience in Egypt and to empathize (reach into their very soul—*nephesh*) with those strangers in their midst, raising to high relief the common humanity of Israelite and stranger bridged by God's love and care for all. This kind of obedience to God requires active participation of memory and moral imagination.

The laws in the Book of the Covenant are found in Deuteronomic Law and protection of widows, orphans, landless, and Levites is specified (Deut 16:11, 14).[70] Provision for them is made through gleaning (Deut 24:19–21) and pledges are protected (Deut 24:17). A social tax that benefits aliens is established in Deut 14:28 (cf. 26:12). In summary, "You shall remember you were a slave in Egypt and the Lord your God redeemed you from there; therefore, I command you to do this" (Deut 24:18). It is God's just love that links the relationship between Israel and the strangers. Natives and strangers are bound by the same laws (Lev 24:22; Num 15:15) and for Israel not to match the holiness of God through its loving and just actions, is to part ways with God.

Strangers (*gērūm*) include those who are from outside the country (see Judg 17:7) and without family or land where they are living and seek protection in their host country because they have no social standing or cultural roots there. Most importantly, in light of present-day xenophobia, the biblical *gērūm* are distinct from travelers or merchants who are just passing through the country (cf. Deut 15:3). All of the laws governing both Israelites and strangers have their origin in God's grace and authority (Book of the Covenant), the love of God as the basis of election (Deuteronomy) and the holiness of God present in God's people (Priestly Laws).

In today's globalized world, it is the rare place where there is no history of war, occupation, colonization, enslavement, or displacement in the reach of human memory. A major step toward reconciliation and healing of xenophobia and other forms of racial injustice today must include understanding the history of the nations, especially one's own. Most families have some memory of "moving," "being expelled," "forced assimilation," or "immigrating"—and being a "stranger" in some form. Alternatively, those who were oppressive colonizers and slave masters have been known to provide protection for former colonists and slaves in times of famine. "The Deuteronomic Law for the community states: 'You shall not abhor an Egyptian, because you were a stranger in his land' (Deut 23:8). So in the third generation the Egyptians may enter the community of God."[71] The memory of suffering in the "heart of the stranger" bears potential for bringing an end to repression in our day. An important role for the Church is to open itself to this memory, and assist others in allowing it to touch their hearts and awaken their vulnerability and move us to act on behalf of the racialized "other."

Xenophobia and the Christian Testament Witness

The New Testament carries forward the memory of Israel's experience as "sojourner," "stranger," and "alien," and this memory motivates Christian inclusivity. In the New Testament, the Greek word *paroikos* is the equivalent of the Hebrew word *gēr,* and is translated as "sojourner" or "resident alien"(Acts 7:6, 13–17; Matt 1:11, 12, 17; Eph 2:19).

Interestingly, the word most often used in the New Testament in relation to the Greek word *philoxenia* meaning "hospitality" is the Greek term *xenos,* which literally means "foreigner," "stranger," or even "enemy." The person who receives the guests is known as *philoxenos,* or a "lover of strangers." For our purposes it is interesting to contemplate the alternative possibility, "love of enemies," for frequently the depth of fears and insecurities move people to perceive the racialized "other" as the "enemy."

In the story of the Good Samaritan (Luke 10:30–37), not only was he good, but also he cared for "an enemy" and in doing so, unlike the Jewish religious leaders, he acted as God, the host, would act.[72] Indeed, Jews and Samaritans were enemies. But the Samaritan's *heart* went out to the injured victim (Lk 10:33). In describing the care the Samaritan offered the victim, Luke reflects the care given by Israel to their Judean captives (2 Chr 28:8–15).

The Samaritan fulfills the law of hospitality, and more. The Samaritan, who had every reason *not* to care for the Jew in the ditch, did so with generosity!

The moral messages one can take from this action are many. First, Jesus shows remarkable disregard for the religious and racial prejudice between Jews and Samaritans merely by including a Samaritan as a positive character in the story. But what is more, that character becomes the moral hero of the story! It was because of the Samaritan's *heartfelt compassion* that he was able to do what was right and just.[73] To feel compassion is to somehow bring oneself and another onto a plane where both have an *equal worth*. The moral wisdom of the heart, not known with the intellect, was what informed his decision to act. To find this common moral worth the Samaritan had to cross both religious and ethnic boundaries. In the end, he was drawn to the deepest and most significant plane, namely, the place of common human dignity. Like the Priest and the Levite, the Samaritan had to prioritize his values, and his self-concept in relation to those values. His lifestyle and self-concept gave him a certain sense of power over those who peopled his world. A long tradition of prejudice against Jews militated against him treating the Jew in the ditch with mutual respect. Yet, his heart was not petrified by fears of loss of personal safety, power, and privilege. Rather, he chose to exercise his moral imagination and to try a different course. He shifted his identity from "the enemy who could yield power over a vulnerable foe," to that of "a neighbor and companion on the human journey." Now the dynamics of power were changed to a sharing of power and mutuality. Though each remained unique and distinct—one serving and one being served, a Samaritan and a Jew—they were of equal worth.

Cultural, ethnic, and racialized pluralism confront us daily. As the Samaritan so clearly showed, the foundational moral experience is reverence for human persons and their environment. Only when we acknowledge our commonality and extend mutual regard to the "other" is any dialogue possible. The biblical call to mutuality, love, and justice points insistently towards a holistic approach to personal morality, a new politics and economics, all based on a full realization of our foundational relationality. In a pluralistic, global, and environmentally threatened age we cannot afford alienation; our survival and salvation depends on it! Indeed, through engagement in dialogue, it may be the "other" who can show us the deeper moral wisdom. Only from a stance of mutuality will we, like the Good Samaritan be able to know reverence for the person and their environment. There is no "other" way!

Islamophobia: Love of Enemy in an Age of Terrorism?

To some extent, in all forms of racism, tribalism and xenophobia fear of the "other" is involved. At the depths of these oppressive exclusions, fear becomes terror and the "other" becomes the enemy. Terror is a primal emotion that operates outside of a person's cognitive structure. Psychoanalyst

Paul Mestancik provides a helpful explanation of "terror" that is best kept in his own words:

> Its primary causes are the threat of annihilation and hopelessness to defend against the annihilation. A person may be seized with terror when he or she is faced with death (which may be other than physical) and has no power to defend oneself. There is also, perhaps, a sense of the irrational in the situation. That is, the person filled with terror may not understand why the outside force involved is making the threat. The threat does not fit into the cognitive structure that forms the basis of a person's understanding of self and world. Terror, as a primal emotion, erupts from underneath the cognitive structure of the person. It is likely to force aside that structure, overpower it at least temporarily, and in extreme cases actually destroy the structure of meaning that has formed the self-understanding of the person. This means that while a community might include in its "world" an explanation of possible terror to its members, in an attempt to keep its terrified members within its cognitive structure, such explanations might or might not suffice to control terror. It may be that incorporating a rationale into the cognitive structure cannot contain terror.
>
> Terror can be distinguished from fear and panic. Fear can be said to be a range of anxieties about threat; indeed terror might be the extreme point on the line. One might then say that terror is an extreme fear of the sort that threatens the cognitive structure. I may fear that I may lose my job or that I may die due to a recently discovered malignancy, but I can easily incorporate that into my cognitive structure ... Panic is related to terror in that it can be said to be a sudden irrational emotion, but one that is likely to subside or disappear; terror, while perhaps equally sudden, does not go away. It becomes a permanent threat—something that I cannot make disappear.[74]

This explains why the first question people in the United States asked on 9/11 was, "But why do they hate us?" Most U.S. Christians perceived themselves as innocent bystanders, and now victims of evil radical Muslim "others" in a world suddenly turned into Hell. Most knew little about the basic tenets of Islam and could only think the worst.[75] They could not separate fear, grief, anger, vengeance, and actual cause and effect. The capacity to maintain the perspective that mainline Muslims are just, loving, peaceful believers in one God was often lost and needed to be reclaimed.[76] This is also pertinent to situations of war and ethnic conflict that erupt into violence.

Dealing with extremes in our perceptions of the "other" requires an equally extreme shift in shaping our moral framework. The hard saying of Jesus to "Love your enemies" (Lk 6:27–36) pushes for such a change.[77] The love he requires is outright and unconditional; there are *no* qualifications. To the contrary, Jesus compels kindness and generosity toward one who is fully capable of inflicting physical and material injury (Lk 6:29–30). Nor is there any indication of acting on a hidden agenda by placating the enemy so they will change their posture, or any hint of psychological gaming, trying to convince oneself that the enemies are not real but only primitive, uncivilized children that can be tolerated. Nor does this love of enemies engage in a competitive spirit by stressing God's overwhelming power to rule the world, ultimately defeating any enemy. As in Lev 19:17–18 (where "neighbor" is the enemy) the only motive for obeying the command to love is to be the desire of God and the need to imitate God's holiness.

Jesus is addressing *all* those who listen to him, whether they are Jews or Gentiles, the poor or the rich, the converted ones or those in need of conversion. Significantly, it is to those who have just experienced his healing power and compassion that Jesus addressed his difficult commands. Thus, they know that he is trustworthy. For those of us who are recovering from terror and other violence, this is an important detail.

Also of major import for us who live in the globalized and terrorized twenty-first century, is that both Jesus and the martyr Stephen ask *God* to forgive the injustices done to them; *they* do not claim to immediately be able to forgive *on their own*. Their words and desire express an inner spiritual and psychological shift; a letting go of their own feeble and ineffective power, and placing themselves in God's hands. This step marks an engagement of God's transforming, healing, and empowering grace and mercy so necessary in recovery from both perpetrating and receiving racialized injustice.

Francis of Assisi also can teach us about overcoming Islamophobia.[78] At a critical point in the history of Western Christianity, when the Saracens (Muslims) held the entire holy land, Francis of Assisi made a bold and life changing move. In a world where Pope Innocent III plotted war for six years, squandered the resources of the entire Church on military preparations, and then led the Fifth Crusade, only to be tragically defeated by the Muslims, Francis began an interfaith dialogue!

Francis made a special journey behind enemy lines to talk with the Sultan, Melek al-Kamil. They spent the first twenty-five days of September 1219 living and praying together. Their conversations ended with Melek al-Kamil giving Francis a horn that was used for the call to prayer, and asking Francis to pray for him, so that by divine inspiration, he might adhere to the religion that was most pleasing to God.

Sadly, on September 26, 1219, the Christian Crusaders stormed the Sultan's forces. Remarkably, the Sultan made no less than five separate offers of peace during that offensive alone, but the Christians refused them all and were ultimately overcome. To make a long story very short, Melek al-Kamil treated his captives with extraordinary generosity and kindness. He continued to offer peace through the 1220s, culminating in the peace treaty of 1229 with Frederick II.

Terror and hatred cannot survive in a world community bonded by trust, mutual respect and a desire to care for "others"; we too can make a difference in our terrified world by making our love concrete. One place for teaching and learning about the concrete expressions of love, justice, and mutuality is the liturgy. Most Catholics do not engage in any other form of catechesis on an ongoing basis.

Liturgical Practices and Preaching: Pedagogical Tools against Racism

Liturgical Practices

One dimension of the liturgy is that in addition to its primary function of worship (doxology), it also functions as a tool of formation (pedagogy). In themselves, liturgical formulations are always social constructions that reflect cultural locations and value systems. The challenge for the worshiping community is to engage in ethically disciplined worship that is unqualifiedly hospitable to *all* who seek Christ. Several general principles illuminate and delimit fruitful liturgical practices for promoting racial justice.

When the Catholic community gathers for worship, it proclaims that God *alone* is God. Through sign and symbol all that would encroach on God's status—nationalism, classism, racism, and militarism—is challenged and set aside. God must be named in an inclusive and varied manner so as to avoid the impression that we positively know God in *only one way*.

In the liturgy we proclaim that God is the Creator, and *all* humans are called to be cocreators with God and the guardians of all of creation. This counters, for example, practices of environmental racism, placing the health of "others" at risk.[79]

The Catholic liturgy commemorates the life, death, and resurrection of Jesus Christ and it links the baptized through a covenant that is both vertical—in relationship with God, and horizontal—in relationship with our neighbors, indeed with all of creation. Or, as Herbert McCabe, OP, puts it, "baptism is not the sacrament of membership of the Church; it is the sacrament of membership of humanity."[80] In worship, Catholics celebrate the Incarnation and the continued presence of Jesus Christ, who in his lifetime, as a Jew born in despised Nazareth, was identified with those who were "other," and he remained faithful to those outcasts—even unto death on the cross.

Catholics claim to share the Eucharistic banquet with *all* peoples here and in the future with God. God's passionate love for and affirmation of the dignity of fallen humanity is offered to us in the Eucharist. In each Eucharist Catholics believe, the Christ becomes present to us. The Eucharist can be understood as a continuation of the Incarnation and the ongoing fruit of the passion. The bread, the wine, and the human—each in their own way are made holy and whole through the presence of Christ. Each communicant is affirmed and given the grace to live into her or his God-given dignity.

In St. Francis of Assisi's understanding, to fail to show proper reverence for Christ present in the Eucharist or Christ present in the human person is to also blaspheme the other. It was Jesus' utter self-emptying love (*kenosis*) that Francis recognized at the core of Christ's influence over the human heart.[81] Human dignity is established in the Incarnation, confirmed through the Passion, and nurtured in the Eucharist. As followers of the Christ who liberates all from sin, Christians are called to liberate one another, spiritually, personally, and institutionally.

The liturgy also celebrates the transforming presence and action of the Holy Spirit, and it creates a foretaste of the Kingdom of God. God's Reign is modeled and experienced in the microcosm when barriers of race, class, culture, age, sex, or ideology are broken down through the power of the Holy Spirit. "The Father of the Poor"—"consoles ... washes what is soiled, waters what is dry, heals what is wounded; bends what is rigid, warms what is cold, guides those lost ... gives the seven sacred gifts."[82] In worship Catholics ritually express their longings for the future, repentance, forgiveness, and reconciliation. There Catholics cry out to God for racial justice and *shalom* and for the assembly to give its "Amen" to that plea. It is the place where Catholics take their first steps forward toward offering themselves, their time and talents to God and the world through the Eucharistic Bread and Wine.

The liturgy sustains and nurtures Catholics in their daily lives of discipleship and ministry. The liturgical gathering is a place to practice the diverse and inclusive lifestyle of the Reign of God. It is the place to be prepared for living out the attributes of love, justice, and mutuality that characterize the Reign of God in the everyday, routine, and the mundane with *all* they encounter.

The worshiping assembly transcends individuality and emphasizes the Christian corporate identity as members of a body of believers within a broader society. There is also the opportunity to participate in making a corporate confession of belief and admission of common brokenness and the sin of institutional racism. And significantly, there is also support for one another in making new beginnings and following through on transforming commitments to open opportunities for leadership and making all dimensions of Church life inclusive and welcoming. This can be a fundamental tool in challenging the insecurities and fears that stand at the heart of intolerance and aggression of racism in all its forms. Being reassured of one's ultimate value before God, and being surrounded by those who believe that *the God who welcomes all* is the ultimate center of value, is vital to sustaining an antiracist stance in a complex, globalized, and ecologically threatened world.

Good liturgy does not take place in isolation, but rather it engages with the culture or cultures of the context in which it is celebrated. The texts, the architecture, the music, the art, the vestments, the arrangement of the worship space—all speak profoundly the values of those inviting the participation of others, or discouraging it. The universal dimension of Christianity is engaged by calling forth an awareness of global realities beyond the local setting, as well. When prayer and teaching is extended beyond the local to the wider world the consciousness and the empathy of the community is shifted to the universal purposes of the creation, the global human family, and the common good.

Preaching

Preaching is perhaps the most critical opportunity for proclaiming the Gospel challenges and resources for racial justice. But preachers need to integrate the Church's social doctrine on racial justice and discuss the issues of racism, tribalism, or xenophobia in their homilies. Clarence Williams suggests that preaching a message that can bring about racial healing begins with the "preacher's finding their voice" in speaking about racial sobriety.[83] There are many texts such as Galatians 2 and occasions such as special national or ethnic celebrations that lend themselves to such preaching.

A most useful insight Williams raises is that preaching on racisms immediately engenders anxiety, based on fear, ignorance, and guilt (FIG).[84] The preacher needs to deal with her or his own feelings of anxiety before any effective preaching on racisms can take place. A major step in overcoming this anxiety is for the preacher to simply break the silence, and begin to talk about racisms. However, breaking the silence involves breaking open the word in a style that is a comfort to their listeners, who have a "FIG-complex" and at the same time helps them to cope with their own politics of niceness that does not allow for talk about the painful topics of racisms.

Breaking the silence can be done by considering the challenge given to Christians that Jesus expressed in Jn 17:11, "that they all may be one just as we are." Certainly his vision is readily like-minded with the vision of the Eucharistic banquet celebrated at each Mass, and the familial image of the Lord's Prayer that precedes the reception of the Eucharist by the faithful.

To fail to oppose racisms in preaching is to scandalously support them by the Church's silence. The saddest moments in Church history were when good people did nothing:

> When Hitler attacked the Jews I was not a Jew, therefore I was not concerned.
>
> And when Hitler attacked the Catholics, I was not a Catholic, and therefore, I was not concerned.
>
> And when Hitler attacked the unions and the industrialists, I was not a member of the unions and I was not concerned.
>
> Then Hitler attacked me and the Protestant church—and there was nobody left to be concerned.[85]

The question for our generation is, will we be complacent and complicit with the nullification of human life and dignity of our day that is racism, tribalism, and xenophobia?

Racism: Ecclesiastical and Institutional Dimensions

The credibility of the Church in the world depends on its modeling racial justice in its own institutional structures and practices. It needs to develop and openly share affirmative action plans, ongoing practices, and strategies of accountability to maintain transparency concerning institutional racial justice. For example, The Catholic Bishops' Conference of England and Wales developed and initiated excellent plans for safeguarding the Church against institutional racisms.[86] Their document, "Diversity and Equality Guidelines," outlines the content for racial justice that needs to be part of the policies and practices for Church parishes and all Church-related institutions and organizations. The guidelines are grounded in no. 29 of *Gaudium et Spes*. They address six areas of diversity: race, gender, disability, religion, belief, sexual orientation, and age; employment practices, representation in Catholic bodies and organizations, volunteer participation in Catholic bodies, positive action, and establish ongoing monitoring and evaluation of their implementation. The intent is that these guidelines witness to the Gospel and that they enable the Church to be respectful, inclusive, and in tune with the spirit and letter of the laws of the European Union, as well as those of England and Wales, while also being respectful of the Catholic ethos of their institutions and organizations. Indeed, the Church's internal law, especially in Canons 208, 220, and 222 no. 2, requires these policies and practices.[87]

Conclusion: "That they all may be one . . ."

The themes addressed here are certainly far from an exhaustive exposé. The intent was to represent some key stepping-stones shaping the pathway toward racial justice, unity of the Christina community, and the global human family. There is no better hallmark for this mandate than Jesus' prayer for unity that expresses his passionate desire that it be so:

> Consecrate them in truth—your word is truth—for I have sent them into the world as you sent me into the world. For their sake, I go to the sacrifice by which I am consecrated, so that they too may be consecrated in truth.
> I pray not only for these but also for those who through their word will believe in me. May they all be one as you Father are in me and I am in you. May they be one in us; so the world may believe that you have sent me.[88]

4

Techniques of Dominance

Central Manifestations of Racism, Tribalism, and Xenophobia

Introduction: Strategic Church Definitions of "Racisms"

Pontifical Justice and Peace Commission

The most thoroughgoing discussion by the Magisterium of racial justice issues is found in the Pontifical Justice and Peace Commission's *The Church and Racism: Toward a More Fraternal Society*. This first-ever Vatican document to deal exclusively with racism is dated November 3, 1988, but it was released on February 3, 1989. Unlike in documents promulgated by many local Churches around the globe, here the Pontifical Justice and Peace Commission gave a more adequate definition of racism in its multiple forms. This approach to defining racism allowed the inclusion of the broader related conflict issues that have often been emptied of the depth of their denigrating capacity because the link to the dynamics of racism are not stressed. In a globalized world, racism can no longer be adequately defined exclusively as biologically rooted and color-coded. The Pontifical Commission outlined no less than nine distinct racisms and it considered all of these in light of the Gospel.

Exclusion and Aggression

Just as racialized aggression is operative paradigmatically in colonialism, in the complex relationships of the globalized world, numerous new situations have emerged where similar dynamics play out.[1] One important new set of circumstances is the unprecedented global reality of displaced peoples on every continent in overwhelming numbers. In his award-winning book, *Migrations*[2] photojournalist Sebastião Salgado documented and gave witness to this phenomenon when he remarked,

People have always migrated, but something different is happening now. For me, this worldwide population upheaval represents a change of historic significance. We are undergoing a revolution in the way we live, produce, communicate, and travel. Most of the world's inhabitants are now urban. We have become one world: in distant corners of the globe, people are being displaced essentially for the same reasons.[3]

Indeed, we need not look far on any continent to see people experiencing the direct and indirect discrimination that is brought about by racialized exclusion and aggression. In Latin America, Africa, and Asia, the indigenous and darker-skinned rural poor have been driven by "development" from their sustainable life on the land to seek safety and survival in the cities. Racialized political shifts have sent millions on the road to escape genocide. In Eastern Europe, the collapse of the Soviet Union released new religious and ethnic wars forcing yet other millions to look for refuge. And when the cities would not or could not accommodate these vulnerable human beings, artificial urban centers were often created in the form of refugee camps or ghettos. Once stripped of their home, jobs, family, and even their legal identity most have not ever recovered. The moral questions this situation raises are legion. But among them certainly are the questions of race and fundamental human dignity. As the Pontifical Justice Commission stated,

> [I]f cases of segregation based on racial theories are the exception in today's world, the same cannot be said about phenomena of exclusion or aggressivity. The victims are certain groups of persons whose physical appearance or ethnic, cultural or religious characteristics are different form those of the dominant group and are interpreted by the latter as being signs of an innate and definitive inferiority, thereby, justifying all discriminatory practices in their regard. If, in fact race defines human groups in terms of immutable and hereditary physical traits, racist prejudice, which dictates racist behavior, can be applied by extension, with equally negative effects, to all persons whose ethnic origin, language, religion or customs appear different.[4]

Global communication allows worldwide interaction even among the poorest and in the most remote places, so it is increasingly impossible for people of dominant and powerful nations of the world to *not know* about the racialized aggression leveled against their fellow human beings. What happens after one knows is indeed the crux of the moral challenge of this massive new development.

Institutional Racism

The Pontifical Commission sees this type of racism as the function of the constitution and laws of a country that sets those persons of European descent as superior to all "others," and then justifies this action by an overarching ideology.[5] Often erroneous interpretations of biblical texts are used as part of the validation of this structure. The Apartheid system of South Africa was one clear manifestation of this type of racism. Clearly, such a thorough penetration of the Apartheid ideology into all dimensions of life and society is well known as one of the most devastating and long-lasting systems of racism the world has known. Though much has now been done to help the black majority as well as other South Africans to recover from Apartheid, even the most cursory research on the present conditions in that country reveals that many still suffer its devastating effects. Sadly, systems similar to Apartheid exist, though perhaps more subtly, such as in the caste mentality that is very much alive, for example, in India and Japan. While the formal national constitutions in both nations prohibit most discrimination, informally and with lax or no enforcement of protective laws, the caste system still survives and has its devastating effects on people such as the Dalit and the Buraku.

Victimization of Aboriginal Peoples

This form of racism is far from new. As we have seen, it was rampant in the Age of Discovery and the colonial period in the Americas and Africa particularly, and it was precisely that moment in history that set in motion many of the dynamics that indigenous people still suffer today. Indeed the Church was often complicit in the practice of racisms during this period, yet overall, some efforts were made to defend the existence of indigenous peoples. However, presently the threats to indigenous peoples' land, human and civil rights, language, customs, and religious traditions are real. Dominant societies in the name of development have ravished the original habitats of many aboriginal peoples and exploited the wealth of that land, often without benefits going to the original inhabitants. There is a crying need to recognize the right of aboriginal peoples to exist, rectify the legal status and rights of these peoples, and to provide for just settlement to their claims to their lands, languages, cultures, and religious traditions. The choice of whether Aboriginal peoples wish to be integrated into the dominant society must truly be theirs.[6]

Religious and Ethnic Disdain and Abolition

In the post-9/11 world, North Americans were made aware of the power of religious discrimination in ways not known quite so overtly for decades. Indeed for many U.S. citizens, to be a Muslim on September 11, 2001, was to have one's life threatened by some, including "Christians" who sought vengeance against the extremists who immolated New York's Twin Towers. Today, a new word—*Islamophobia*—is part of the common global vocabulary. In France, Denmark, or England, third and fourth generations of non-Christians whose ancestors came as immigrant workers to assist in the post-World War II rebuilding of Europe are still set aside in ghettos and live with limited rights.

However, Christians have also been, and still are, discriminated against. In areas of the world where Christians are in the minority, they are at times subject to religious laws such as Islamic Shariah or, as in India, when Dalits convert from Hinduism to Christianity, they lose their right to scheduled caste preference. In some parts of the world, full citizenship requires membership in the dominant religious tradition.[7]

Tribalism and Ethnocentricity

Ethnic identity gone wrong has been at the heart of tragedies such as Rwanda and Burundi or in the former Yugoslavia, Serbia, and Croatia.[8] This God-given gift of identity and belonging (based on common ancestry, memories of a shared past, kinship, religion, language, culture, shared history, and land) when allowed to blind people to their common and foundational reality as a human being like all other human beings, is the source of all sorts of human misery. Injustices and indignities such as political and economic corruption leave some persons with power, sufficient resources for living, opportunities and rights that allow them privileged places, because they cut off the very means of gaining life's necessities from those they define as "others." Tribalism is one devastating example of this exclusive identification.[9]

Social Racism

The dominant majority in any society has often gained its position and maintained it at great cost to "other" groups in the society. There are numerous theories to explain this phenomenon, but the effect is that masses of people are driven from their land, deprived of their livelihood, or kept within the economic control of large corporations and, sometimes through discriminatory laws and at times at gunpoint, without regard for their rights. Such cases can be seen in the corporate plantations in Central America,[10] oil company holdings in Colombia[11] or in topless mountains of the coal producing regions of West Virginia and Kentucky in the United States.[12] Migrant workers are often exploited to the extent that they become virtually enslaved by employers who hold their "illegal" status over them or keep them ignorant of their rights. As the Pontifical Commission puts it, "There is no great difference between those who consider 'others' their inferiors because of their race and those who treat their fellow citizens as inferiors exploiting them as a workforce."[13]

Spontaneous Reprehension and Xenophobia

The vast numbers of upheavals whether caused by wars, natural disasters, or economic shifts have compelled millions of people to seek asylum or a better life beyond their homelands. Large numbers of "strangers" immigrating into otherwise settled areas of the world have been the occasion for increased nationalism. At times, fear combined with patriotic fervor has motivated the formulation of legitimate political parties such as the National Front that overtly support a racist and xenophobic agenda and even violence against those considered as "others." Behaviors accompanying xenophobia range from ostracizing the "others" to violent efforts to drive them out of "our country." Fear, as well as restrictive policies and laws, keep the newly immigrated peoples isolated and they find it more difficult if not impossible to become integrated into their new country and culture. Their struggle thus seems to fulfill the accusations by their bigoted detractors that the immigrants are inferior.[14]

Anti-Semitism

In spite of the post-Holocaust efforts by Christians and other people of goodwill, the Jews are still the target of prejudice and violence of all sorts. The continued warring between Palestinians and Israelis provides the occasion for even the most nonpoliticized Jews in places far from the Middle East to be drawn into the crosshairs of those who seek to do harm. Many countries still have laws that place extraordinary restrictions on Jews, especially those seeking to immigrate.[15]

Genetic Manipulation

Though the United Nations and other prestigious bodies assert that there is no scientific basis for racial discrimination, the destructive pseudoscientific theories of race have not been totally abandoned.[16] New biotechnologies also loom as possible tools for those who "might seek to produce human beings selected according to racial criteria or any other characteristic. This would give rise to the resurgence of the deadly myth of eugenic racism, the misdeeds of which the world has already experienced."[17] There are similar possibilities for the racist use of sterilization or abortion campaigns such as the processes used in the "One Child" campaign in China.[18]

Archbishop of Chicago

In the U.S. context, the same categories outlined by the Pontifical Justice and Peace Commission could be used to define the manifestations of racisms. Yet, because of the particular constitutional and legal system in place in the United States (and other democracies), racist strategies have morphed into more subtle yet equally effective and denigrating means of discrimination. When dealing with these more subtle forms of racism, the Church, and all people of goodwill can find the four categories of racism—Spatial, Institutional, Internalized, and Individual—as set forth in Cardinal Francis George's

Dwell in My Love useful. Since the Archdiocese of Chicago is primarily an urban setting, the four categories reflect an urban socioeconomic context.

Spatial Racism

In most major U.S. cities, the inner urban population has become predominantly African Americans, Hispanics, and newly arrived immigrant groups. On the other hand, in the suburban or in gentrified areas of the city, populations tend to be predominantly affluent white people. This segregation usually affects the membership in Catholic parishes, as well. The impact of this segregation is devastating, creating economic disparities and undermining the moral basis of the society. Situations like this are clearly contrary to the biblical vision of the "one human community" and the U.S. national ideal of equal opportunity for all. All dimensions of the economy are affected by spatial racism—housing, employment, finance, education, infrastructure, transit, trade, and commerce.[19]

Institutional Racism

While civil rights legislation as well as the U.S. Constitution serves to make any overt discrimination on the basis of race illegal, the development of institutions in the United States has been for the large part the purview of white males. As the cardinal observes, "Patterns of racial superiority continue as long as no one asks why they should be taken for granted."[20] The dominant group has control of the way things are done, and "white privilege" goes undetected since people presume things are the way they should be. In reality, "white privilege" allows those of lighter skin color or those the dominant society holds as "superior" to continue to benefit from the system that was created without the contribution or needs of people of color in mind. The questioning eye can easily spot such discrimination in the U.S. judicial and political systems, social clubs, hospitals, universities, major corporations, labor unions, sports teams, or the arts. The Church is also vulnerable to these same unquestioned systemic violations of human dignity, as seen for example in the disproportionately low numbers of clergy, religious, or lay leaders of color. At times, genuine efforts to be inclusive of people of color have been made, however no real change in the institution has occurred because there has been no accompanying change in the organizational structures or dynamics of power and authority. At other times, the voiced needs of the long-standing minority community have been totally ignored, or viewed as exceptional anomalies.

Internalized Racism

As the song from *South Pacific* reminds us, "You've got to be taught to hate and fear ... before you're six, or seven, or eight ... you've got to be carefully taught."[21] On the other side, one also needs to be taught *that* one is hated and *that* people are afraid of you. There is ample evidence that children as young as four years of age already know the racial scripts of their society.[22] Deplorably thousands of people of all ages are schooled in their alleged inferiority and they live a lifetime without knowing that affirmation of their God-given human dignity is, in truth, the norm. This is internalized racism—to be educated and socialized into truly believing one is inferior as insinuated in every moment of one's existence in a racialized society. People of color come to see themselves through the eyes of the dominant culture. They know little if anything positive about their own history or culture, rarely see people like themselves in leadership roles, and apply to themselves nearly exclusively negative stereotypes of their people that the dominant culture has created.

Individual Racism

The form of racism that is best known is the belief in the superiority of the dominant group (white people) that is perpetuated in both conscious and unconscious ways in society. This "superiority complex" manifests itself in racial slurs, racial hate crimes, and numerous overt or subtler ways of disparaging the dignity of another person one perceives as inferior. The insecurities and fears of the unknown "other" are often at the root of racist behaviors, and people most frequently assign superior status to their own people, while holding those outside their group as inferior.

Having reviewed the primary ways in which the Church defines and understands racism, as well as the conflict situations that most often have racialized components, we now turn to the social sciences to assist in understanding prejudice and discrimination as the techniques of dominance.

Insights from the Social Sciences: Defining Prejudice and Discrimination

Prejudice

Philip Mason viewed prejudice as a judgment "based on a fixed mental image of some group or class of people and applied to all individuals of that class without being tested against reality."[23] The belief is arbitrary, fixed, generalized, and unfavorable. The categorical nature of prejudice violates any semblance of rationality. The inflexible dimension of prejudice distinguishes it from being simply an error in thought and subject to change if given sufficient evidence to the contrary. At times, though rarely, the prejudicial person may allow for an exception. But rather than allowing the exception to impinge on their erroneous position, the rarity of the exception is stressed, to bolster the erroneous position that indeed, the majority of instances prove the accuracy of the general original judgment. The content of the judgment is its negative aspect.

Stereotypes

Without some form of generalizations about life situations, people, and behavior, no learning would be possible and life would be chaotic. However, the vast difference between role generalizations and stereotypes is that the latter are oversimplified, groundless, and invalid assumptions most often based on hearsay and social myths. The proponents of stereotypes fail to see how they themselves share many of the same characteristics as those they judge to be negative traits in "others," and they do not see how the behaviors of the dominant social groups contribute to creating the very traits disparaged in "others."

In spite of the usual inflexibility of stereotypes, several studies have shown that as major social shifts occur, stereotypes are modified.[24] In the United States, such shifts have been observed in the perceptions of African Americans by white students after they had contact with one another on a college campus; the image of German Americans and Japanese Americans prior to World War II and after, or the perceptions of Russians by Americans after the Cold War ended.[25] Interestingly, though they became more positive, stereotypes remained nonetheless. Another interesting factor is that not infrequently, when two groups of people understand themselves as being in competition with each other, the very same traits that they see as positive among themselves will be applied only in degrading terms in the "other" group.[26]

Among the most responsible for shaping stereotypes in a society are parents, teachers, and those in control of the media.[27] People tend to tune in to media that are compatible with prior perceptions that are already conveyed in other social settings. In the end, the effectiveness of the media in conveying the same message to all people is uncertain.[28] An awareness of how stereotypes work is essential for any efforts to control and eradicate racisms.

Social Distance

Prejudice involves both the mental perceptions of ethnic groups and the feelings toward them. These cognitive and affective dimensions of prejudice when taken together form what social scientists call social distance. Social distance can be thought of as the degree of intimacy one allows oneself to experience toward the "other." Factors considered to determine one's sense of social distance include physical characteristics, religion, class, or ideology.[29] There is always pressure to conform to the norms and standards set by society, as a whole. However, what *people say they would do* in a situation and *what they actually do* are often two different things.[30] When confronted face-to-face with a decision concerning a judgment involving social distance, that social pressure can play either negatively or positively for the socialized and racialized "other." The ability to empathize with the "other" and act on that empathy makes all the difference.

Discrimination

There are numerous definitions for discrimination; however, one of the most adequate is that given by Joe R. and Clairece Booher Feagin: "[A]ctions or practices carried out by members of dominant groups, or their representatives, which have a differential and negative impact on members of subordinate groups."[31] The discrimination takes place not only in the behaviors themselves, but also through the various structures and methods involved. Though discrimination is related to prejudice, it is something distinct; one may be present without the other. Most often, however, they are mutually reinforcing. Discriminatory actions as well as prejudice are applied against individuals on the basis of membership in groups, as well as to collections of group members. Persons or groups of persons are denied something positive based not on their capacities, abilities, merits, or behavior but because of their membership in a group negatively judged. Discriminatory actions range from derogatory name-calling and racial slurs to lynching and genocide. The common denominator is that the subjects of discriminatory actions are persons judged on the basis of random negative criteria that define their membership in a group of those with like characteristics, and not morally justifiable criteria or value.

Individual Discrimination

People who act intentionally as individuals to limit or block the participation or reception of persons judged negatively as "other" take part in discrimination. They most often are motivated by prejudicial attitudes. Within institutions, it is possible for individuals to act in a discriminatory manner unintentionally when focusing their motives on the requirements (spoken or unspoken) of the rules of the institution. Nonetheless, the moral responsibility for the actions falls to the individual, and the negative effect of the discriminatory action is the same regardless of the motive.

Institutional Discrimination

As the Pontifical Justice and Peace Commission discussed, direct institutional discrimination is based on policies, laws, and structures purposefully that legally establish a normative system of discrimination against groups of people negatively defined as "other."[32] Indirect institutional discrimination is also possible when the effect of policies, laws, and structures is to unjustly bar people from necessities or opportunities that hold them at a clear and permanent disadvantage or eliminate their participation entirely.[33] Also there is the reality of "side by side discrimination" where one form of direct and intended discrimination effectively precipitates another set of discriminatory activity.[34] The intended discriminatory practices of selling houses to people of color or of a certain national origin in only one area of a city can effectively result in those persons having a disproportionate disadvantage for job opportunities available in the suburbs (unintended discrimination), when the reason for building in the suburbs was that it could be done at a lower cost.

It is also true that much of the unintentional discrimination that takes place in institutions is also unconscious. Usually those who do unintended discrimination would never consider themselves racists. In fact, they think of themselves as at times "bending over backwards" to give "them" opportunities. What those in authority in institutions often fail to consider is that they may simply be unaware of many factors known within a group being considered, and they fail to see the situation and its context from the perspective of that group. Thus, unintentional discriminators frequently become "victim blamers" asserting that the problems within a particular group are what hold that group back, and not discriminatory practices of the dominant majority.[35]

Three Complementary Theories

It is widely agreed that prejudice and discrimination are not innate in humans, and there are numerous theories explaining how and why people behave in an unjust and discriminatory fashion. Even when some groups become antagonistic toward one another, there are varying degrees of commitment to and behaving out of the animus. Prejudice and discrimination are learned patterns and prototypes for thought and actions. The most prominent theories for understanding racial prejudice and discriminatory actions fall into the three categories of psychological theories, normative theories, and power-conflict theories. We will examine each one in turn.

Psychological Theories

Having already discussed the concept of "scapegoating" we have some insight into what psychologists call the frustration-aggression theory for explaining racism. According to this explanation, people build up frustrations over some negative dimension of their life, and they simply "displace" their feelings of frustration onto some vulnerable group of people by doing negative and harmful things to them. Since they are not able to confront the actual source of their frustration, they take out their frustration on the easiest target. According to the psychologist Gordon Alport, racial, religious, or ethnic groups are easy targets for such displacement because they are always available and can be readily characterized.[36]

While this explanation is convincing, it has its limits. We know that not all people deal with their frustrations through this kind of scapegoating and displacement. The theory fails to account for why frustration at times is directed at the real source of the frustration, and at other times, it might be directed inward. Also the theory does not explain why discrimination is directed toward one vulnerable group and not another. Most significantly, the displacement through aggression is not all that satisfactory for the long term. At best, scapegoating is a momentary solution and far from an ultimate resolution because it fails to eliminate its real source of the frustration and, thus, it recurs.

Another psychological theory for explaining racial prejudice and discrimination focuses on the authoritarian personality of those who discriminate. After the World War II, psychologists studied those Nazis responsible for the "Final Solution" and discovered that one thing they held in common was a strict authoritarian upbringing.[37] The key to this theory is the reality that those who experience strict authoritarian upbringing tend to be highly conformist, disciplinarian, cynical, intolerant, and preoccupied with power. Such people were attracted to the Nazi movement because, among other things, it required submission to a powerful leader. Authoritarian personalities are comfortable with conservative values, and are highly resistant to change. Thus, they are likely to have prejudicial thoughts and behave in a discriminating manner when given the chance.

While this theory accounts for some important dimensions of prejudice and discrimination, it fails to explain how the prejudices come about in the first place. Nazi ideology appealed to many ordinary people and to varying degrees. This theory does not adequately account for all of the more subtle manifestations of prejudice and discrimination. It seems that particular situations and contexts are also important when seeking a cause for prejudicial and discriminatory behavior. For the Holocaust to have taken place as well as for other forms of racism to take hold as a socially acceptable way of being, behaving, and structuring a society or institution, considerably large numbers of people need to conform to and comply with behavioral demands that place one or more groups at a permanent place of inferiority. In other words, normal ordinary people are often involved in racism and discriminatory behaviors, both consciously and unconsciously. Some accounting of this is needed for an adequate theory of racial prejudice and discrimination.

Normative Theories

Situational norms are important and often overlooked influences on human behavior. These norms set the pattern for what is expected of people within a given context or situation, and people usually comply with them even though they would rather do or say something that resists conforming to them. In his classic 1964 study, Frank Westie explained normative theory this way:

Individuals are prejudiced because they are raised in societies which have prejudice as a facet of the normative system of their culture. Prejudice is built into the culture in the form of normative precepts—that is, notions of what "ought to be"—which define the ways in which members of the group ought to behave in relation to the members of selected outgroups.[38]

This normative theory suggests that the key to prejudicial attitudes and discriminatory behavior is education and socialization.

Socialization includes the numerous ways people (especially children) learn to conform to the expectations of society, ranging from those clearly set forth in educational programs to those subtly taught by example or modeling and that are learned through affective and intuitional sensibilities. Most of the learning takes place in families or among peers. Children as young as four years old can distinguish the meaning of racial terms and use them in demeaning ways.[39] The children quickly and thoroughly learn through family, peers, the media, and the social and political context in which they live that there are advantages and sanctions for being or not being part of he dominant majority group. The latter is true, even in cases where a child's immediate family makes explicit efforts to teach the child in an egalitarian and multicultural manner.

Those groups that have influence on people, especially children, are known to sociologists as reference groups. People aspire to become or become like those in their reference group. Family members, teachers, and others have the ability to shape and influence children's beliefs and values and are models of thought and actions. Reference groups provide the security of belonging and a framework for identity. As a person's reference group changes, her or his attitudes and actions change as well.[40] All of this suggests the vital influence of role models and the importance of exposing children to those who value all human persons as of equal worth. Also those role models and teachers need to promote empathy with those who suffer and confidence in their own moral identity as a vital part of their guidance.[41]

In his classic 1949 study, sociologist Robert Merton identified how attitudes and behaviors toward persons of various ethnic groups change with a shift in social context.[42] He came up with four paradigmatic types by linking the prejudicial attitudes or the lack thereof with the propensity to either engage or refrain from discriminatory actions. While in reality, most people function at either higher or lower degrees in both their behavior and attitudes, the types illustrate well the potential effects of social norms.

As expected there was one group, the unprejudiced nondiscriminators, who accepted all peoples as equals and refrained from discriminating behaviors against ethnic minorities. At the other extreme, there was a second group, the prejudiced discriminators who did not hesitate to claim their supremacy and act out their prejudicial beliefs when an opportunity presented itself.

Less predictable were the third and fourth groups. The third group, that Merton called "timid bigots," was prejudiced nondiscriminators who, though they maintained prejudiced beliefs and attitudes toward ethnic minorities, were influenced by situational norms and did not act out in discriminatory behaviors. Merton's fourth group, the unprejudiced discriminators, was also influenced by situational norms and though they held beliefs in human equality, they gave in to discriminatory behaviors in contexts where to do otherwise was to experience social sanctions.

What is vitally important for those who would work to eliminate racisms of all sorts is that Merton's study and numerous other studies have shown that while prejudice and discrimination are often practiced together that is not necessarily the case. Beyond that, it is the reality that prejudice follows discrimination to justify it—not the other way around. An historical example is readily found in the unjust discrimination that accompanied colonization. It is also seen in patterns of ethnocentrism and in xenophobia. The fundamental task for those seeking racial justice is not only to change attitudes, but also to change behavior. Thus, public policies, institutional structures, rules of evaluation for promotion, and advancement in employment that set various levels of sanctions on behavior are so significant. While morality as such cannot be legislated, laws and rules do set both boundaries and standards for all to strive for. On one hand, the boundaries, rules, and laws set parameters to safeguard and protect the value and equality of all human life. On the other hand, they set a minimum goal requirement that people do *at least* certain things, exist in certain ways, and do not prohibit others from acting and existing.

Power-Conflict Theories

After reviewing psychological theories and normative theories that attempt to explain prejudicial attitudes and discriminating behavior, we are still left with the question concerning the origins of these phenomena (prejudice and discrimination). The racialized manifestations of xenophobia and tribalism perhaps most readily illustrate power-conflict theories. The rise of xenophobia surrounding the unification of Germany and the wider struggle in Europe can be largely explained by power-conflict theory. Also the tribalism and ethnocentricity that has again emerged in Eastern Europe and in postcolonial Africa find coherence with this approach. Simply put, the interests of friendly groups like "us" are pitted against the interests of "others" different from us or "them." The occasion of this conflict differs, varying among economic, social, or political incidents, but patterns are similar. Discrimination and prejudice are the means of shifting the dynamics of power and the associated advantages and domination from one group (them) to another group (us) or ensuring that the power and advantages do not shift from "us" to "them." In all instances, the parties involved do not readily perceive it as possible or acceptable that mutual benefit can be achieved by a sharing of power and advantages.

As we saw, the paradigmatic cases of colonialism and slavery are examples of prejudice justifying discrimination for economic advantage. The need for large numbers of cheap laborers and the desire to lay hold of land and wealth was justified by the often brutal discrimination of enslavement and even genocide—death being the ultimate exertion of power over one conceived of as inferior.

The conversations between the former Exalted Cyclops of the Ku Klux Klan, C.P. Ellis and Ann Atwater, a black militant civil rights organizer provide a less extreme example of this theory.[43] Ellis was among the working poor, living in Durham, North Carolina, in the 1960s. He perceived the pressures for equal opportunity and full exercise of civil rights by African Americans as a threat to his newly achieved status and greater economic security as a proprietor of a gas station and he was determined to not allow anything take that away. Across town was an equally single-minded poor community worker, Ann Atwater, who was determined to take back the full freedom from discrimination and better economic opportunities for the "poor black folks" who lived in Durham. In a series of arranged meetings orchestrated by the AFL-CIO and the U.S. Department of Health, Education, and Welfare, the two leaders and their followers came together. In the end, Atwater and Ellis became cochairs of a committee that worked to change the quality of education and conditions in the Durham schools that would enable and ensure the future economic well-being of all of the people in the city.

In their discussion of various theories concerning economic structures and processes that try to explain racial discrimination, Omi and Winant name three main approaches: market relations, systems stratification, and class conflict.[44] Market relations approaches place causes of racial conflict in the realm of exchange, systems of stratification deals with distribution issues, and processes of class conflict deal with issues of production.

Market Relations. The market relations approach claims that the forces of the market if left uninhibited will eliminate all racial discrimination. However, proponents of this theory hold that there are three sources of disruption of market equilibrium. First, there is irrational prejudice or "the taste of discrimination" that is prevalent among some people. Second, there are monopolistic practices that grant privileges and that create incentives for maintaining and transferring racial inequality. Third, there are disruptive state practices that interfere with the equilibrium of the market. What are seen as the solution for these disruptions are simply the pressures of the market itself. If those participants in the market currently holding the advantage wish to achieve the greatest advantage, they need to allow the market to be truly free. Likewise, if those participants in the market currently without advantage desire to gain economic advantage, they too must let the market work, by wisely participating at crucial times and ways, such as buying, selling, or perhaps boycotting certain products. In the view of the proponents of this approach, the central problem is not race per se; rather, other problems of the market are the real cause. Racial politics and ideologies of inequality often mask the fact that concrete avenues for advancement are blocked.

Stratification. Stratification theories deal with the social distribution of resources, chiefly economic in nature. The chief proponent of this theory,

William Julius Wilson detached class categories from racial categories.[45] Addressing conditions in the United States, he claimed that prior to 1965 the "life chances" of black people were determined by racial stratification. After 1965, however, they have been shaped by class; a small privileged class now exists whose opportunities are equivalent to those of whites with similar skills. Now, there also exists a massive underclass, which is relegated to permanent marginality, and he called for state action to ameliorate the class cleavage.

As Omi and Winant point out, Wilson can be faulted on several counts.[46] He was overoptimistic about the changes following the civil rights legislation of 1965. He misjudged the electoral dynamics and the charges of reverse discrimination brought particularly by white males. Also the ties of middle-class blacks are most often to lower-class blacks, not to the upper class because of the racialized social and political structures of these U.S. systems. Education and job opportunities for lower-class blacks are dependent on the dominant (white) majority. The black middle-class works in industries and economic sectors that depend on the lower class for viability.

Class Conflict. Class conflict theory asserts the centrality of the "social relations of production" in structuring classes and the class relationship.[47] Class conflict infers racially oriented political interests from economic ones. Race and its function can be viewed in two opposing tendencies, each found in the labor market. In segmentation approaches, the conception of racially based inequalities in production relations has the effect of "divide and rule." In exclusion approaches, a split labor market is seen as the source of inequalities.

According to Michael Reich, a proponent of segmentation theory, "Capitalists benefit from racial divisions whether or not they have individually or collectively practiced racial discrimination."[48] Class divisions remain primary, and racially based organization is considered part of a false consciousness and not in tune with the real problem, which is class conflict. In the 1970s, the class segmentation theory began to lose credibility because it failed to explain why race contributed to the split labor market; indeed race and class are distinct, yet related issues. As Omi and Winant assert, "Racial dynamics must be understood as determinants of class relationships and indeed class identities, not as mere consequences of those relationships."[49]

In Edna Bonacich's exclusion approach, the workers of the dominant ethnic group benefit most from prejudice and discrimination in the labor market. She sees three categories of people in the capitalist market: business people, high-paid workers, and low-paid workers. Those who control certain jobs that pay better are in conflict with those who are paid less. Since employers seek to hire workers at the lowest wage possible, it is the immigrants who are often willing to work to survive in their new context that are hired. Those threatened most by the cheap labor force are those of the dominant ethnic group working in the better jobs, since the wage differential will not increase due to the lower wage limits of immigrants. Thus, higher paid laborers discriminate against migrants or others willing to work at the lowest wage level.

In Bonacich's words, the racially discriminatory movements that clash because of the threat to the wage differential are not racially or nationalistically motivated per se, but "the product of historical accident which produced a correlation between ethnicity and the price of labor."[50] This kind of analysis was visible in the rhetoric of many in Germany[51] and throughout Europe in the 1980s and 1990s at the high point of right-wing political activity and even violence against immigrants.

While these theories addressing the economic elements of conflict are certainly cogent, they are not without problems. All of them fail to address the concrete politics and ideologies of race. As Omi and Winant point out, "[S]egmentations and splits must be understood politically and ideologically, rather than as 'objective' systems of division within the labor market, and beyond this, within the working class as a whole."[52]

Conclusion

Prejudice and discrimination are complex and the various theoretical explanations reviewed here only begin to tap into explaining their existence and the accompanying dynamics and consequences. As we have seen, each theory sheds a bit more illumination on particular dimensions of the problem. While theories of competing interests need to be included, competing interests are not always the best primary consideration when seeking resolution and ending prejudice and discriminatory behavior. Indeed, as numerous programs and processes of conflict resolution show, what is most necessary is to persuade the parties of their common interests, their common life needs, indeed their common humanity.[53]

There will no doubt always be a need for external social and legal sanctions to hold the minimum standard of racial justice. But much can and must be done to shape the moral imagination and inspire true love, justice, and mutuality in our relationships with our fellow human beings. Elsewhere in this text, I have pointed to studies and resources such as the work of Timothy E. O'Connell, that indicate important ways in which people can be formed and educated to be moral and empathetic persons who can live together in racially just relationships. As we are humans living in a globalized and ecologically threatened world, our future temptation will no doubt be that peoples and nations attempt to hold onto disproportionate wealth and power, allowing millions to needlessly suffer and die as is the case in Darfur. Yet, the ecological and spiritual reality and the major moral traditions of the world show us otherwise. The vision of a racially just world needs to be drawn from those traditions and illuminated by the testimony of one who saw the world as few have been privileged to see it.

Viewed from space, Earth is but a small blue and white marble whirling through the cosmos. This image is indicative of the ontological reality that everything and everyone on earth is related. To name any fellow passenger on our planet as "other" is to operate out of a false consciousness and to risk the very survival of the planet. Listen to the witness of one astronaut, Russell (Rusty) Schweikart, upon his return to Earth,

> [Earth] is so small and so fragile and such a precious little spot in the universe that you can block it out with your thumb, and you realize on that small spot, that little blue and white thing, is everything that means anything to you—all of history and music and poetry and art and death and birth and love, tears, joy, games, all of it on that little spot out there that you can cover with your thumb. And you realize from that perspective that you've changed, that there's something new there, that the relationship is no longer what it was.[54]

As human persons, there is no denying the reality that we and all beings on this Earth are—for good or for ill—stuck in the same *oikos* (home), with all of our individuality, unity, diversity, and universality. Frequently, our differences tempt us to name our companions as deviants, immoral, or abnormal, in absolute terms. All too many times in the history of humankind, we have attempted such banishment, to live only to experience the reality of our inseparability. At the height of such attempts stands the *Shoah*. Yet, similar dynamics are played out in the daily and less heinous indifference humans extend to one another and toward Earth itself.

But the moral wisdom from the sages of history calls us to something much different. Like siblings who often can't get along, and who are sent to their common bedroom by a wise mother to "work it out," so too, we are compelled by the new (yet ancient) moral paradigm and potential dire consequences of our pluralistic and ecologically threatened age to find a way to work it out with one another, or perish. There is no "other." All are our fellow travelers on this planet; there is no "away" to which we can banish one another and still flourish.

The formal moral norm of mutuality calls all humans to concreteness in solving all hostile alienations.[55] Mutuality is an ecumenical moral norm that harmonizes beautifully with the notions of interdependence and unrationed reverence that permeate major religions of both east and west. Mutuality points insistently toward a holistic approach to personal morality, a new politics and economics, all based on a full realization of our foundational relationality.

The challenge I extend is for a movement from assuming power over to assuming power with—a movement to mutuality—a foundational starting point for moral discourse about racism, tribalism, and xenophobia. Attention to the formal norm, mutuality, militates against the kind of moral reasoning and debate that constructs distinctions of absolute inferiority and superiority, marginalizes individuals, generates categories of behavioral and moral deviance and abnormality, effectively constructing the "other." I submit that in a pluralistic, global, and environmentally threatened age, we cannot afford such alienation. It is from only a stance of mutuality that we will be able to know the Foundational Moral Experience—reverence for the person and their environment.[56] In my view there *is* no "other" way!

5

Racism, Tribalism, and Xenophobia

Challenges for the Future

Introduction

As these pages have illustrated, the realities of racism, tribalism, and xenophobia are certainly not new, nor are efforts to eradicate these sins from the human heart, and the social, political, and economic systems of the world. As Simone Campbell, national coordinator of NETWORK, recently put it, the pages of history concerning racism are

> like a pad of paper where someone wrote very hard on the first sheet and the indentation is seen all the way through the pack. The ink may not be there, but the message is still clearly visible. Even after turning all of the pages, and the expenditure of all this effort, our institutional work to be anti-racist in our beings is just that—work![1]

Indeed the deepest perennial challenge of antiracism is to do the work from the grassroots of families and neighborhoods through the highest realms of global systems to attain and maintain the most advantageous social identity for all human beings, namely as one created in the divine image and as a being of inviolable dignity. And perhaps even more challenging is that the former dimension of identity also requires that each human concretely treat all others with profound respect, always and everywhere.

Social Identity

In an ecologically threatened and globalized world, there can be no "in-group" and "out-group" if any one group (humans) is to thrive. But making this a reality requires a shift in consciousness and the way most people think. Indeed, psychologists have shown that all people want to think highly of themselves. Thus, they want to identify with the "in-group," that is, the "winners," rather than with the real or perceived "others," or the "losers."[2] To not behave in this manner requires a conscious choice. As shown in another study, researchers found that if a person identifies with an "in-group," one will associate pleasant words and images with that group, and unpleasant words and images with the "out-group."[3] When applying these observations to the real world, for example, the Southern Poverty Law Center found that in the U.S. context, terms such as *American* were more likely to be linked with European faces than they were with Asian faces. With information like this in tow, it is possible to train oneself to check one's behavior and to not act out of one's biases.

Another useful insight for establishing social identity comes from yet another recent study.[4] In the case where two racially integrated teams opposed each other, the focus of identity shifted away from "racial differences," to a "team identity." The important point is that when mixed groups share a common goal, biases are significantly reduced. Other useful analyses show that when a person is embarrassed or feels guilty about wrongfully stereotyping another person, that experience motivates them to change their thinking and behavior.[5] Thus, doors are open for the work of the Church and other people of goodwill to seek ways to bring this knowledge into practical and pastoral practices. The challenge is to constantly reinforce concretely, a global identity as "one human race."

However, it is also important to recognize that human beings have a need for intimate belonging, as well. Indeed, it has been the experience of the Church in Africa, for example, that while stressing the renewed identity of Christians as "the Family of God" it is important not to discount the value of the peoples' traditional tribal and clan identities. Here it is helpful to recall the work of anthropologist Judith Nagata concerning the reality of "multiple identities."[6] The status and value of particular intimate identities need to be balanced with a sense of the common good of all and not excluding anyone as "other," depriving them of the necessities and requirements of a life with dignity. The Church is challenged to continue to assist mature Christians and other people of goodwill to grow into this social identity, which requires engagement with others different from oneself, for the benefit of all; indeed, this is the vision of genuine Christian community.

Institutional Racism in the Church: Structures and Leadership

Sadly, due to the Church's past complicity in racism and its continued status as part of the dominant culture in many contexts, its teaching concerning racism, tribalism, and xenophobia is often suspect. If this is to change, the Church itself needs to make changes both internally and in the way it deals with the "others" of the world. One recent example will illustrate this challenge.

In 2004, the United States Conference of Catholic Bishops published "A Research Report Commemorating the 25th Anniversary of *Brothers and Sis-*

ters to Us," by James C. Cavendish and his seven expert associates.[7] The document reported the results of a study of the progress toward achieving the recommendations given in the 1979 pastoral on racism, *Brothers and Sisters to Us*. Briefly stated, the results are mixed. On the one hand, the bishops are to be congratulated for their concern and follow-up. On the other hand, one wonders why so little has changed in twenty-five years. The report provides analysis of all seven of the recommendations, but here I use only three samples from the report to illustrate.

Concerning "Speaking Out against Racism," it was discovered that white Catholics exhibited diminished support for government policies aimed at reducing racial inequality.

The second recommendation involved "Sharing in Responsibility and Decision Making." The findings reported that blacks are represented in most ministerial positions in the Church in the expected proportions given that they represent about three percent of all U.S. Catholics. However, blacks are still underrepresented among priests, sisters, lay pastoral ministers, and diocesan directors of religious education. Among Catholic Charities' full-time paid staff, minorities are overrepresented in the general population, but they are still underrepresentative of the minorities they serve.

The data on the recommendation about "The Continuation and Expansion of Catholic Schools in the Inner Cities and Disadvantaged Areas" indicated that the percentage of Catholic schools in inner-city neighborhoods remained about the same over the twenty-five years. However, there has been a decline in the enrollment of black children in those schools, while at the same time there has been an increase in the Hispanic and Asian enrollment. It was also reported that the rate of segregation in Catholic schools was often greater than in the area's public schools. Tuition costs keep black enrollment in Catholic colleges and universities at about a six percent rate. While black students represent about eight percent of the enrollment in Catholic schools, black teachers are only three percent of the faculty, and in Catholic colleges and universities only two percent of the full-time faculty is black.

The conclusions drawn from information such as this were summarized in the report and deserve to be quoted at some length:

> Church leaders must renew their commitment to speak out against racism so as to raise people's awareness of the systemic nature of this form of evil. ... This reality should lead Catholic leaders to devote more attention and resources to eliminating employment discrimination, fostering vocations, and developing programs that will provide [b]lacks and other minorities with the kind of confidence, skills, and expertise necessary to hold ministerial, teaching, and administrative positions throughout the Church.

But addressing racism and underrepresentation of minorities is not enough. Evangelization of minorities requires developing homilies, liturgical rituals, symbols, music, pastoral programs, and educational curricula that reflect upon the community's life, history, and culture. Pastoral leaders, therefore, must make every effort to ensure not only that these practices and institutions are sufficiently inculturated, but also that they are fully accessible to those who wish to participate in them. Only then will [b]lacks and other racial minorities be able to enjoy their rightful place at the table.[8]

White Privilege and the Dominant Gaze

The Church is but one global institution whose leadership has been and remains predominantly white males. As Peggy McIntosh's 1988 classic essay, "White Privilege: Unpacking the Invisible Knapsack,"[9] pointed out, being light complected (especially if male) provides numerous unearned privileges that the world's darker complected (and female) peoples cannot have or take for granted. Simply stated, white privilege can be defined as the psychological advantage that one can be confident that one's perceptions of the world will be deemed correct and credible, that one's viewpoint will set the standard for all others, and that one will never have to answer for one's entire ethnic group or disprove a negative stereotype of them. As McIntosh already pointed out nearly twenty years ago, there are very real and at times life threatening or life-changing implications for having or not having such advantages.

Closely associated with white privilege is the capacity to hold the "dominant gaze."[10] The "dominant gaze" is the cultural lens through which the powerful, dominant group views a society, and then judges that racism is only an individual matter. This view fails to grasp the structural and institutional racisms perpetuated by those in power. All humans are seen along a complexion color spectrum (white to black) that is readily divided into "white" and "nonwhite" and then value and power are assigned to those of lighter skin tones.

Among all the magisterial statements related to racism, tribalism, and xenophobia examined for this volume, only two of the documents addressed these phenomena. It seems that, deplorably, the Church often stands as an example of white privilege. If it is to be a credible teacher of racial justice, it must openly recognize the reality and the dynamics of white privilege and the dominant gaze. This acknowledgment will require a conscious letting go of power so that others may take up the power, participation, and credibility that is rightfully theirs.

Theologically, there is no better example of this relinquishment than Jesus, the Son of God, letting go of his godly status to live out the fullness of the reality of God in human form (Phil 2:1–11). And lest anyone miss the point, there is the concrete example of the Eucharistic scene in the Gospel of John—where Jesus, knowing full well who he was, took the towel and began to wash the disciples' feet (Jn 13). Perhaps the greatest challenge to the Church is to bring its own house in order through a graceful and grace-filled recognition and relinquishment of white privilege among its members, in its structures, and in its organizations and institutions.

Engaging Practices of Intercultural Communication

The process of letting go of power and the taking up of power by and among diverse groups demands that people become skilled in intercultural communications. At minimum, this requires that Christians, especially Church leaders and ministers, learn to deal with the complexities of religion and religiosity, interactions between immigrants and dominant cultures, issues of age and gender, and the significance of intercultural communication, itself.[11] Those in the dominant culture cannot presume that minority culture people can automatically or easily articulate their experiences or needs in terms readily understood by dominant culture people.

Robert Schreiter suggests three goals for effective interactions in the one multicultural Church: recognition of the other, respect for cultural differences, and healthy interactions among cultures. He suggests that effective ministry in a multicultural church that is not racist, requires special attention to language because it is so central to identity, self-expression, and interactions. According to Schreiter, customs around special events, holidays, and holy days, especially Christmas and Easter, are also important cultural expressions that can easily also serve as occasions for sharing and dialogue among various cultural groups in a parish. And finally, he holds that the material aspects of a culture are important, especially dress and food since they bring people together. Schreiter summarizes, "Respect for the differences will be shown when changes in a parish become habitual or permanent rather than one event ... if certain festivals such as Tet or Our Lady of Guadalupe become regular features of the parish calendar, the message to the parish people is that difference is here to stay."[12] While much can be done by local parishes, the support and combined resources of dioceses or even from the Church at the national level is needed for effective multicultural ministry.

Indigenous Peoples

Indigenous peoples from across the globe are under increasing pressures from dominant nations and globalized corporations seeking to overtake their land and develop the natural resources available from those regions. In June of 2006, the United Nations Human Rights Council adopted a Draft Declaration of Rights of Indigenous Peoples that comprehensively addressed individual and collective rights, cultural rights and identity, and rights to health, education, employment, and language. The Draft Declaration also ensured indigenous peoples' right to remain distinct as it is upheld in the UN Charter and the Universal Declaration of Human Rights. Sadly, as of this writing, this document languishes amid bureaucratic entanglements. While such a document is not legally binding, it would have an impact on the obligation of member nations to respect the rights of indigenous peoples around the globe.

Historically, the Church has a mixed record concerning indigenous peoples. Following the lead of Pope John Paul II, recently the Church has renewed its commitment and used its considerable influence on behalf of indigenous peoples. The issues of the right to exist, rights to traditional lands, to the resources of their lands, and the preservation of indigenous languages and cultures will continue to be issues for decades to come. The Church's challenge is to strengthen its denunciation of all forms of racism perpetrated against indigenous peoples and to concretely support their efforts for respect and autonomy amid growing acute concerns of ecological crises and global climate change.

Migrants, Refugees, and Asylum Seekers

As was noted in the previous chapter, across the globe, people are literally on the move in unprecedented numbers as migrants, refugees, and asylum seekers. As vulnerable "others" they frequently encounter xenophobia and other forms of racism. Indeed, the history of race and racisms shows that frequently the contact with unfamiliar populations gives rise to myths about "others" that become the absolutes of racisms.[13] Given the deep complexities of the global situations at the root of these massive human movements, the Church will be challenged for decades to care for the dignity of these peoples.

Practical knowledge and better understanding of the realities of specific peoples is needed, especially among not only those who minister to the migrants, refugees, and asylum seekers but also by "ordinary people in the pew." The complexities and trends, issues, and links among sending and receiving countries must be studied. The Church needs to form networks with NGOs, migrant groups, and people of goodwill who will support and address the situations of these vulnerable peoples to ensure their fair and just treatment. The Church must also continue to raise its voice to challenge legal barriers that prevent refugees from legally working and which foster grounds for illegal employment. Without legal employment opportunities, refugees are exploited by low wages and given no health, safety, or social protections. With renewed zeal, the Church must engage in efforts to make real its desire proclaimed in no. 29 of the *Church on Racism* that: "Within a given state, the law must be equal for all citizens without distinction."

Sexualizing of Racism

To date, no Church document has discussed the reality that racism is a structure of both desire and disgust. The psychological and physical fascination and repulsion dynamics involved in constituting the racialized "other" construct each other into a neurosis called racism. This is seen most vividly when racial differences are understood in forms of blood and lineage. Racialized women's bodies become the disgusting conduits of male entitlement. As a specified group is deemed inferior, women of that group are uniquely at risk. R. Lenten vividly explains,

> Because women bear the next generation of a collectivity, they are put uniquely at risk as members of a group targeted as "racially inferior." Taking into account the construction of women as ethnic and national subjects, the definition of genocide must be gendered, to include political projects involving slavery, sexual slavery, mass rape, mass sterilization, aimed, through women at "ethnic cleansing" and the elimination or alteration of a future ethnic group, catastrophes, genocidal or otherwise ... target women in very specific ways due to their social, ethnic, and national construction.[14]

From another perspective, as white male privilege is threatened by competition from other men, the demasculization of other men of racialized communities intensifies with increased efforts to deny them their rightful place in the world of work, as citizens, or in society. Often, failure in the public sphere to wield "heterophallic" power, effectively results in loss of self-respect, and that loss cycles into a "false machismo," leading racialized men to put down or brutalize women,[15] These realities are often fed by age-old myths of the hypersexed black male, which is easily transformed into a version of any racialized male. The Church is challenged to deal with these issues with a more clear and connected teaching relating sexuality, gender status, race, and physical difference in an embodied morality.

The Racialization of Consumption and Distribution of Goods, Services, and Assets

Numerous pastoral letters and encyclicals dealing in economic justice have been promulgated. However, only passing references have been made linking the inability of the poor to consume the necessities of life with racism. Access to food or the inability to have proper nutrition, for example, is a function of structural inequalities in the global economy. According to Amartya Sen, hunger is determined by social status, not the absolute levels of the food supply.[16] Thus, from the absence of grocery stores in urban neighborhoods to the economic power of some nations to bask in abundance while others languish in human-made famine, access to food can be traced to the indelible racialized patterns of colonialism and empire that have existed in the world since the nineteenth century.[17] Racialized class relations are redrawn through various means. "The diffusion of economic relations does not detract from their bite, or from the simultaneous deepening of racism and class exploitation."[18] The challenge for the Church is to make explicit the role of racialized relations in economic injustices, to assist Christians and other people of goodwill in understanding this reality, and to find concrete ways to confront it.

The New Slavery

Just as the world economy formerly allowed for overt racism, tribalism, and xenophobia to prosper within nations, these evils are now readily able to take on vast global proportions because of the general and expansive portability and commodification of human labor and human persons. One small example of this global challenge is the new slave trade. Where the old slavery of the sixteenth to nineteenth centuries included the legal ownership of slaves, a high initial purchase cost of a slave, low profits for slave traders, a shortage of potential slaves, the social obligation to maintain the enslaved, and a long-term relationship between the enslaved and their owner, today's system requires none of that. The new slave trade normally operates with impunity and in spite of laws prohibiting it. Willing slave owners are able to purchase people at very low cost, traders become wealthy because of the volume of their business, there is a surplus supply of impoverished destitute people who are potential slaves, and owners have short-term relationships with their slaves who are considered utterly disposable. The Church has addressed most of these factors in relation to human rights in general, but the reality is not accurately conveyed without the consideration of racism as a factor in determining who in the present day are the enslaved and who the slave owners are. Here again, the reality of racism and its pervasive reach needs attention from the Church, and the moral authority of the Church needs to be raised against this evil.

Conclusion

These nine areas presenting major challenges to the Church in the future are certainly not exhaustive. The reality is that while the universal Church has made a good beginning with the more recent promulgation of the *Church and Racism* (1988) and the *Contribution to the World Conference Against Racism* (2001), there is still a need for a more thoroughgoing integration of a consciousness of the influences of racism on other issues and an understanding of how racism impacts the way the Church needs to approach its social agenda.

Increasingly theologians are publishing their reflections on racism and white privilege, as well as developing pastoral tools to bring the tenets of social teaching and doctrine to the faithful in workshops, retreat experiences, cross-cultural learning exercises, and interfaith dialogue. The outlines of the social teaching documents on racism, tribalism, and xenophobia collected in this text are intended to aid in these reflections and efforts. This work toward conversion and transformation is vital if anything more is to come of these present-day teachings than came from the words of the popes and bishops of the Age of Discovery. It is also encouraging that many local bishops and conferences of bishops are speaking out and raising their voices in denunciation of racism. Sadly, the majority are still silent on racism, however. Certainly, words are limited in their affect if the life of the Church and its members does not reflect what is taught. Across the globe, the Church has begun to address racism, tribalism, and xenophobia. But it has only begun! With God's grace, perhaps someday, we will come close to fulfilling the deep desire of Jesus "[t]hat they may be one" (Jn 17).

PART II
CHURCH DOCUMENTS ON RACIAL JUSTICE

Introduction

How to Read a Church Document on Racial Justice and Related Issues

Most documents promulgated by the official Church are never read by ordinary Catholics, who are often the very people who could most thoroughly and concretely bring such teachings to life. The all too familiar saying, "The social teachings of the Church are its best kept secret," bears witness to this. Ironically, often the more controversial a topic or issue is, the less likely ordinary Catholics know what their bishops teach about it. There are numerous reasons for why this is the case. Indeed, two common reasons are, first, that the documents are written in a style and vocabulary that only theologians and ethicists can decipher. Second, the documents often do not move beyond describing the rather depressing state of some major issue, and there is no pastoral follow-through establishing pastoral guidance or strategies for concrete action by the People of God and other persons of faith and goodwill. Thus, the documents are readily written off as being irrelevant to the real lives of real people and are left to collect dust on some ecclesial bookshelf.

These difficulties have been addressed in various ways by pastoral leaders.* The following chart is a process of analysis that has proven useful with ordinary "people in the pew," as well as with college and theology students preparing for ministry in the Church. Here I will briefly comment on each step of the process. What one takes from reading a Church document is in many ways the function of one's ability to ask critical questions, and not necessarily on the level of one's formal education or academic prowess. The questions listed here are not intended to be exhaustive of the relevant

---

*Kevin J. O'Neil, "A Method for Reading Church Documents in Moral Theology," *New Theology Review* 19/2 (May 2006) 63–72.

How to Read a Church Document on Racial Justice and Related Issues

I. Context and Background of the Document

    A. Social Conditions
    B. Conditions in the Church

II. The Central Problem or Issue That Is the Focus of the Document:
A Description from Expert Sources outside the Church

III. The Document You Are Studying

    A. Provide a General Outline of the Text
    B. How is the central problem/issue defined?
        1. Is this definition adequate? Why / why not?
        2. Discuss the advantages of defining the problem this way. Who benefits; who loses?
        3. Discuss the disadvantages of defining the problem this way. Who benefits; who loses?
    C. What solutions to the problem/issue are proposed?
        1. Is this solution adequate? Why / why not?
        2. Discuss the advantages of resolving the problem this way. Who benefits; who loses?
        3. Discuss the disadvantages of resolving the problem this way. Who benefits; who loses?
    D. How was the document received?
        1. Within the institutional Church?
        2. By the people in the pew?
        3. The wider general public?

IV. In what ways, if at all, does this document continue to be relevant today?

---

queries.* The intent is to provide some starting points for reading a Church document and finding its relevance for the ordinary person, and to discover the possibilities for actively engaging with its teaching and bringing it to bear on their reality.

I. Context and Background of the Document

The context in which a document is written includes the authors of the document and their point of view. Who are the authors? Why did they

---

*Joe Holland and Peter Henriot, *Social Analysis: Linking Faith and Justice*, Revised and Enlarged Edition, (Maryknoll, NY: Orbis Books, 1983). See R.F. Broderick, MSC and Cora Richardson, MSHR, et al., *Love Your Neighbour: Christian Social Analysis*, Training for Community Ministers, no. 27 Lumko Series (Delmerville, South Africa, 1989). Also Fran Wijsen, Peter Henriot, Rodrigo Mejía, eds., *The Pastoral Circle Revisited: A Critical Quest for Truth and Transformation* (Maryknoll, NY: Orbis Books, 2005).

choose to write on this topic? To whom is the document addressed? Where are the authors located geographically or socioeconomically in relation to the topic and issues they address? What is their experience of the topic and what informs what they say, and why? What are the author's theological or theoretical preferences or biases?

A. Social Conditions

Where in the world was the document written? Where is the location of the people (subjects) involved with the topic and its issues? What are the demographics of the location? What is the racial or ethnic character of the place? What are the cultures represented in the area? What does the social class structure look like? What social problems are in the region that affect the topic addressed in the document? What is the psychosocial atmosphere in the area like—are people generally positive or negative, depressed or hopeful? What is the economic profile of the locale? What is the state of the health of the economy? What is the status of the environment in the community? What are the economic problems people face? Is there a healthy relationship between the local, regional, and global economies? What is the political profile of the locale? What are political leaders like? Who are the "informal" leaders in the area? What institutions, groups, media or other factors influence people in the region?

B. Conditions in the Church

What is the religious profile of the area? Are Catholics and Christians in the majority or minority? What is the relationship of the Church and other faith groups? What is the relationship of the Church with nonbelievers? What is the health of the local Church? Are relationships among the laity, clergy, religious, and the bishop credible and amicable? How is the Church perceived by the local people?

II. The Central Problem or Issue That Is the Focus of the Document: A Description from Expert Sources outside the Church

A careful reading of the document will usually uncover the central problem or issue the authors seek to address. However, in order to gain perspective on what the document states, it is often helpful to consult with an outside source concerning the matter. The response to this inquiry may involve some research in a library or interviews with local leaders, professionals, officials, or government archives and resources.

III. The Document You Are Studying

A. *Provide a General Outline of the Text*

Depending on the style of the document, this step may not be necessary. Increasingly magisterial documents have useful headings that guide the reader. Even if headings are provided, it is useful to survey the document before reading the text, glancing at the headings. This activity can readily provide a sense of the flow of the text, and can help bring coherence about the author's understanding of the topic.

Sections IIIB and C of the Chart Are Self-Explanatory

D. *How was the document received?*

This is perhaps the most difficult information to determine. Sources to examine for evidence of the reception of a document include the Catholic press—diocesan newspapers, national newspapers, magazines, and Web sites of Catholic organizations, religious order newsletters or web pages. The secular media often include reports of religious events and many newspapers have a religion section. News magazines also occasionally provide articles on Church documents. Naturally, different kinds of publication and various media have different audiences. Thus, one may need to search out several different kinds of sources to uncover the reception by various audiences: the institutional Church, the people in the pew, or the general public. The unfortunate reality is that Church teaching documents often receive little if any coverage in places where ordinary people get their news. A mention in a Sunday parish bulletin may be the most coverage any document gets beyond academia or chancery halls.

IV. In what ways, if at all, does this document continue to be relevant today?

Here is an opportunity to engage the moral imagination and a process of theological reflection on the current state of affairs in the reader's context. Such reflection is best done in the context of a group and guided by someone trained in utilizing a social analysis process such as the classic "Pastoral Circle" or a similar method. Often, when the circumstances in which the document was written have changed, or when a document authored in one context is read in another setting, readers can uncover new insights and ideas for action. One benefit of reading Church documents from various parts of the world is that while there is much in common in the Church across the globe, Christians can learn much from the unique perspectives each culture offers. Even a brief foray into this kind of reading and sharing shows the Spirit of God is active throughout the Church! This is not to say that there is no room for improvement in the drafting of the magisterial teaching documents.

Recent Catholic Episcopal Teaching on Racism*

In his classic analysis of some twenty episcopal documents published by the bishops of the United States, Bryan N. Massingale noted ambiguity in how the bishops defined racism, how they interpreted the meaning of racism, and the means they posed for the eradication of racism. This in part accounts for why the Church's voice has often not been effective against racial injustice.

The importance of recalling this work by Massingale again here is to stress that not all magisterial documents are equally helpful in providing theological warrants and grounding or for giving guidance to resolve the pressing evil of racial injustice. The way a problem is defined in large part determines the solution advocated. The more nuanced the definition, the more adequate the recommendations for rectifying racial injustice will likely be. As Massingale illustrated, most bishops addressed racism only at the level of personal sin and neglected the institutional and structural dimensions, because they did inadequate social analysis and theological and social ethical reflection on racism.

While certainly there is relatedness between personal and social sin, the measures taken to deal with personal sin will not adequately serve in the public forum. As we have seen, racisms today take on many forms—personal prejudice, exclusion and aggression against immigrants and asylum seekers, instructional policies, genocide of aboriginal peoples and ethnic cleansing, structural "white privilege," economic frameworks, ethnic stereo typing, religious hatred, anti-Semitism, and more. While certainly personal sin is involved in all of this, if the Church is to speak and act in relevant ways the analysis brought to these issues must be evident in the teaching documents the Church publishes. Thus, it is necessary for Christians who wish to make a difference guided by Catholic magisterial teaching to read the documents with a critical eye. And there is a challenge to the Magisterium to provide more adequate and nuanced teaching to guide all People of God in the work of racial justice.

---

*Bryan N. Massingale, "James Cone and Recent Catholic Episcopal Teaching on Racism," *Theological Studies* 61/4 (December 2000) 700–730.

Papal, Conciliar, and Vatican

1. *Mit Brennender Sorge:* On the Church and the German Reich

POPE PIUS XI, 1937

To the Venerable Brethren The Archbishops and Bishops of Germany and other ordinaries in peace and communion with the Apostolic See, 1937

Full text of document available at: http://www.vatican.va/holy_father/ pius_xi/encyclicals/documents/hf_p-xi_enc_14031937_mit-brennender-sorge_ en.html

Abstract

Pope Pius XI protested Nazi persecution of the German Catholic Church and their violations of the Reich–Vatican Concordat. Warning against the deification of race, nation, and state and urging Catholics to be faithful, he stressed that "God-given rights" and "human nature" are without borders. He also defended the canon of the "Old Testament" as part of the Christian biblical heritage against those promoting anti-Semitism.

Historical Note

This encyclical was smuggled into Germany, printed secretly, and distributed to the clergy and read from all Catholic pulpits throughout the Third Reich on Palm Sunday, March 21, 1937. Some critics fault Pius XI for not directly condemning the Nuremberg Laws of 1935 that stripped German Jews of their rights, and for referring to Jews as those who were "constantly straying" from God and who had crucified Christ. As time passed, however, Pius XI's critique of the Nazis intensified. In fact, he commissioned *Humani*

Generis Unitas that directly denounced racism and persecution of Jews by advocates of racial purity. Unfortunately, Pope Pius XI died of a heart attack on February 9, 1939. It is doubtful he ever saw the final document. It was never published, only surfacing to receive scholarly attention in the 1970s.

Discussion Questions

1. Discuss the circumstances and the conditions of the Concordat between the Holy See and the Third Reich.
2. Should Pius XI have articulated a more direct criticism of Nazi policies and laws, comments against the Nuremberg Laws of 1935, for example? Why or why not?
3. Research the impact of the reading of this document on Palm Sunday, March 21, 1937.

Excerpts from the Text

8. Whoever exalts race, or the people, or the State, or a particular form of State, or the depositories of power, or any other fundamental value of the human community—however necessary and honorable be their function in worldly things—whoever raises these notions above their standard value and divinizes them to an idolatrous level, distorts and perverts an order of the world planned and created by God; he is far from the true faith in God and from the concept of life which that faith upholds.

9. Beware, Venerable Brethren, of that growing abuse, in speech as in writing, of the name of God as though it were a meaningless label, to be affixed to any creation, more or less arbitrary, of human speculation. Use your influence on the Faithful, that they refuse to yield to this aberration. Our God is the Personal God, supernatural, omnipotent, infinitely perfect, one in the Trinity of Persons, tri-personal in the unity of divine essence, the Creator of all existence. Lord, King and ultimate Consummator of the history of the world, who will not, and cannot, tolerate a rival God by His side.

10. This God, this Sovereign Master, has issued commandments whose value is independent of time and space, country and race. As God's sun shines on every human face so His law knows neither privilege nor exception. Rulers and subjects, crowned and uncrowned, rich and poor are equally subject to His word. From the fullness of the Creators' right there naturally arises the fullness of His right to be obeyed by individuals and communities, whoever they are. This obedience permeates all branches of activity in which moral values claim harmony with the law of God, and pervades all integration of the ever-changing laws of man into the immutable laws of God.

15. In Jesus Christ, Son of God made Man, there shone the plentitude of divine revelation. "God, who at sundry times and in divers manners, spoke in times past to the fathers by the prophets last of all, in these days hath spoken to us by His Son" (*Heb*. i. 1). The sacred books of the Old

Testament are exclusively the word of God, and constitute a substantial part of his revelation; they are penetrated by a subdued light, harmonizing with the slow development of revelation, the dawn of the bright day of the redemption. As should be expected in historical and didactic books, they reflect in many particulars the imperfection, the weakness and sinfulness of man. But side by side with innumerable touches of greatness and nobleness, they also record the story of the chosen people, bearers of the Revelation and the Promise, repeatedly straying from God and turning to the world. Eyes not blinded by prejudice or passion will see in this prevarication, as reported by the Biblical history, the luminous splendor of the divine light revealing the saving plan which finally triumphs over every fault and sin. It is precisely in the twilight of this background that one perceives the striking perspective of the divine tutorship of salvation, as it warms, admonishes, strikes, raises and beautifies its elect. Nothing but ignorance and pride could blind one to the treasures hoarded in the Old Testament.

16. Whoever wishes to see banished from church and school the Biblical history and the wise doctrines of the Old Testament, blasphemes the name of God, blasphemes the Almighty's plan of salvation, and makes limited and narrow human thought the judge of God's designs over the history of the world: he denies his faith in the true Christ, such as He appeared in the flesh, the Christ who took His human nature from a people that was to crucify Him; and he understands nothing of that universal tragedy of the Son of God who to His torturer's sacrilege opposed the divine and priestly sacrifice of His redeeming death, and made the new alliance the goal of the old alliance, its realization and its crown.

2. *Gaudium et Spes:* Pastoral Constitution on the Church the Modern World*

VATICAN COUNCIL II, 1965

Full text of document available at: http://www.vatican.va/archive/hist_councils/ii_vatican_council/documents/vat-ii_cons_19651207_gaudium-et-spes_en.html

Abstract

Because each person is called to a unique relationship with God, the Church is interested in them and their development. All factors related to

---

*The Preface, Part I, and Chapters 1 and 2 most directly address the topics of racial justice.

fundamental human dignity, including racial and religious discrimination, are central concerns of the Church. Here the stage is set for the Church to engage in interfaith dialogue and, even nonreligious perspectives.

Historical Note

Pope Paul VI promulgated *Gaudium et Spes* on December 7, 1965, as the last of the sixteen Vatican Council II documents. The council concluded the following day.

Discussion Questions

1. Compare the Church's thought on human beings prior to Vatican II with the understanding articulated in *Gaudium et Spes*.
2. Beyond the fact that "race" is listed as a criterion of unjust discrimination in no. 29, in what ways does *Gaudium et Spes* support racial justice?

Excerpts from the Text

27. Coming down to practical and particularly urgent consequences, this council lays stress on reverence for man; everyone must consider his every neighbor without exception as another self, taking into account first of all his life and the means necessary to living it with dignity, so as not to imitate the rich man who had no concern for the poor man Lazarus.

In our times a special obligation binds us to make ourselves the neighbor of every person without exception, and of actively helping him when he comes across our path, whether he be an old person abandoned by all, a foreign laborer unjustly looked down upon, a refugee, a child born of an unlawful union and wrongly suffering for a sin he did not commit, or a hungry person who disturbs our conscience by recalling the voice of the Lord, "As long as you did it for one of these the least of my brethren, you did it for me" (Matt 25:40).

Furthermore, whatever is opposed to life itself, such as any type of murder, genocide, abortion, euthanasia, or willful self-destruction, whatever violates the integrity of the human person, such as mutilation, torments inflicted on body or mind, attempts to coerce the will itself; whatever insults human dignity, such as subhuman living conditions, arbitrary imprisonment, deportation, slavery, prostitution, the selling of women and children; as well as disgraceful working conditions, where men are treated as mere tools for profit, rather than as free and responsible persons; all these things and others of their like are infamies indeed. They poison human society, but they do more harm to those who practice them than those who suffer from the injury. Moreover, they are supreme dishonor to the Creator.

28. Respect and love ought to be extended also to those who think or act differently than we do in social, political and even religious matters. In fact, the more deeply we come to understand their ways of thinking through such courtesy and love, the more easily will we be able to enter into dialogue with them.

This love and good will, to be sure, must in no way render us indifferent to truth and goodness. Indeed love itself impels the disciples of Christ to speak the saving truth to all men. But it is necessary to distinguish between error, which always merits repudiation, and the person in error, who never loses the dignity of being a person even when he is flawed by false or inadequate religious notions. God alone is the judge and searcher of hearts, for that reason He forbids us to make judgments about the internal guilt of anyone.

The teaching of Christ even requires that we forgive injuries, and extends the law of love to include every enemy, according to the command of the New Law: "You have heard that it was said: Thou shalt love thy neighbor and hate thy enemy. But I say to you: love your enemies, do good to those who hate you, and pray for those who persecute and calumniate you" (Matt 5:43–44).

29. Since all men possess a rational soul and are created in God's likeness, since they have the same nature and origin, have been redeemed by Christ and enjoy the same divine calling and destiny, the basic equality of all must receive increasingly greater recognition.

True, all men are not alike from the point of view of varying physical power and the diversity of intellectual and moral resources. Nevertheless, with respect to the fundamental rights of the person, every type of discrimination, whether social or cultural, whether based on sex, race, color, social condition, language or religion, is to be overcome and eradicated as contrary to God's intent. For in truth it must still be regretted that fundamental personal rights are still not being universally honored. Such is the case of a woman who is denied the right to choose a husband freely, to embrace a state of life or to acquire an education or cultural benefits equal to those recognized for men.

Therefore, although rightful differences exist between men, the equal dignity of persons demands that a more humane and just condition of life be brought about. For excessive economic and social differences between the members of the one human family or population groups cause scandal, and militate against social justice, equity, the dignity of the human person, as well as social and international peace.

Human institutions, both private and public, must labor to minister to the dignity and purpose of man. At the same time let them put up a stubborn fight against any kind of slavery, whether social or political, and safeguard the basic rights of man under every political system. Indeed human institutions themselves must be accommodated by degrees to the highest of all realities, spiritual ones, even though meanwhile, a long enough time will be required before they arrive at the desired goal.

3. The Church and Racism: Toward a More Fraternal Society

PONTIFICAL JUSTICE AND PEACE COMMISSION, 1988*

Full text of document available at: http://www.inaword.com/svd/church%20and%20racism.pdf

Abstract

Racism continues to plague today's world. Here different manifestations of racism are examined and Catholic principles of human dignity and solidarity are reaffirmed. The Church's role is to change hearts and offer a place for reconciliation toward facilitating structural change.

Historical Note

Released February 10, 1989, this is the first Vatican document dealing exclusively with racism. Following Pope John Paul II's September 1988 visit to Southern Africa, it reflects his concern about Apartheid and addresses the relation between evangelization and colonization in light of the approaching quincentenary of Columbus' voyage to America.

Discussion Questions

1. Why does our Christian faith reject racism?
2. What are ways to "inculturate" the Gospel, that is, to make the Gospel more effective in the culture of this country and of other countries?

Excerpts from the Text

II. Forms of Racism Today

8. Today racism has not disappeared. [...] The victims are certain groups of persons whose physical appearance or ethnic, cultural, or religious characteristics are different from those of the dominant group, and are interpreted by the latter as being signs of an innate and definitive inferiority, thereby justifying all discriminatory practices in their regard. If, in fact, race defines a human group in terms of immutable and hereditary physical traits, racist prejudice, which dictates racist behavior, can be applied by extension, with equally negative effects, to all persons whose ethnic origin, language, religion or customs make them appear different.

---

*See Edward P. DeBerri, et al., eds., *Catholic Social Teaching: Our Best Kept Secret*, Fourth Edition (Maryknoll, NY: Orbis Books, 2001) 96–98, 226.

9. The most obvious form of racism, in the strictest sense of the word, to be found today is institutionalized racism. This type is still sanctioned by the constitution and laws of a country. It is justified by an ideology of the superiority of persons from European stock over those of African or Indian origin "colored," which is, by some, supported by an erroneous interpretation of the Bible. This is the regime of apartheid or of "separate development." [...]

10. In some countries, forms of racial discrimination still persist with regard to aboriginal peoples. In many cases, these peoples are no more than the remaining vestiges of the original populations of the region, the survivors of veritable genocides carried out in the not too distant past by the invaders or tolerated by the colonial powers. It is also not uncommon to find these aboriginal peoples marginalized with respect to the country's development.

11. Other States still have varying traces of discrimination legislation which limit to one degree or another the civil and religious rights of those belonging to religious minorities, which are generally of different ethnic groups from those of the majority of the citizens. On the basis of such religious and ethnic criteria, even though they are granted hospitality, the members of these minorities cannot, if they request it, obtain citizenship in the country where they live and work.

12. Some mention must also be made of ethnocentricity. This is a very widespread attitude whereby a people has a natural tendency to defend its identity by denigrating that of others to the point that, at least symbolically, it refuses to recognize their full human quality. This behavior undoubtedly responds to an instinctive need to protect the values, beliefs and customs of one's own community, which seem threatened by those of other communities. However, it is easy to see to what extremes such a feeling can lead if it is not purified and relativized, through a reciprocal openness, thanks to objective information and mutual exchanges. The rejection of differences can lead to that form of cultural annihilation which sociologists have called "ethnocide" and which does not tolerate the presence of others except to the extent that they allow themselves to be assimilated into the dominant culture. [...]

13. It is not an exaggeration to say that, within a given country or ethnic group forms of social racism can exist. For example, great masses of poor peasants can be treated without any regard for their dignity and their rights, be driven from their lands, exploited and kept in a situation of economic and social inferiority by all-powerful land owners who benefit from the indifference or active complicity, of the authorities. These are new forms of slavery which are frequent in the Third World. There is no great difference between those who consider others their inferiors because of their race, and those who treat their fellow citizens as inferiors by exploiting them as a work force. In such situations, the universal principles of social justice must be applied effectively. Among other things this would also prevent the over-privileged classes from sinking to actual racist feelings toward their own fellow citizens and finding in them a further alibi for maintaining unjust structures.

14. The phenomenon of spontaneous racism is still more widespread, especially in countries with high rates of immigration. This can be observed among the inhabitants of these countries with regard to foreigners especially when the latter differ in their ethnic origin or religion. The prejudices which these immigrants frequently encounter risk setting into motion reactions which can find their first manifestation in an exaggerated nationalism—which goes beyond legitimate pride in one's own country or even superficial chauvinism. Such reactions can subsequently degenerate into xenophobia or even racial hatred. These reprehensible attitudes have their origin in the irrational fear which the presence of others and confrontation with differences can often provoke. Such attitudes have as their goal, whether acknowledged or not, to deny the other the right to be what he or she is and, in any case, to be "in our country" [...]

15. Among the manifestations of systematic racial distrust, specific mention must once again be made of anti-Semitism. Anti-Semitism has been the most tragic form that racist ideology has assumed in our century with the horrors of the Jewish "holocaust." It has unfortunately not yet entirely disappeared. As if some had nothing to learn from the crimes of the past, certain organizations, with branches in many countries, keep alive the anti-Semitic racist myth, with the support of networks of publications. Terrorist acts which have Jewish persons or symbols as their target have multiplied in recent years and show the radicalism of such groups. Anti-Zionism—which is not of the same order, since it questions the State of Israel and its policies—serves at times as a screen for anti-Semitism, feeding on it and leading to it. Furthermore, some countries impose undue harassments and restrictions on the free emigration of Jews.

16. There is widespread fear that new and as yet unknown forms of racism might appear. This at times is expressed concerning the use that could be made of techniques of artificial procreation through in vitro fertilization and the possibilities of genetic manipulation. Although such fears are still in part hypothetical, they nonetheless draw the attention of humanity to the new and disquieting dimension of man's power over man and thus to the urgent need for corresponding ethical principles. It is important that laws determine as soon as possible the limits which must not be surpassed, so that such "techniques" will not fall into the hands of abusive and irresponsible powers who might seek to "produce" human beings selected according to racial criteria or any other characteristic. [...]

In order firmly to reject such actions and eradicate racist behavior of all sorts from our societies as well as the mentalities that lead to it, we must hold strongly to the convictions about the dignity of every human person and the unity of the human family. Morality flows from these convictions.

Laws can contribute to protecting the basic application of this morality but they are not enough to change the human heart. The moment has come to listen to the message of the Church which gives body to and lays the foundation for such convictions.

4. Contribution to World Conference Against Racism, Racial Discrimination, Xenophobia and Related Intolerance

PONTIFICAL COUNCIL FOR JUSTICE AND PEACE, 2001*

Full text of document available at: http://www.vatican.va/roman_curia/ pontifical_councils/justpeace/documents/rc_pc_justpeace_doc_20010829_ comunicato-razzismo_en.html

Abstract

The *Contribution* notes an increase in racism and discrimination since 1988. It emphasizes the Church's appeal for personal conversion, and for requesting and granting pardons for past actions. Education's role in combating racism, namely teaching the value of human dignity and promoting solidarity and the common good is stressed. Strategies of "positive action" are also recommended. See especially nos. 2, 3, 4, 6, 7, 8, 12, 13, 17, 18, and 21.

Historical Note

The Pontifical Council for Justice and Peace used the world conference on racism held in Durban, South Africa, in 2001 to republish *The Church and Racism* (1988), and issue its corollary. The *Contribution* cites Pope John Paul II extensively, especially his Jubilee Year (2000) requests for pardon for the Church's complicity in racism and discrimination.

Discussion Questions

1. Why does the Vatican stress the importance of forgiveness when speaking about discrimination? What does the process of forgiveness consist of?
2. What kinds of educational experiences help to defeat racism?
3. Why is affirmative action condoned and what limits are put on it?

---

*See Edward P. DeBerri, et al., eds., *Catholic Social Teaching: Our Best Kept Secret*, Fourth Revised and Expanded Edition (Maryknoll, NY: Orbis Books, 2003), 125–128.

Excerpts from the Text

The Catholic Church's Requests for Pardon

6. The Christian should never make racist claims or indulge in racist or discriminatory behaviour, but sadly that has not always been the case in practice nor has it been so in history. In this regard, Pope John Paul II wanted to mark the Jubilee of the Year 2000 by *requests for pardon* made in the name of the Church, so that the Church's memory might be purified from all "forms of counter-witness and scandal" which have taken place in the past millennium. [...] A *purification of memory* then becomes necessary. [...]

7. In this context, during the Jubilee Year, a Solemn Mass was celebrated in Saint Peter's Basilica in Rome on 12 March 2000, in the course of which special prayers confessing faults and requesting pardon were offered. Among the particular intentions, there were confessions for faults committed in relations with the people of Israel, as well as for actions contrary to love, peace, the rights of peoples, cultures, and religions. [...] Having already asked pardon of the peoples of Africa for the slave trade Pope John Paul II took up this theme again on his visit to Senegal, when he visited the "House of Slaves" on the island of Gorée on 22 February 1992; the Pope wanted to make "an act of expiation" and ask pardon of the American Indians and of Africans deported as slaves.

Pardon as the Only Path to National Reconciliation

8. The request for pardon concerns the life of the Church first of all. It is still legitimate however to "hope that political leaders and peoples, especially those involved in tragic conflicts, fuelled by hatred and the memory of often ancient wounds, will be guided by the spirit of forgiveness and reconciliation exemplified by the Church and will make every effort to resolve their differences through open and honest dialogue." In fact, in recent years, in Africa, Latin America, Eastern Europe or Asia, at the end of international, inter-ethnic or civil wars, or with the fall of military or communist dictatorships, legislation has been passed in order to seek the truth and identify those responsible. [...]

11. As an act of gratuitous love, forgiveness has its own demands: the evil which has been done must be acknowledged and, as far as possible, corrected. The primary demand is therefore respect for *truth*. Lying, untrustworthiness, corruption, and ideological or political manipulation make it impossible to restore peaceful social relations. Hence, the importance of procedures which allow truth to be established. [...]

12. From the legal point of view, all persons (individual or corporate) have a right to equitable *reparation* if personally and directly they have suffered injury (material or moral). The duty to make reparation must be fulfilled in an appropriate way. As far as possible, reparation should erase all the consequences

of the illicit action and restore things to the way they would most probably be if that action had not occurred. When such a restoration is not possible, reparation should be made through compensation (equivalent reparation). [...]

The Fundamental Role of Education in the Struggle Against Racism and Discrimination

13. The international community is aware that the roots of racism, discrimination, and intolerance are found in prejudice and ignorance, which are first of all the fruits of sin, but also of faulty and inadequate *education*. To take a main theme of the Durban Conference, the role of education, understood as a "good practice to be promoted" in the struggle against these evils, is fundamental. In this regard too, the Catholic Church recalls her very extensive active role "on the ground," in educating and instructing young people of every confession and on every continent through many centuries. [...] For, in the Church's view, "all people of whatever race, condition, or age, in virtue of their dignity as human persons have an inalienable right to education. This education should be suitable to the particular destiny of the individuals ..."

Positive Discrimination as a Means of Counteracting Racism and Forms of Discrimination

18. Regarding "good practices to promote" and more especially what is called "positive discrimination" or "affirmative distinctions," it is well known that the *International Convention on the Elimination of All Forms of Racial Discrimination*, of 21 December 1965, envisages in Article 1, 4 the possibility of adopting special measures "for the sole purpose of securing adequate advancement of certain racial or ethnic groups or individuals requiring such protection as may be necessary in order to ensure such groups or individuals equal enjoyment or exercise of human rights ..." (the Holy See ratified this Convention in 1969; [...] "So far as the *International Convention on the Elimination of All Forms of Racial Discrimination* is concerned, the Holy See takes special pleasure in reiterating its support of the Convention as the Catholic Church considers it its duty to preach the equal dignity of all human beings, created by God in His image"). [...]

5. The Compendium of the Social Doctrine of the Church

PONTIFICAL COUNCIL FOR JUSTICE AND PEACE, 2005

Full text of document available at: http://www.vatican.va/roman_curia/pontifical_councils/justpeace/documents/rc_pc_justpeace_doc_20060526_compendio-dott-soc_en.html

Abstract

God-given human dignity is the starting point for all Christian reflection on race and racism. The notion of race is not defined here, but the fundamental equality of persons is emphasized. There is one human family and all nations must seek the common good of all peoples. Jesus Christ is the prototype and foundation of the new humanity. The laity in particular is charged with promoting human rights within a human and civil culture. See nos. 144, 431, 433, and 557 that directly address racism.

Historical Note

On October 25, 2004, Cardinal Renato Raffaele Martino, president of the Pontifical Justice and Peace Council, held a press conference in Rome to announce the release of the Church's first *Compendium*. It brings together complex epistemological questions inherent in the nature of the Church's social doctrine. The *Compendium* gives a universal and unified dimension to a set of teachings to serve over time amid the rapid social, political, and economic changes in the world.

Discussion Questions

1. Compare your understanding of the basis for human dignity and that expressed in no. 144.
2. How would you explain to a friend what it means that "Jesus Christ is the prototype of the new humanity?" What implication does this hold for racial justice?
3. Research the use of the phrase "human person integrally considered" in Catholic social teaching. What does this have to do with racial justice? Explain.

Excerpts from the Text

D. The Equal Dignity of All People

144. *"God shows no partiality"* (Acts 10:34; cf. Rom 2:11; Gal 2:6; Eph 6:9), *since all people have the same dignity as creatures made in his image and likeness* [281]. The Incarnation of the Son of God shows the equality of all people with regard to dignity: "There is neither Jew nor Greek, there is neither slave nor free, there is neither male nor female; for you are all one in Christ Jesus" (Gal 3:28; cf. Rom 10:12; 1 Cor 12:13, Col 3:11).

Since something of the glory of God shines on the face of every person, the dignity of every person before God is the basis of the dignity of man before other men [282]. Moreover, this is the ultimate foundation of the radical equality and brotherhood among all people, regardless of their race, nation, sex, origin, culture, or class.

b. Jesus Christ, prototype, and foundation of the new humanity

431. *The Lord Jesus is the prototype and foundation of the new humanity.* In him, the true "likeness of God" (2 Cor 4:4), man—who is created in the image of God—finds his fulfillment. In the definitive witness of love that God has made manifest in the cross of Christ, all the barriers of enmity have already been torn down (cf. Eph 2:12–18), and for those who live a new life in Christ, racial and cultural differences are no longer causes of division (cf. Rom 10:12; Gal 3:26–28; Col 3:11).

Thanks to the Spirit, the Church is aware of the divine plan of unity that involves the entire human race (cf. Acts 17:26), a plan destined to reunite in the mystery of salvation wrought under the saving Lordship of Christ (cf. Eph 1:8–10) all of created reality, which is fragmented and scattered. From the day of Pentecost, when the Resurrection is announced to diverse peoples, each of whom understand it in their own language (cf. Acts 2:6), the Church fulfils her mission of restoring and bearing witness to the unity lost at Babel. Due to this ecclesial ministry, the human family is called to rediscover its unity and recognize the richness of its differences, in order to attain "full unity in Christ." [873]

II. The Fundamental Rules of the International Community

a. The international community and values

433. *The centrality of the human person and the natural inclination of persons and peoples to establish relationships among themselves are the fundamental elements for building a true international community, the ordering of which must aim at guaranteeing the effective universal common good.* [880] Despite the widespread aspiration to build an authentic international community, the unity of the human family is not yet becoming a reality. This is due to obstacles originating in materialistic and nationalistic ideologies that contradict the values of the person integrally considered in all his various dimensions, material and spiritual, individual and community. In particular, any theory or form whatsoever of racism and racial discrimination is morally unacceptable. [881]

The coexistence among nations is based on the same values that should guide relations among human beings: truth, justice, active solidarity and freedom. [882] The Church's teaching, with regard to the constitutive principles of the international community, requires that relations among peoples and political communities be justly regulated according to the principles of reason, equity, law and negotiation, excluding recourse to violence and war, as well as to forms of discrimination, intimidation and deceit. [883]

557. *The social and political involvement of the lay faithful in the area of culture moves today in specific directions. The first is that of seeking to* *guarantee the right of each person to a human and civil culture* "in harmony with the dignity of the human person, without distinction of race, sex, nation, religion, or social circumstances" [1168]. This right implies the right of families and persons to free and open schools; freedom of access to the means of social communication together with the avoidance of all forms of monopolies and ideological control of this field; freedom of research, sharing one's thoughts, debate, and discussion. At the root of the poverty of so many peoples are also various forms of cultural deprivation and the failure to recognize cultural rights. The commitment to the education and formation of the person has always represented the first concern of Christian social action.

Africa

6. Africa Will Arise!

SYMPOSIUM OF EPISCOPAL CONFERENCES OF AFRICA AND MADAGASCAR, 1997

Full text of document available in: *Catholic International*, 8/8 (August 1997) 355–359.*

Abstract

This pastoral letter addressed the ongoing crisis of violence in the Great Lakes Region of Africa that resulted in the slaughter of over 800,000 persons in Rwanda, Burundi, and Zaire (Democratic Republic of the Congo). The bishops distinguish "ethnicity," as a gift of God, and "ethnocentrism," as a perversion of ethnicity and an instrument of exclusion of others. They discuss the root causes of the violence, challenge the international community, and ask the bishops of the affected regions to follow their recommendations.

Historical Note

The Hutu and the Tutsi are two ethnic groups who share a long and violent history together, dating back to nineteenth-century colonial times. These peoples share the same language, intermarry, and have many common cultural features. In 1990, the Tutsi Rwandan Patriotic Front (RPF) invaded Rwanda from Uganda and tried to overthrow its Hutu-led government. Peace accords were signed in 1993 and a coalition government was formed. Sadly,

---

*All quoted text is from this source.

in April 1994, a plane bearing the presidents of both Rwanda and Burundi was shot down and both presidents were killed. In the following 100 days, Hutus terrorized Rwanda killing over 800,000 Tutsis. The Tutsi RPF retaliated and routed the Hutu government in fourteen days. No country came to the aid of the Tutsis or UN Peacekeeping Force that was overwhelmed by the violence and that withdrew when ten of their forces were killed. Some 1.7 million Hutu guerrillas fled into Zaire, but continued to fight from there. In 1998, a rebellion instigated by Rwanda and Uganda ousted Zaire's president. Amid all of this thousands of refugees were created, massacres continued, and the international community basically did nothing.

Discussion Questions

1. Locate the Great Lakes Region of Africa on a map. Research the tribal groups and languages of the area.
2. Has this part of Africa yet "risen"? What social, economic, and political changes have taken place?
3. Has there been reconciliation between the warring parties of the Great Lakes Region? What has contributed to and what has detracted from establishing peace and racial justice in the region?

Excerpts from the Text

5. We have also identified the following as some of the many causes of this human tragedy:

- excessive ethnocentrism and particularism arising from pride, jealousy, greed, and selfishness;
- domination and oppression of one group by another that trigger off interminable violence;
- prejudice and stereotyping that breed contempt, disdain, and closing in on oneself;
- colonialism which has created artificial nations or rather callously separated ethnic groups for selfish economic interests and political egoism of the Metropole;
- support given by industrial nations to different ethnic groups or warring factions by supplying them arms for financial gains at the price of decimating or exterminating African populations;
- manipulation of the ideology of ethnocentrism in order to gain and retain power;
- spirit of vendetta and the inability to forgive, forget and be reconciled;
- disdain for traditional structures of reconciliation used for settling disputes and conflicts;
- poverty which drives people to seek their livelihood by any means, fair or foul;
- denial of the God-given and inalienable rights of others.

We have also come to realize with regret that at times the irresponsible conduct of some pastoral agents have, consciously or unconsciously, contributed to aggravating the situation.

9. By our baptism, we become sons and daughters of God, brothers and sisters of Christ, members of the Church-as-Family. We receive a new identity. Indeed the Christian identity is totally different from ethnic identity. It is, therefore important to deepen that which we have already become by our baptism and to be conscious of this fraternity that knows no boundaries.

In the Church-as-Family, it is Christ that is the center and it is he who gives cohesion to our communion. This is manifested in the mutual respect and collaboration, growth in sharing the joys and the sorrows, in the reciprocal love which enables us to love even our enemies.

10. Having listened to our brothers from the Great Lakes Region, we wish to affirm that even though ethnocentrism shows its atrocities in this tragedy, ethnicity in itself does not connote a negative attitude. On the contrary, ethnicity indicates a gift of God which makes us different one from the other for our mutual enrichment. It is God who makes each one what he is. Ethnicity gives us our social and cultural identity, as well as our security. The individual finds his roots and values in his ethnic group.

18. We appeal to you priests, religious men and women, catechists, leaders of small Christian communities and other pastoral workers, not to let your painful experiences destroy your apostolic fervor. On the contrary, you should see it all as your part of the cross of Christ which he has unequivocally asked us to take up daily and follow him, if we are his true disciples. Please, be healed of your inner wounds and dedicate yourselves to your noble pastoral ministry.

7. Christ Our Peace (Eph 2:14)

SYMPOSIUM OF EPISCOPAL CONFERENCES OF AFRICA AND MADAGASCAR, 2000

Full text of document available at: http://www.sceam-secam.org/

Abstract

The bishops address the developments and problems in Africa and in the Church of Africa since the 1995 Synod on Africa and reflect on the hopes and potential of Africans to resolve problems for the common good. The Church's role as the Family of God is to model, witness, and teach the ways of Christ, the source of peace. The bishops chide the unresponsive wealthy and powerful nations of the world, especially former colonizers and those that conduct "wars by proxy."

Historical Note

Since the Synod on Africa, seventeen of the fifty-three African countries saw armed conflicts and the international community virtually ignored them all. Government structures left by colonizers are inadequate for dealing with current needs. While the gross domestic product (GDP) growth rate necessary to sustain real development is 7 percent, Africa's overall growth rate was 2.5 percent. The external debt of Africa was $349 billion. Of the 191 countries studied by the World Health Organization, thirty-five African countries were listed among the bottom fifty, and seventeen were among the last twenty. The Church in Africa grew one percent in population to 116,664,000; priestly vocations increased by 18 percent to 19,654. Forty-nine new dioceses were created between 1994 and 2000.*

Discussion Questions

1. Research some of the dimensions of colonialism in Africa.
2. Why did the international community fail Africa?
3. Can Africans resolve their own problems? Why or why not?
4. Is the "Church as the Family of God" a realistic goal for the Church in Africa amid its vast diversity of cultures, regions and language groups?

Excerpts from the Text

34. Africa has entered a period of profound change in managing conflicts. Attempts have been made, here and there, to regulate and lessen conflicts. In spite of the concept of noninterference in the internal affairs of states, Africa is coming, with the support of the international community, to control some crises (Liberia, Sierra Leone, Burundi). In Africa's numerous conflicts, several forms of conflict resolution have been adopted, such as force (ECOMOG), embargo, intimidation, even the threat of destabilisation.

35. We note with satisfaction the emergence of a more informal system of managing conflicts and tensions, built on specific diplomatic activities. Some African heads of state and important persons have involved themselves in this. [...]

36. In an Africa whose future is endangered by conflicts of all sorts, the "do ut des," that is the "give and be given," is one of the bases of conflict resolution. This idea of compromise allows the protagonists of a violent clash to "save face," to avoid giving the impression of being defeated. The "give and be given" arises not only from psychology, but from the idea of

---

*This data is cited in Cardinal John P. Schotte, "Africa: A Changing Continent Since the Celebration of the Special Assembly for Africa," http://www.afrikaworld.net/synod/schotte2.htm, Accessed July 14, 2006.

sharing, or recognition. Many conflicts persist in Africa because the minimum compromise has not been found which would lessen the claims of both, while assuring each a "place in the sun."

37. Some regimes are politically trapped because of personal antagonism, clan rivalry or ancestral hatred consciously maintained. The refusal to share and the will to wield power exclusively, often against all common sense, gives rise to insoluble situations that the passage of time only makes worse. Things are complicated further when under the pretext of refusing impunity, one really tries to settle scores. The "do ut des" is then perceived to be favoring impunity. Impunity arises out of justice, but the "do ut des" is at its best a form of charity, of love of neighbor. The common good and the greater interest of the nations are part of the ethical basis of social justice.

If justice requiring impunity is sometimes recommended, love which takes account of the interests of the poor and innocent victims of bloody conflicts should often prevail. If the interest of the people requires that one does not judge or condemn, why insist on justice? Here arises the concept of the 'Pardon' as a solution to bitter and intractable conflicts.

38. The 'Pardon' demands, in the light of the intractability of certain problems, and after a full analysis of the requirements of the common good of the whole population, a complete "return to the same level." All political actors have to agree to transcend the past to build the future together. This is difficult, but also heroic, and the only way to resolve some intractable problems.

Far from being an easy compromise, the "give and be given" solution, when it is not limited to political leaders or elites and genuinely aims at the common good and makes dialogue and tolerance triumph over hate and revenge, is the highway to peace.

39. However, for this to occur, all the people—the whole nation—must be involved ... not just the summit which ignores the base. But the "give and be given" can't do away with every demand or Justice. The International Court on Rwanda exists to show the necessity of dealing ruthlessly with known perpetrators of genocide and heinous crimes and mass executions. Justice from such an international court has a cathartic effect which cannot be underestimated. It deals exemplarily with the guilty now to prevent such atrocities in the future. In a legal process culminating in a trial, there is an educative element which must not be overlooked. [...]

40. A third element must be taken into account in reparation and in the "give and be given" process. The settlement which is effected should be effective, educative, totally geared to solving problems of peace and development, a wide-ranging development which takes into account the suffering of the people and tries to alleviate it. A deal cannot be agreed just for the sake of completing a deal, but to bring into play ideas and concepts, practices and plans, and to build a society of unity, justice, and peace.

8. On Tribalism

BISHOPS OF CAMEROON, 1996

Full text of document available by writing to the National Episcopal Conference of Cameroon, Yaounde. Request a photocopy from: Princeton Theological Seminary Library.

Abstract

Six years after the bishops issued their pastoral letter, *Economic Crisis Afflicting Our Country* (1990), Cameroon's crisis had deepened. The bishops identified rampant tribalism as a root cause, and they elaborated its destructive effects throughout Cameroonian society.

Historical Note

Cameroon had a long, postcolonial struggle for national unity, having been controlled by France, Germany, and Britain. In 1996, following turbulent reform efforts, a new constitution was adopted, giving the president considerable power and mandating regional and local elections.

Discussion Questions

1. Research the social, economic, and political conditions in Cameroon in 1996 and compare them to conditions today.
2. How do the bishops define tribalism? Is tribalism found elsewhere in the world beyond Africa? Explain.
3. Compare and contrast the characteristics of "tribalism" and a healthy ethnic identity. Can a person change from one way of viewing her or his ethnicity to another? What might cause such a change?

Excerpts from the Text

3. The basis of tribalism, which we have just enumerated, naturally lead people to adopt egoistic and individualistic positions characterized by a tendency to fall back on their own ethnic groups, which is what we are seeing these days. When a citizen fails to find in State institutions that which he expects as of right—job security, immediate and fair settlement of court cases, protection from assaults, etc.—he naturally turns to "*his own people.*" Blood ties, a common language, reference to the same customs, and

all that unites a group, provide a natural cultural support that is reassuring. But these are reactions we should all fight to overcome.

4. The harmful effects of this tendency to withdraw to *"to one's own people" become evident when such parental ties are brought* to bear on economic as well as the political life of the nation; thus going beyond the legitimate framework of the extended family. In his Post-Synodal Apostolic Exhortation Ecclesia in Africa, the Holy Father extensively condemns the evil effects of such behavior, by pointing out that:

- tribalism endangers both the peace and the pursuit of the common good of the entire society
- tribalism hinders open and constructive dialogue among different ethnic groups
- tribalism encourages ethnic hatred and impedes the construction of national unity; it may even produce political disorder and cause civil war.

This evil finds fertile grounds especially in the political interests of some ambitious citizens who stir up tribal feelings of the weaker folk to gain political power which enables them to use the common good to their own advantage. Are those preaching tribal idolatry really out to protect their tribe or to enrich themselves as quickly as possible? To be rich can be legitimate and even Christian. But to become rich in a dishonest way requires restitution before reconciliation with God is possible.

5. To love one's tribe is a good thing; it is to love oneself, which the Gospel recommends (Mk 12:31). However, attachment to one's tribe becomes a real evil when one excludes others, persecutes them, deprives them of their rights, assassinates them, instigates one ethnic group against another for personal, political, or economic ends. Thus we see these days anonymous tracts, bearing clearly tribalistic messages sometimes supported by biblical quotations, circulating in our country, inciting one group to rise up against another, under the pretext of self defense and of the "protection of the minorities." There is no better way of distorting the message of Sacred Scripture! Newspaper articles have even echoed these tracts with the same intention. The audiovisual media have at times magnified the same message in national and official languages. The Bishops have already expressed their disapproval of such manipulation of public opinion by saying: *"Tensions aroused and sustained by unscrupulous and often veiled interests are threatening the stability of public institutions, social harmony and the peace of families."* (Pastoral Letter on the Economic Crisis, no. 14)

7. To prevent similar tragedies from befalling our country, the first remedy is for us to become aware, on a personal as well as collective level, of the great diversity of our people. [...] Cameroon's diversity constitutes its richness, not its weakness. To be proud of the exceptional variety of the languages and cultures that make up our country, and to convince our children to do the same, is a noble reaction.

It is even more noble to express admiration for the greatness of others. Every one of our ethnic groups has its own splendors, its own values and its own richness which it can bring to light and share with others. It has been said several times over that Cameroon is Africa in miniature, a fact we should rightly be proud of as nothing would be more unrealistic and dangerous than to claim that we did not have differences. The danger, however, lies in saying one thing and doing another thing altogether, in other words, officially acclaiming the richness and human variety of the nation while privately and secretively systematically denouncing our neighbors' particularities. And that is precisely what is happening in the privacy of family conversations and even in school today. There, no doubt, lies the hidden source of danger and sin: "For it is from the heart that come evil ideas." (Mt 15:19)

15. To you, Christians, know that "*you are the salt of the earth and the light of the world.*" (Mt 5:13–14). A Christian cannot claim to be a disciple if he nurtures in himself racism, tribalism or hatred for another human being, whoever he or she may be. [(Mt 5:45–48) is quoted here.]

9. Evangelization in Kenya

CATHOLIC BISHOPS OF KENYA, 2004

Full text of document available at: http://www.evangelizatio.org/portale/adgentes/chieselocali/chieselocali.php?id=47

Abstract

Following upon John Paul II's Apostolic Exhortation *Ecclesia in Africa* that the African Church become the "Family of God," the bishops invite all Catholics to recommit themselves to Jesus Christ; to overcome the divisions of race, ethnicity, class, and nation; and to work for justice, peace, and reconciliation.

Historical Note

This pastoral was released at the Kenyan bishops' meeting, St. Thomas Aquinas Seminary in Nairobi, April 20 to 23, 2004, following years of corrupt government, tribal violence, and land disputes resulting from British colonial land leases given to the Maasai and others. The election of President Mwai Kibaki was seen as a sign of hope. Early in January 2004, a constitutional conference was convened to revise the constitution, but Kibaki's coalition divided over reducing the president's powers and establishing an executive prime minister. The government withdrew from the conference.

Discussion Questions

1. Research the social, political, and economic developments in Kenya since 2004.
2. What techniques and strategies can parents and teachers use to help youth identify with their tribal or ethnic group, and yet understand him- or herself as a member of the "Church as the Family of God"?
3. What can Christians and people of goodwill outside of Kenya do to support Kenyans in their efforts to sustain themselves as a Family of God building a good nation?

Excerpts from the Text

Church—Family of God

The Church, as a community of God's people, looks at the Trinity as the full expression of love between the Father, the Son and the Holy Spirit. The family is the central structure of human life. Jesus was born in a human family; with his incarnation, Jesus became a member of a human family. As members of a human family we are different and have different roles, the Church has different ministries and gifts. We make unity in diversity. This is the richness of the Church. In the Old Testament and in many African cultures, brotherhood and sisterhood was based on blood relationship. In the light of the New Testament, the new Family of God is not an association of clans or ethnic groups but a brotherhood and sisterhood beyond the frontiers of blood relationship, clan, ethnic group, or race. For Christians, "brothers and sisters" are those reborn with water and the Spirit in Baptism. These are the disciples of Jesus who hear the Word of God and keep it: "Whoever does the will of my heavenly Father is my brother, and sister, and mother."

By Baptism we enter into God's family. We receive God's life and Spirit. We are no longer slaves. We are God's children, and we can call God "Abba, Father." Being members of God's family, we are heirs; and as we share Christ sufferings, we share also his glory. Those who are particularly in need are considered as "brothers" and "sisters" regardless of their religion, race, status: "Whatever you did for one of these least brothers of mine, you did for me." Jesus, by becoming a member of the human family, becomes the "firstborn among many brothers." Jesus, the Son of God, "is not ashamed to call us brothers" and he has become like his brothers in every way except sin, that he might be a merciful and faithful high priest. In this family of God, St Paul exhorts: "Let love be sincere; hate what is evil, hold onto what is good; love one another with mutual affection; anticipate one another in showing honor. Do not grow slack in zeal, be fervent in spirit, serve the Lord. Rejoice in hope, endure in affliction, persevere in prayer."

Peace and Social Responsibility

In a world where conflicts are a sad reality, the Catholic Church—together with all people of goodwill—wishes to build PEACE. In his message at the beginning of this year 2004, Pope John Paul II reiterated his appeal: "to reach peace, teach peace…If peace is possible it is also a duty." As we plan for a new evangelization of Kenya and a deepening of our faith, we must be educated practically to the great value of peace—a peace based on solid principles.

1. "Blessed are the peacemakers, for they will be called children of God."
2. Truth, Justice, Love, and Freedom are the four pillars on which Peace is built.
3. To build peace we must first of all respect the Dignity of the Human Person. We witness constant harassments. Often the poor and ignorant are victims of blatant injustices. It is our Christian duty to show respect for all: (a simple person boarding a matatu, a patient in hospital, or an "ordinary" citizen requesting a service in a public office) without distinction of social class, religion, race, sex or age. Those who have professions must act in accordance with the ethics and spirit of that profession. The poor, the weak, the sick will always need special attention, as they cannot defend themselves.

10. A Message to All Catholics in Southern Africa

SOUTHERN AFRICAN BISHOPS' CONFERENCE, 2003

Full text of document available at: http://www.catholic-ct.org.za/about/messagetoallthecatholicsinsouthernafrica.htm

Abstract

Ten years after the official end of Apartheid in South Africa, the Church remained far from being racially unified. The scars of South Africa's traumatic Apartheid and violent history are deep. The pastoral letter announced a bold and concrete practical pastoral plan for working through the most difficult racial issues Catholics hold and that prevent their coming together. The plan consisted in convening facilitated seminars in eight regions of South Africa that focused on three aims: (1) to raise awareness and facilitate discussion about race relations within the Church, (2) to create safe spaces for people to share their experiences and dialogue about racism and general race relations in their daily contexts, and (3) to help evaluate past and present experiences and mistakes in the Church with integrity so as to promote healing and corrective action. The bishops participated in each of the seminars explaining the Church's concern about the state of race relations in the Church and society.

Historical Note

The Catholic Church in South Africa originated in 1652 as a "settler church" and was viewed as an "unwelcome guest" by the Calvinist Dutch majority. The Catholic hierarchy's priority was to establish bridges with the Afrikaners "for the Church's safety." As late as 1964, there was disagreement over the Catholic position for publicly challenging Apartheid between Bishop Hurley, who held it was "unchristian and immoral," and Bishop Whelan, who denied it was immoral, though deplorable. Only in 1977 in its "Declaration of Commitment" did the South African Catholic Bishops' Conference shift to a position of black equality. This legacy still haunts the Church.

Discussion Questions

1. Research the Apartheid system of South Africa.
2. Racialized structures feed people's prejudices. What kind of social structures can support the disbursement and elimination of prejudices?
3. What conditions contribute to creating "a safe space" in which people can share their experiences and dialogue about racism and general race relations in their daily contexts?

Excerpts from the Text

The Vision of God Is a Community of All Peoples

This plan of God for all people (Is 25:6–10) is especially apt to describe a vision for all our peoples in Southern Africa growing together into one community.

Let us examine ourselves. Parish Pastoral Councils, Associations and small Christian communities should ask themselves the following:

- What examples of God's love do we experience in our communities, which reflect God's vision for people?
- What evidence do we see in our communities of the vision held out in the Pastoral Plan?
- What do we do in our efforts to tolerate the needs of other cultures in our community?
- Are we Catholic enough in the fullest sense of that name which calls us to be embracing and all encompassing?

We Are Called to Continue Christ's Mission to Create Unity

The gospel message calls us to reach out and create one human community in which all find an experience of belonging to the same human family. Our church with its many groupings, structures, and networks places us in a unique position to work at overcoming these barriers. [...]

We urge you all to look for ways to bring people of different cultural and ethnic traditions into greater fruitful contact with each other. The call is to go further than casual and superficial acquaintance, to work together and to build up real family relationships in the one family of the Church.

In particular we, as Bishops, feel challenged to assist people in overcoming the uneasiness they feel with each other. This uneasiness often results in their not participating in church or civic activities when there is a difference in cultural and ethnic expressions, for example in:

- Burials;
- Holy Masses on special occasions, e.g. ordinations and pilgrimages;
- Parish bazaars; and
- Associations and sodalities.

We seek your support and assistance as we pledge ourselves to work together with you in promoting this climate for greater social interactivity.

Conclusion

The difficulties, which we still experience in many of our church communities, are a reflection of the difficulties experienced as a nation. [...]

We would like to quote again from *Community Serving Humanity*, published in 1989:

"In Southern Africa we have inherited a legacy of barriers. These are the racial barriers erected by a political policy that fed on people's racial prejudices... There can be no meaningful search for community that does not strive to remove those barriers. Discrimination whether based on race or on sex, is found not only in society but also in our Church communities. In pursuing the theme of *Community Serving Humanity we* must therefore give special attention to demolishing these barriers, removing discrimination, and fostering a genuine experience of equality before the Lord." (no. 16)

In the name of the Lord we call on you, Beloved Sisters and Brothers, to reach out to one another in church services and in the life of the parish, despite differences of language and culture. Succeeding in this will mean more than building a new South Africa; it opens the door to the Kingdom of God among us.

11. I Was a Stranger and You Welcomed Me

CATHOLIC BISHOPS OF ZAMBIA, 2001

Full text of document available at: http://www.catholiczambia.org.zm/PastoralLetterB.pdf

Abstract

Though the Church of Zambia is a welcoming church, increased flows of refugees have sparked growing attitudes of xenophobia and racism. The bishops challenge Zambian Catholics to reflect on this trend and reject its influence. Rather, Christians must warmly welcome the stranger in Christ's name, supporting them in a dignified way. See especially nos. 1, 6, 7, 10, 11, 12, 13, 18, 19, and 21.

Historical Note

This letter commemorates World Refugee Day 2001 and the UN World Conference against Racism, Racial Discrimination, Xenophobia, and Related Intolerance in Durban, South Africa. Surrounded by conflict-ridden nations, a steady flow of refugees entered Zambia from the 1960s to the present.

Discussion Questions

1. What is the relationship between racism, immigrants, and asylum seekers?
2. Discuss the psychosocial dynamics and needs of a migrant or an asylum seeker? What can the Church do to help meet the needs of such persons?
3. What might cause a Christian to fail to "welcome" a "stranger?"

Excerpts from the Text

Growing Xenophobia

10. The first issue is the increase of negative feelings towards outsiders among the Zambian people, clearly fostered by a xenophobic campaign developed by some elements of the mass media. Let us remember the words of the Holy Father on this matter:

> *The mass media can play an important role, both positive and negative. Their activity can foster a proper evaluation and better understanding of the problems of the "new arrivals," dispelling prejudices and emotional reactions, or instead, it can breed rejection and hostility, impeding and jeopardizing proper integration* (John Paul II, Message WMRD, 1998).

12. We are obliged to note that any criminal accusation must be addressed exclusively against the subjects in the case and must be followed by prosecution in court according to the Law. General criminalization of a social group is an expression of racism and xenophobia completely contrary to the Law of God and to the tradition of hospitality that the Zambian people have always honoured.

13. With this public remark we fulfill the command of John Paul II:

It is necessary to guard against the rise of new forms of racism or xeno-phobic behaviour, which attempt to make these brothers and sisters of ours scapegoats for what may be difficult local situations. When an understanding of the problem is conditioned by prejudice and xeno-phobic attitudes, the Church must not fail to speak up for brotherhood and to accompany it with acts testifying to the primacy of charity (John Paul II, Message WMRD, 1996).

18. Consequently, we call on the Zambian people to offer such long-term refugees opportunities to participate in all aspects of our social life, so that they can integrate themselves into our society and rebuild their lives in safety and stability. Against the xenophobic statements that are continuously served up for public opinion, we call the attention of the Zambian people to the great potential for contribution to the country's development that would result from integration of long-term refugees with whom we enjoy mutual familiarity.

19. This call has a special meaning for the Zambian Catholic faithful and their pastors. It is our duty to keep our congregations, social services, justice and peace work, and developmental initiatives open to those who desire a place where they can feel part of us, protected and welcomed in a communion of fraternity, the Family of God. Whatever their origin or religion, this is requested from us by our faith, as the Pope remarks:

Catholicity is not only expressed in the fraternal communion of the baptized, but also in the hospitality extended to the stranger, whatever his religious belief, in the rejection of all racial exclusion or discrimination, in the recognition of the personal dignity of every man and woman and, consequently, in the commitment to furthering their in-alienable rights (John Paul II, Message WMRD, 1999).

21. Finally, we call on the authorities to reconsider their policies and to develop legal schemes which allow refugees to recover their full rights when they are forced to stay in Zambia due to the continuation of conflict or persecution in their countries of origin. We also call on the authorities to step up their efforts to protect refugees and asylum seekers from any abuse or arbitrariness resulting from the restriction of their rights by the Law.

Asia

12. Consultation on "Indigenous/Tribal Peoples in Asia and the Challenges of the Future"

OFFICE OF EVANGELIZATION, FEDERATION OF ASIAN BISHOPS' CONFERENCES, 2001

Full text of document available in: Franz-Joseph Eilers, ed., *For All the Peoples of Asia,* Vol. 3 (Quezon City, Philippines: Claretian Publications, 2002) 227–229.*

Abstract

The Church is committed to assist the indigenous and tribal peoples in preserving their way of life and culture. The Gospel enlightens all cultures and the best means of preserving what is good in any culture is through evangelization. The Church is committed to assist indigenous and tribal peoples of Asia.

Historical Note

The consultation was held in Pattaya, Thailand, from December 14 to 18, 2001. The consultation was to respond to John Paul II's call in his Apostolic Exhortation, *Ecclesia in Asia*, for the Church of Asia to defend indigenous cultures as part of its evangelizing mission. The forty-two participants included representative indigenous and tribal people, as well as thirteen bishops from seven of the FABC conferences.

---

*All quoted text is from this source.

Discussion Questions

1. Why is it important for the Church to affirm the right of indigenous peoples to exist?
2. What kind of training can the Church provide to help indigenous peoples to preserve their way of life by defending threats to it?

Excerpts from the Text

4. The traditional way of life of indigenous/tribal peoples is threatened by ecological destruction of the habitat in which they live, by displacement and alienation from their lands, by globalizing market forces that make it impossible for them to compete, and by insensitive development projects carried out by governments which sometimes even refuse to recognize their identity as a people. Against these threats, we affirm the right of indigenous/tribal peoples to remain who they are and to decide their own priorities in the development process. In this, we unite ourselves with the words of Pope John Paul II in his *Apostolic Exhortation Ecclesia in Asia*: The Church proclaims "an attitude of deep respect for their traditional religion and its values; this implies the need to help them to help themselves, so that they can work to improve their situation and become the evangelizers of their own culture and society" (EA, 34).

5. [...] Education is the key to well-being and the solution to the many problems that afflict indigenous/tribal peoples.

6. The Church's task includes helping people to preserve and express their identity in the face of modernization, urbanization and exploitation, and to keep alive and promote their cultural traditions. [...] At the same time, the Church must defend the right of indigenous/tribal people to become Christ's disciples without being thereby cut off from their ancestral roots.

7. Our concern for indigenous/tribal peoples in Asia must involve the whole Church. [...]

8. The best way to preserve what is good in any culture is to evangelize that culture. If we want to preserve the riches of indigenous/tribal cultures, we must strive to bring the Gospel to those peoples who have not yet been blessed by the Good News of Jesus Christ. It is indigenous/tribal Christians themselves who can best evangelize their own people, but the encounter between the Gospel and indigenous/tribal peoples does not end at baptism. True inculturation occurs when a people bring together, under the guidance of the Holy Spirit, the Gospel teaching with their own cultural values. To this end, we recommend:

  i. that our dioceses foster formal and non-formal education of indigenous/tribal peoples making provision also for sociopolitical education programs so that they can analyze the situation in which they live, protest injustices, train future leaders, and grow in political awareness of the need for committed and effective civic life,

ii. that we encourage and participate in programs in which the values and traditions of indigenous/tribal peoples can be celebrated in song, dance, drama, storytelling etc.,

iii. that "Associations of Tribal/Indigenous Peoples" be formed in order to build solidarity through interaction with similar groups, to spread awareness of the causes of indigenous/tribal peoples, and to promote their concerns in Christian circles and structures,

iv. that the Holy Father create a Pontifical Council for Indigenous/Tribal Peoples' Concerns or at least a Desk for Indigenous/Tribal Peoples within the Sacred Congregation for the Evangelization of Peoples,

v.   that the FABC establish an Office for Indigenous Peoples' Concerns, or at least an Indigenous/Tribal Concerns Desk within an existing FABC Office; in doing so, we strongly endorse the similar recommendation made at the 1995 Hua Hin consultation on Indigenous/Tribal Peoples.

13. Statement on Caste

CATHOLIC BISHOPS' CONFERENCE OF INDIA, GENERAL BODY MEETING, TIRUCHIRAPALLY, 1982

Full text of document available at: http://www.dalitchristians.com/html/CBCI_Tiruchirapally010482.htm

Abstract

The bishops categorically held that neither "caste" nor a "caste mentality" have any place in Christianity. They appealed to the constitution of India and sought enforcement of its ideal provisions of "Liberty, Fraternity, and justice for all without discrimination of caste or creed." They called on Catholics to reflect on the compatibility of caste and the Eucharist, and they held that any exclusion of fellow Christians based on consideration of caste is intolerable. The statement was drafted by members of the Dalit Welfare Committee, Bishops Patrick D'Souza, Alan de Lastic, and Thomas Fernando.

Historical Note

The Indian bishops met in Tiruchirapally, from January 4 to 14, 1982. They participated in a workshop on the "problem of caste" in Indian society. By unanimous decision, they agreed to publish a statement boldly condemning and confronting the current situation of caste and caste mentality pervasive in Indian society and among Christians, in particular.

Discussion Questions

1. Research the structure and origins of the caste system in India.
2. What is your impression of the terms the Indian government and the bishops use to name the special categories of people?
3. How effective have the efforts of the Indian bishops been in eradicating the caste mentality from the Church itself?

Excerpts from the Text

Notwithstanding all these efforts, much yet remains to be done within the Church and outside particularly in the eradication of what is known as the "caste mentality" which often finds expression in actions that are manifestly unchristian and even affects, in some areas the sphere of religious practices. The tensions arising from the caste mentality are not confined to the oppression of the lower castes by those of the higher castes but are also found within the castes themselves.

We state categorically that caste, with its consequent effects of discrimination and "caste mentality," has no place in Christianity. It is, in fact, a denial of Christianity because it is inhuman. It violates the God-given dignity and equality of the human person. God created man in his own image and likeness. He accepts and loves every human being without distinction. He so loved the world that He sent His only Son, Jesus Christ, who became fully man and died to save all men. "In Christ Jesus you are all sons of God there is neither Jew nor Greek neither slave nor free for you are all one in Christ Jesus" (Gal 3, 26–28). Thus, human dignity and respect are due to every person and any denial of this is a sin against God and man. It is an outright denial of the Fatherhood of God which, in practice, renders meaningless the brotherhood of man.

Catholics, in particular, are called to reflect on whether they can meaningfully participate in the Eucharist without repudiating and seriously striving to root out caste prejudices and similar traditions and sentiments both within the Church and outside. It is intolerable that caste should be a determining factor in membership of pastoral or parish councils and other Church associations; and even worse, in ecclesiastical appointments and posts of responsibility in religious Congregations.

The National Consultation referred to above has made some concrete suggestions relating particularly to those belonging to the backward classes, e.g., removal of all forms of segregation, greater fraternizing on a social level and so on. Special provision, perhaps on a priority and guaranteed basis, should also be made for them in the matter of admissions to educational institutions, where particular attention should be paid to them, through remedial and coaching classes, if necessary.

Caritas India, which has already opted in favor of projects to assist the backward classes, is urged to step up its programs in this line so as to remedy the helplessness resulting from economic, social and other causes. In all cases, our efforts must be directed towards removing the sense of inferiority under which they have been laboring for centuries and towards strengthening their feeling of being free citizens of India.

In particular we call upon pastors and religious superiors to provide positive encouragement towards the promotion of vocations from the backward classes to the priesthood and the religious life.

The issue of caste and its consequent evil effects is not a peripheral one for the Church or, indeed, for society at large. Delay in facing it—or sometimes even a refusal to do so—is more than a question of human rights. It is betrayal of the Christian vocation. We can no longer watch complacently while millions of our brothers and sisters are denied the rights that flow from their dignity as human beings and children of God.

14. Message for Liberation and Development of Dalit Christians

CATHOLIC BISHOPS' CONFERENCE OF INDIA, 1998

Full text of document available at: http://www.dalitchristians.com/html/CBCI_Varansi032198.htm

Abstract

The statement is made in preparation for the Jubilee year—*Yesu Krist Jayanti 2000*. The bishops again denounced the caste system and Dalit discrimination, admitting their efforts to eliminate these were ineffective, even in the Church. They outlined an action plan for all dioceses and a special ten-point plan for development of Dalit Christians.

Historical Note

Since the 1982 bishops' statement condemning the caste system, increased efforts by Catholics and religious groups raised awareness of Dalits, and they begin to assert their rights. But violent reprisals against the Dalits followed. The bishops' 1992 statement supported the Dalits in their socioeconomic concerns, equality within the Church, and proper respect from upper-caste Catholics. In 1997, the CBCI Commission for Scheduled Castes/Tribes and Backward Classes asked the Hierarchy to urge the state at all levels again to grant the Dalits their rights and to introduce legislation in Parliament restoring the rights denied since 1950, when Christians of Scheduled Caste Origin were removed from the list (paragraph 3 of the constitution). The CBCI also joined other Christian and religious groups in numerous appeals for justice for Christians, especially the Dalits.

Discussion Questions

1. What keeps the caste system alive and well in India, even though it has been illegal for years?
2. Has the bishops ten-point plan been effectively implemented? Why or why not?

Excerpts from the Text

Action Program

5.1 First of all there needs to be a faith-based vision that enables us to see Jesus in the poor, the Dalits and Tribals so that there is a change in our attitude towards them. This must become evident to them in our policies and practices and day-to-day interactions.

5.2 Non-formal education to consciences [conscientize], train, organize and empower the poor, the Dalits and the tribals must be given top priority in our social apostolate.

5.3 We should make every effort to liberate the poor from the clutches of dishonest practices by upholding the values of honesty and dignity in public life. We should refuse to collaborate in any way with those who indulge in corrupt practices of bribery, discriminatory favoritism etc.

5.4 The church must take a clear stand against caste discrimination and declare it a sin. This must be taught in Catechism and homilies and any form of discrimination must be completely stopped, wherever it exists, be it among the priests, in religious communities, in practices of selection of candidates for priesthood and religious life and in the sphere of administration. We propose this as a goal to be set in motion powerfully and immediately so that we can present to the Lord and proclaim to the world that we are fully reconciled and transformed Christian community at the dawn of the third millennium.

5.5 Our liturgy should challenge us to build relationships as members of one family, foster fellowship and solidarity leading to active concern and equality. There should be no sign of any discrimination in places of worship, cemeteries etc. Our liturgy should also challenge us to face the realities of the world with a sense of mission. The Word that we celebrate should become the giving event for the world. Our celebrations of popular devotions such as novenas and prayer sessions should have a mission thrust.

5.6 Our institutional services must cater increasingly to the poor and there must be reservations both in admission and in employment for the Dalits and tribals.

5.7 Following the example of the first Christians who shared generously with the poor, we *should make* personal and institutional sacrifices, whatever they may cost us, for the poor, the Dalits and the tribals of today. Only then will we become truly the Church of the poor. This is the New Way of Being Church that we want to usher in as we enter the third millennium.

10-Point Program for the Integrated Development of Dalit Christians

1. In places of worship and burial grounds Christians of Scheduled Caste Origin (CSCO) should be treated on a footing of equality and there should be no discrimination.
2. Opportunities should be created in the dioceses to enable CSCO to join seminaries, convents and religious congregations in numbers.
3. In order to create leadership in their ranks, CSCO should be encouraged to become members of Parish Councils, Parish Finance Committees, Diocesan Pastoral Councils, Multi-Purpose Social Service Societies and other Church related organizations, and entrusted with responsible positions.
4. In matters of admission to Catholic Teacher Training and Industrial Schools, preference should be given to the students belonging to the CSCO.
5. Special coaching classes should be conducted to improve the educational standards of the students who are weak in their studies to enable them to improve their performance.
6. Preference should be given CSCO in matters of appointment in the educational institutions, Social Service Societies and other Church sponsored organizations and projects.
7. In the Diocesan Social Service Societies, developmental projects should be exclusively designed to promote the economic development of the CSCO and members of these should be chosen to involve actively in the execution of such projects and in the training programs connected therewith.
8. To encourage high education, particularly technical and professional education among CSCO, the Diocesan and Religious Congregations should jointly create a Scholarship Fund as a source of encouragement to deserving students.
9. A SC/ST/BC Commission should be created in each diocese immediately to monitor the programs meant for these people.
10. In the CSCO struggle to obtain their rights and privileges from the Central and State governments the Church in India should actively support their programme in this regard.

15. Toward Overcoming Buraku Discrimination: The Fundamental Position of the Catholic Church toward the Buraku Issue

Committee for Buraku Issues, Catholic Bishops' Conference of Japan, 1992

Full text of document available in Japanese by writing the Committee for Buraku Issues, Catholic Bishops' Conference of Japan, at: info@cbcj.catholic.jp

Abstract

The bishops recognize that despite their past efforts, discrimination against the Buraku is still rampant in Japanese society. They call for concrete efforts to abolish this discrimination within the Church and in Japanese society.

Historical Note

The Report of the Dowa Policy Council (1965) called Dowa discrimination against the Buraku "a most serious and important social problem," and challenged Japan to rectify Dowa civil and human rights. A 1990 survey showed that the Buraku experienced discrimination within the Church, as well. Little progress was made to remedy discrimination since the 1987 pastoral, "Let Us Live Together with Joy."

Discussion Questions

1. Research the history and the present living conditions of the Buraku.
2. What progress has been made to integrate the Buraku into the mainstream life of the Japanese Church?
3. How is the Buraku discrimination a concern of the whole Church?

Excerpts from the Text*

Dear brothers and sisters in Christ,
This message is for all who are interested in the discrimination issue in the hope to overcome the Buraku discrimination.

Introduction

1. It is extremely lamentable that there is a minority group discriminated against and suppressed existing in this world in which we live. In his previous message on peace, "There Is No Peace without Respect for the Minority," John Paul II emphasized that we should respect the right of the minority in order to embody the peace on earth.[†]

---

*Translated from Committee for Buraku Issues Catholic Bishops' Conference of Japan, http://www5b.biglobe.ne.jp/~catburak/jinken%20date.htm, Accessed December 23, 2006.

†Message of His Holiness John Paul II for the celebration of the World Day of Peace, January 1, 1989, http://www.vatican.va/holy_father/john_paul_ii/messages/peace/documents/hf_jp-ii_mes_19881208_xxii-world-day-for-peace_en.html

In Japan, there are various minority groups being discriminated against. Their existence itself has become the painful plea to our consciousness. Especially, the existence of Buraku discrimination rooted in our cultural and historical traditions, and the cry of those discriminated against in various circumstances including employment and marriage, challenges the Catholic Church in Japan and questions the consciousness of our souls.

Our consciousness tells us that discrimination is an evil and unacceptable act as a human being. Further, the Bible declares that discrimination is sin.

For instance, the Apostle James says: "My brothers, show no partiality as you adhere to the faith in our glorious Lord Jesus Christ. For if a man with gold rings on his fingers and in fine clothes comes into your assembly, and a poor person in shabby clothes also comes in, and you pay attention to the one wearing the fine clothes and say, 'Sit here, please,' while you say to the poor one, 'Stand there,' or 'Sit at my feet,' have you not made distinctions, among yourselves and become judges with evil designs?" (Jas 2:1–4)

As a representative of the Catholic Church in Japan, the Bishops Committee on Society of the Catholic Bishops' Conference of Japan comes to clarify the fundamental opinions, positions and decisions against Buraku discrimination. We ask for your understanding and support regarding this matter.*

Discrimination among Us

2. While there are various discriminations that exist in contemporary Japanese society, the Buraku discrimination is profound, deep-rooted, and peculiar to Japanese society "built upon the social class system which has been formed through its historical development."† To this day, numerous efforts have been taken to solve the Buraku discrimination. However, the discrimination over marriage, employment, and education still exist in contemporary Japan. Not only that, we have to face the reality that the discrimination exists in our Church itself.**

---

*The Bishops Committee on Society is one of the committees composed by Japanese Catholic bishops and deals with social issues.

†The 1965 Report on the Dowa Policy Council states, "[T]he so-called Dowa problem is a most serious and important social problem deriving from the fact that a segment of the Japanese people, owing to discrimination based on a class system formed in the process of the historical development of Japanese society, is placed in such an inferior position economically, socially and culturally that their fundamental human rights are grossly violated even in present-day society and that, in particular, their civil rights and liberties, which are ensured to all people as a principle of modern society, are not fully guaranteed in reality" (1:1). Therefore, "[I]ts urgent solution is the responsibility of the country as well as our nation's challenge" (Preamble).

**The report on the opinion survey regarding the Buraku issue within the Church in 1990 indicates that the discriminatory environment exists in the Church the same as in the secular society. Contact addresses are found at http://www5b.biglobe.ne.jp/~catburak/address.htm

Discrimination Must Be Conquered

3. It has been the consistent teachings by the Catholic Church that any kind of discrimination would go against the will of God. The Second Vatican Council says as follows: "All human beings are created as an image of God and equipped with equal nature and origin, redeemed by Jesus Christ, and given the same calling and purpose from God. Thus, it has to be strongly recognized that all the people are fundamentally equal ... Regardless whether it is based on social, cultural, gender, ethnic, skin color, position, language or religious difference, any kind of discrimination towards fundamental human rights goes against the will of God, therefore, that needs to be overcome and eradicated" (*Universal Human Rights Declaration*, 29). Our Japanese Catholic Church reaffirmed our motto, "Go along with those in the marginalized position," as our fundamental attitude at the first ecumenical conference in 1987. Because, this attitude itself is the way of life of Jesus Christ, founder of the Church, and his fundamental teaching.*

Church Must Strive to Abolish and Solve Buraku Discrimination

4. The Catholic Bishops' Conference of Japan had already established the Committee for Buraku Issues in 1984 and has been grappling with the Buraku discrimination. In hope of further development of these efforts, we plead to all brothers and sisters in Japan with renewed resolution for this cause. Each one of us who belongs to the Japanese Catholic church has to strive to overcome and eliminate Buraku discrimination according to each circumstance.

First, we have to overcome the discrimination existing among us. To do that, we have to recognize the discrimination within the Church and acknowledge the fact that we do discriminate. We should also acknowledge that we do discriminate under the influence of society. This means that the Church community itself needs to convert. In other words, we must revisit and transform the way in which the church exists as well as its organization, systems, customs, liturgies, weddings and funerals, religious education, and so forth. By making daily conversion and walking the path of liberation from discrimination, we believe that the Church can better contribute to a transformation of the society according to the teachings of the Bible as well as the abolishment for the Buraku discrimination.†

Things to Do to Overcome and Abolish Buraku Discrimination

5. What can we do concretely for the Church community to convert? First, it is important to pray for overcoming and abolishment of the Buraku

---

Let Us Live Together with Joy, Catholic Bishops' Conference of Japan, 1987.

†The report by Bishops' Conference of Japan at the Second National Incentive Convention for Evangelization (NICE), *Catholic Weekly*, July 19, 1992.

discrimination. At the same time, we have to collaborate together for the embodiment of this task. Therefore, we would like to ask your understanding and cooperation in the following points.

1. As soon as possible, each diocese will make an effort to establish the organization which specifically deals with the Buraku discrimination (for instance, a "Buraku committee").
2. We also would like to ask each religious order and missionary community to make the same effort.
3. In the Catholic schools, we request the establishment of a human right curriculum which deals with the discrimination issues including Buraku discrimination.

Achieving these goals requires many to make efforts, cultivate patience and understanding. The Committee for Buraku Issues of the Catholic Bishops' Conference of Japan is a special organization established to support the effort [to overcome and solve the problems of] the Buraku discrimination across the country in Japan. We hope that you continue to find us as a good partner for each diocese, religious order, missionary community and Catholic school regarding the Buraku discrimination and strive to provide beneficial information and support.*

Dear brothers and sisters in Christ, "You are called for freedom." (Gal 5:13) Freedom means that we are relieved from discrimination among ourselves. May the Lord Jesus Christ's blessing, God's love, communion of the Holy Spirit be with you all. Amen.

September 18, 1992 Catholic Bishops' Conference of Japan, Bishops Committee on Society

16. Indigenous Peoples and the Church: Journeying toward the Jubilee

CATHOLIC BISHOPS' CONFERENCE OF THE PHILIPPINES, 1999

Full text of document available at: http://www.cbcponline.net/documents/1990s/1999-great_jubilee.html

Abstract

The bishops praised the passage of the Indigenous Peoples Rights Act (IPRA) in 1997, and called for its immediate and full implementation.

---

*The Japanese Catholic Committee for the Buraku Issue has been working on the Buraku discrimination issue under the Committee for Bishops Committee on Society.

Historical Note

On October 29, 1997, President Fidel V. Ramos finally signed Republic Act 8371, commonly known as the IPRA, into law. It had been in the legislative process through three congresses for over a decade. It was considered a landmark reaffirmation of the rights of indigenous peoples giving them the justice that was long overdue. However, the successor to Ramos, Joseph E. Estrada, did not give priority to the implementation of the law nor was the necessary budget allocation made. Instead the new president politicized the process resulting in continued injustices for the indigenous peoples.

Discussion Questions

1. Research the Philippines Indigenous Peoples Act of 1997. In what ways has that act been effective toward establishing and sustaining racial justice?
2. What has the Philippine Church done to fulfill the bishops' promise to assist in the implementation of this law?

Excerpts from the Text

As we approach the Great Jubilee 2000, we are overjoyed with the call of the Lord of Creation to implement the spirit of Jubilee: 'the *strengthening of faith and of the witness of Christians*. It is therefore necessary to inspire in all the faithful a *true longing for holiness*, a deep desire for conversion and personal renewal in a context of ever more intense prayer and of solidarity with one's neighbor, especially the most needy.' (TMA 42)

In the context of the Philippine situation we are made aware, among other things, of the deprivation of the lands suffered by the Indigenous peoples which comprise 10% of our population. In a Pastoral Statement in 1993, "the Church deplores and condemns the present treatment by government and big business of the indigenous peoples in their disregard of the latter's rights to their ancestral domain."

Our concern here must be to actively support, promote and accelerate the process of law on their behalf, and be on their side so that their ancestral domains, their cultures, rights and the integrity of their environment be defended, preserved, and promoted. (PCP II, 379)

We are happy that in 1997 the Indigenous Peoples Rights Act (IPRA) was signed into law to rectify the unjust situation. Though not perfect, the law offers a good start for the IPs to secure their ancestral domains and protect their culture and identity.

We are now alarmed that some groups are working against IPRA.

We recall the statement of Pres. Joseph Estrada on December 10, 1998 on the Protection of Human Rights. *"Isa sa mga prayoridad ko ay ang kapakanan ng may sampung milyong katutubong Pilipino o indigenous peoples na nabibilang sa hanay ng mahihirap sa ating bansa. Ipapatupad ko nang lubusan ang Indigenous Peoples Rights Act or IPRA na kumikilala sa kanilang karapatan sa mga ancestral lands.*" We are committed to protect these rights through the implementation of the IPRA and the ratification by the Senate of ILO Convention 169, or the Indigenous and Tribal Peoples Convention.

We call on all the Indigenous Peoples to unite and fight for their rights. We call on all people of good will who take to hearts the spirit of Jubilee to help the Indigenous Peoples regain their distinct place in our nation. The full joys of the Jubilee will never be ours unless we restore justice to the Indigenous Peoples.

Europe

17. Statement on the Rise of Racist Political Parties in Europe

CATHOLIC BISHOPS' CONFERENCE OF ENGLAND AND WALES, 1994

Full text of document available from the Committee for Community Relations, Catholic Bishops' Conference of England and Wales, 39 Eccleston Square, London SW1V 1BX

Abstract

The bishops denounce racism as intrinsically evil and condemn the parties that promote racist ideology as a political philosophy and foment racial violence.

Historical Note

On September 16, 1993, Derek Beackon, a candidate of the British National Party (BNP) won a by-election victory in the Milwall ward on the Isle of Dogs, E. London. The BNP was the largest openly racist organization in Britain since its split from the National Front in 1982. The European Parliament's Committee on Racism and Xenophobia described the BNP as an "openly Nazi party whose leadership have serious criminal convictions ... the BNP are uninhibited in their racist style and report unabashedly on their members stabbing black people." Against this background of the increase in racist *political* parties and organizations across Europe the bishops made this statement.

Discussion Questions

1. Why might a Christian think of supporting a racist candidate or political party?

151

2. What evidence exists that the action of the Church raising its voice against racist political parties or candidates is effective to any degree?
3. What actions should the Church take in the face of racist political parties or candidates? What can one person do?

Excerpts from the Text

Racism is intrinsically evil, and especially destructive when it expresses itself in organisations and political parties explicitly committed to a racist ideology and engaged in fomenting violence against ethnic minorities. All people share with Christians an obligation not to support such organisations under any circumstances.

We recognise that some people may vote for such parties out of frustration or despair rather than deeply rooted prejudice. People in circumstances of poverty and disadvantage are vulnerable to manipulation, and all political parties, therefore, have a responsibility to be clear and unequivocal in their refusal to collude with racism.

The increase in the activities of racist organisations and political parties raises a number of fundamental issues which must be seriously addressed:

a. Article 4(b) of the *International Convention of the Elimination of All Forms of Racial Discrimination* states that overtly racist organisations and political parties should be banned. Government must now seriously consider whether such action is not called for, despite concerns for freedom of speech and association.
b. Those elected to public office are obliged to represent the genuine needs and interests of all their constituents. If this obligation can be easily ignored, minority ethnic communities will be effectively denied democratic representation.
c. If candidates of overtly racist parties are permitted to run for public office, responsible authorities must ensure that black and ethnic minority communities are free from intimidation and able to exercise their right to vote.
d. All political parties constantly need to re-examine and re-state their commitment to policies which will eradicate discrimination.

It is likely that, in order to address such issues adequately, new legislation will be required or existing legislation will have to be strengthened.

It is essential that all citizens are able to walk the streets and participate in democratic processes without fear or intimidation and in safety.

18. Serving a Multi-Ethnic Society

COMMITTEE FOR RACIAL RELATIONS, CATHOLIC BISHOPS' CONFERENCE OF ENGLAND AND WALES, 1999

Full text of document available at: http://www.catholicchurch.org.uk/ccb/catholic_church/catholic_bishops_conference_of_england_and_wales/publications

Abstract

In this document, the bishops provide a framework and a mandate for Catholic organizations and institutions to make a self-evaluation of their service to a multi-ethnic community. The bishops are clear that all Catholic organizations and institutions will be held accountable for their actions according to these standards.

Historical Note

On April 22, 1993, black youth Stephen Lawrence was brutally murdered in Eltham, in southeast London. Nobody was convicted of his murder. Numerous allegations of incompetence and racism were brought against the Metropolitan police officers in charge of the case. In February 1999, Sir William Macpherson of Cluny reported to Parliament the findings of his investigation into the case. A central issue was "institutional racism." The Macpherson report delivered a damning assessment of the "institutional racism" within the Metropolitan police and policing generally. It was "the collective failure of an organisation to provide an appropriate and professional service to people because of their colour, culture or ethnic origin." Many of the commission's seventy recommendations aimed specifically at improving police attitudes to racism. The bishops mandated this review in light of these events.

Discussion Questions

1. What instances of institutional racism are you aware of?
2. What policies do the organizations to which you belong—clubs, parish, diocese, business, sports teams, for example—guard against institutional racism?
3. What can you do to challenge institutional racism?

Excerpts from the Text

The gospel values which underpin our work call us to the service of all, especially the poor and marginalised. Events surrounding the death of Stephen Lawrence and the Report of the subsequent Inquiry, have highlighted the reality of 'institutional racism' and our common obligation to address it.

Institutional racism is a form of structural sin and primarily a sin of omission. The Macpherson Report defined it as (46.25):

> "The collective failure of an organisation to provide an appropriate and professional service to people because of their colour, culture or ethnic origin. It can be seen or detected in processes, attitudes and behaviour which amount to discrimination through unwitting prejudice, ignorance, thoughtlessness, and racist stereotyping which disadvantage minority ethnic people."

Knowing that institutional racism exists in some of the key institutions of our society, we cannot assume that Catholic organisations and institutions are unaffected. In such a situation, we become culpable if we fail to take stock and examine carefully the nature of the service we offer.

This is, therefore, an opportune time to review our work in order to determine whether it reaches out to the whole community, including minority ethnic groups who might be in danger of being excluded. We hope that Catholic organisations will use the Jubilee Year as the time to undertake such a review.

The Review

To carry sufficient authority, the review should normally be initiated by those responsible for the governance of an organisation. They will establish its basic parameters and give someone in senior management the task of ensuring that the review is carried out. As far as possible, everyone in the organisational community should be invited to be part of the process.

The organisation will want to ensure that the perspectives of minority ethnic communities are fed into all stages of the review.

The following are some questions that organisations might ask themselves in order to facilitate the process of review.

1. What are the organisation's objectives? [...]
2. Is it a diverse organisation? [...]
3. Whom does it serve? [...]
4. What services does it offer? [...]
5. Does the organisation have a multi-ethnic ethos and image? [...]
6. Is it committed to equal opportunities? ...
7. Is training available for management, staff and clients? [...]
8. What other positive action might bring about change? [...]

The Outcome of the Review

Ideally, the review will produce agreement concerning a strategy for the future. The strategy will normally take the form of an action plan which includes specific targets, timetables and monitoring of outcomes. The strategy must carry the full authority of those responsible for governance, and management must be committed to its effective implementation.

A report of the review, including an outline of the agreed strategy for the future, will benefit the organisation itself. However, these reports could also be useful to others involved in similar exercises.

To enable an exchange of information to take place, reports can be sent to the Committee for Community Relations. The Committee, while respecting any requests for confidentiality, will undertake to act as a clearing house for sharing information, experience and lessons learned. As part of this process, a Conference will take place in November 2000. The Committee will report back to the Bishops' Conference in Low Week 2001.

19. Diversity and Equality Guidelines

CATHOLIC BISHOPS' CONFERENCE OF ENGLAND AND WALES, 2005

Full text of document available at: http://www.catholicchurch.org.uk/index .php/ccb/media/files/cbcew_publications/diversity_and_equality_guidelines (Use Search at the sidebar)

Abstract

As part of the European Union dealing with the widespread burgeoning issues of immigration, xenophobia, and racism, as well as its internal national policy standards against all forms of discrimination in its member nations, England and Wales passed legislation to comply. The bishops welcomed these efforts, brought their policies in line with the law, while safeguarding Catholic ethos.

Historical Note

Since the end of World War II, immigration has mushroomed in Europe generally, and England and Wales in particular. In the former British colonies poverty, economic crises, violence, and hope of a better life drew the "children of the empire" home to the exemplary, "civilized motherland." Over night the population diversified in culture, language, religion, and complexion. Numerous often violent conflicts occurred.

Discussion Questions

1. What guidelines are necessary to ensure racial justice in employment? Housing? Education? Church organizations? Civic groups? Others?
2. Do you agree with the Church's position on "positive action" (also known as "affirmative action" or "just opportunity")?

Excerpts from the Text

Policy Statement

> All human beings are endowed with a rational soul and are created in
> God's image; they have the same nature and origin and, being redeemed
> by Christ, they enjoy the same divine calling and destiny ... forms of
> social or cultural discrimination in basic personal rights on the grounds
> of sex, race, colour, social conditions, language or religion, must be
> curbed and eradicated as incompatible with God's design. *(Gaudium
> et Spes, 29)*

The fundamental truths of Christianity, in common with other faiths,
include the dignity and equality of all human beings. All of us are created
in the image of God, are loved by God and are part of one human family.
Thus every human being deserves respect and has fundamental rights.

This belief articulated by the Second Vatican Council, must be reflected
in the vision and lived out in the practice of Catholic organisations and institutions. This is not an easy task. We live in a world which is complicated,
diverse and unequal. Respecting diversity and promoting equality is complex
and challenging.

Legislation in the [United Kingdom] deals with diversity and equality in
six areas: race, gender, disability, religion and belief, sexual orientation,
age (by end 2006). With a growing number of agencies and organisations involving, employing and serving more and more people, we must understand
and comply with current legislation and good practice and reflect this in
all we do.

This document sets out the policy of the Catholic Bishops' Conference
of England and Wales. Our view is that those responsible for, or working in,
Catholic organisations and institutions have twin duties. The first is to witness to the Gospel by striving always to be inclusive, respectful of the human
dignity of all and in tune with the spirit as well as the letter of the law. The
second is to safeguard and uphold the Catholic ethos and identity of the
organisation in question.

In carrying out these twin duties, Catholics should always keep in mind:

- Our first obligation is to the values of the Gospel and the teachings of
  the Church
- It is fundamental to this teaching that every person deserves respect
- Catholic bodies should publicly acknowledge their commitment to
  both diversity and equality
- While people have a right to their private and family lives, at the same
  time a Catholic organisation needs to cultivate and preserve an ethos
  appropriate to its vision, mission and values and this will make demands on all involved in the organisation

- We value the contribution that talented and committed people, with different life experiences and abilities may be able to make in the life of the Church
- In a society in which relationships are increasingly fractured and complicated, it is only to be expected that this may at times be reflected in the lifestyles of those who serve the Church
- Where there is tension between discrimination law and the right of a Catholic institution to safeguard its ethos, Catholics should seek advice

We, the bishops of the Church, commend this policy to all the faithful as an expression of faith and witness in today's society. With this policy statement we have issued Guidelines demonstrating our determination to set an example of respect for all God's people and their contribution to the human community.

As we take up this challenge, we must remain true to our own faith and traditions. We expect the freedom to live according to these, just as we recognise the same rights for other faith communities. Above all, we are called to be neighbour, friend and partner to all men and women, as we struggle together to create a more just society.

20. Declaration of Repentance

CONFERENCE OF BISHOPS OF FRANCE, 1997

Full text of document available at: http://www.bc.edu/research/cjl/meta elements/texts/cjrelations/resources/documents/catholic/french_repentance.htm

Abstract

The Catholic Bishops of France take responsibility for the decisions made by their predecessors during World War II regarding anti-Semitic activities and their silence during the Holocaust. The bishops account for the Church's failures, and own the deep suffering the Church's complicity inflicted on the Jews. The legacy of these past failures is a whole generation with "a heavy inheritance" of responsibility to make reparations and heal wounds.

Historical Note

The Conference of Bishops of France published this public apology on the fifty-seventh anniversary of the passage of anti-Semitic laws by the collaborationist Vichy government during the Nazi occupation of France, September 30, 1997.

Discussion Questions

1. Research the role of the Catholic Church in France concerning the "Jewish Question" prior to and during World War II.
2. Does an apology of this sort do anything more than salve the conscience of the guilty? Explain.
3. What relevance does such an apology hold for racial justice?

Excerpts from the Text

For the most part, those in authority in the Church, caught up in a loyalism and docility which went far beyond the obedience traditionally accorded to civil authorities, remained stuck in conformity, prudence and abstention. This was dictated in part by their fear of reprisals against the church's activities and youth movements. They failed to realize that the church, called at that moment to play the role of defender within a social body that was falling apart, did in fact have considerable power and influence, and that in the face of the silence of other institutions, its voice could have echoed loudly by taking a definitive stand against the irreparable.

In the process which led to the Shoah, we are obliged to admit the role, indirect if not direct, played by commonly held anti-Jewish prejudices, which Christians were guilty of maintaining. In fact, in spite of (and to some extent because of) the Jewish roots of Christianity, and because of the Jewish people's fidelity throughout its history to the one God, the "original separation" dating back to the first-century became a divorce, then an animosity and ultimately a centuries-long hostility between Christians and Jews.

There can be no denying the weight of social, political, cultural and economic factors in the long story of misunderstanding and often antagonism between Jews and Christians. However, one of the essential points in the debate was of a religious nature. This is not to say that a direct cause-and-effect link can be drawn between these commonly held anti-Jewish feelings and the Shoah, because Nazi plans to annihilate the Jewish people has its sources elsewhere.

To the extent that the pastors and those in authority in the church let such a teaching of disdain develop for so long, along with an underlying basic religious culture among Christian communities which shaped and deformed people's attitudes, they bear a grave responsibility. Even if they condemned anti-Semitic theologies as being pagan in origin, they did not enlighten people's minds as they ought because they failed to call into question these centuries-old ideas and attitudes. This had a soporific effect on people's consciences, reducing their capacity to resist when the full violence of national-socialist anti-Semitism rose up, the diabolical and ultimate expression of hatred of the Jews, based on categories of race and blood, and which was explicitly directed to the physical annihilation of the Jewish people. As Pope John Paul II put it, "an unconditional extermination... undertaken with premeditation."

Nevertheless, while it may be true that some Christians—priests, religious, and lay people—were not lacking in acts of courage in defense of fellow human beings, we must recognize that indifference won the day over indignation in the face of the persecution of the Jews and that, in particular, silence was the rule in face of the multifarious laws enacted by the Vichy government, whereas speaking out in favor of the victims was the exception.

Today we confess that such a silence was a sin. In so doing, we recognize that the church of France failed in her mission as teacher of consciences and that therefore she carries along with the Christian people the responsibility for failing to lend their aid, from the very first moments, when protest and protection were still possible, as well as necessary, even if, subsequently, a great many acts of courage were performed.

This is the fact that we acknowledge today. For, this failing of the church of France and of her responsibility toward the Jewish people are part of our history. We confess this sin. We beg God's pardon, and we call upon the Jewish people to hear our words of repentance.

This act of remembering calls us to an ever keener vigilance on behalf of humankind today and in the future.

21. Joint Statement on the November Youth Riots

JACQUES DAVID, BISHOP D' EVREUX; JEAN-FRANÇOIS BERJONNEAU,
SECRETARY OF THE PRYSBTÉRAL COUNCIL AND PERSON IN CHARGE
FOR THE CROSSROADS OF THE CITIES; AND PAUL MAGNAN, ORGANIZER OF
THE CROSSROADS OF THE CITIES PROJECT, 2005

Full text of document available at: http://www.cef.fr/ (French)

Abstract

Following the November 5, 2005, statement of the Conference of Catholic Bishops of France Plenary Assembly, Lourdes, and the ongoing youth riots all over France, Bishop D' Evreux, Jacques David and the leaders of the *Crossroads of the Cities Project* issued this joint statement that was to be read in all the Catholic churches during Advent 2005. Holding small group meetings to discuss the statement and the issues involved was also encouraged.

Historical Note

In France, the persistence of xenophobic and neocolonialist attitudes and the strong belief that equal treatment for all is an adequate response has prevented state institutions from vigorously tackling racial discrimination with appropriate policies. There is ethnicization of social relations at work, school and in the neighborhoods, and the specific harms suffered by long-settled postcolonial immigrants and their children are neglected. The latter are the easy scapegoats of a perceived general societal malaise, and for this they are easily criminalized. Only if people become more open about rights to the city and more tolerant of ethnic expressions in public space will current timid attempts at inclusion in France gain force.

Discussion Questions

1. What is the root cause of xenophobia?
2. What can the Church do to prevent xenophobia? What can you do?
3. What can be done to defuse xenophobia once it is rampant in a community or nation?

Excerpts from the Text

For more than fifteen days, certain cities of our country have been touched by demonstrations of violence. Our department also knew serious events at that time.

In the Madeleine, in Evreux and, in a less proportion, other cities, cars were burned. People were wounded. Tradesmen saw their work tools damaged. Fear was propagated.

By this message we first want to express our friendship and our active solidarity with all those who were in one way or another affected by this violence. In these districts, Christians of all cultural origins, gather; celebrate their faith in Jesus Christ in parochial communities and movements of Catholic Action. They are builders of fraternity and express by their engagements that the love of Christ is without borders.

Also in solidarity with those who were touched by these events, we want to express that we are at their sides to support them in the prayer and to seek with them all that can restore the bond and restore trust between the various inhabitants of these districts.

Like Paul the apostle said: *"If a member suffers, all the members share his suffering."*

Yes, this situation concerns us all, the Catholics of this diocese. It is revealing fractures which cross our company. It constitutes an alarm for all.

It again reveals and causes us to examine the realities which constitute everyday life of a number of inhabitants of these districts: unemployment of long duration, breakdown of the families, absence of a future for the young people, deterioration of the social bond.

This is why, beyond the emotion caused by these events and the echoes given in the media, in fact the communities of our diocesan Church have to take the time to reflect, in the light of the Gospel, and to distinguish in what ways they are concerned with this situation.

We cannot leave mistrust or fatalism to gain our hearts. As it is written in the foreword to the booklet of the Crossroads of the Cities Project: *"We have to overcome any fear that will hold us apart, or any feeling of resignation which would consist in thinking that there is nothing to be done. As in the Gospel, the Risen Christ invites us to work together so that any exclusion moves back and so that the dignity of any person is recognized."*

This is why we ask the communities of the diocese to consider 3 questions:

1. Which image do we have of these districts?

When we recall cities like the Madeleine and Netreville with Evreux, Boutardes or Valmeux in Vernon, the Acacias or the Red House with Louviers, the Large Terminal with Valley of Reuil, which images come to mind?

Do we focus ourselves on the handicaps (exclusion, unemployment, insecurity)? Or are we attentive to those proud peoples who live in these districts, to locate the richness of family solidarity, community life, basic fraternity in the meeting of people of different cultures?

In this time of the Advent which prepares us to welcome the birth of Jesus in the poverty of a cattle shed, let us realize that Christ continues to be born in these districts through the bonds which are woven there.

2. Do our behaviors hold account of solidarity with people of these districts?

Without living there, we however have to make choices about who will have an impact on the life in these districts.

How do we influence our elected officials so that the social housing construction is carried out in certain communes?

Which attitude do we have when, in conversations, discriminatory remarks are made with respect to such or such category of population?

Does it sometimes occur to us to intervene when we hear about a refusal to recruit someone, because of the origin or the place of dwelling of the applicant for work?

The small omissions can have serious consequences on the life of our brothers and the poorest sisters. It is necessary for us in many circumstances to recall this word of the Gospel

"All that you did not do for one of these small ones who are my brothers, neither did you do it to me." (Mt 25, 45)

3. Which effective meetings do we have with inhabitants of these districts?

In the same city, Christian communities located in different districts can coexist without meeting and really knowing one another.

Which initiatives can we take for a true meeting with the Christians of these districts, to listen to them speak to us about their life, in the way in which they live their faith, their hopes, their sufferings?

How can Christians, who are engaged in district associations, raise the challenges posed by unemployment and the degradation of the social bond with other citizens with different convictions, and find places for the poor and unemployed within our communities? How is their way of life taken into account in the celebrations, the life and the mission of our parishes?

Which meetings will we have with believers of other religions and in particular with the Muslims to overcome fears and to improve our breaking bread together in the districts?

With Christ we are the people of unity. This unity inseparably relates to the communion which connects us with God and fraternity with all men and, in particular, with those which are touched by precariousness. With the confidence we have in Christ we pledge to be the servants in our cities of the meeting and renewal of confidence!

Jacques David, Bishop D' Evreux
Jean-François Berjonneau, Secretary of the Presbyterial Council; Person in charge for the Crossroads of the Cities Project
Paul Magnan, Organizer of the Crossroads of the Cities Project
During the time of the Advent, the Catholic communities are invited to convene meetings to think of the questions which are put here, in the light of the Word of God. ✝J.D.

22. Human Dignity Is Unimpeachable

A STATEMENT FOR "THE WEEK OF THE IMMIGRANT" BY KARL CARDINAL LEHMANN, PRESIDENT OF THE GERMAN CONFERENCE OF BISHOPS, 2003

Full text of document available at: http://www.dbk.de/ (German)

Abstract

The German bishops continued their support of the annual "Week of the Immigrant" they began in 1975, which became a national event. They reiterated the condemnation of racism and xenophobia elaborated in their joint statement with the German Protestant Churches (1997). The bishops call for continued interaction of diverse peoples in ordinary ways to foster peaceful and mutual understanding.

Historical Note

This statement was given at a press conference on September 23, 2003, in Hanover, Germany. The tone of the term *ausländischen Mitbürger* is significant in that it indicates a "fellow-citizen, or co-citizen." The German bishops have been heavily involved in their own initiatives, and ecumenical efforts to deal with the xenophobia that produced violence in Germany in response to an unprecedented flow of immigrants into Europe. As Lehmann noted, in 2003, seven people had been killed and hundreds victimized by xenophobic violence.

Discussion Questions

1. Research the development of the "Week of the Immigrant" in Germany.
2. What celebrations or commemorations are held in your area to draw attention to the needs of immigrants?
3. How is the Church in your region serving the needs of immigrants? Is this adequate?

Excerpts from the Text

When we are opening today for the 25th time the "Week of the Immigrant"—this time under the theme "Human Dignity Is Unimpeachable"—we are doing this in a specific context. Racism and xenophobia have become visible again in our country to a frightening extent. This year alone we have already to mourn seven dead and several hundred others who have become victims of xenophobia.

From its beginning, it was the aim of the "Week of the Immigrant" to reach better understanding and reduce prejudices through contacts and encounter on a personal and neighborly level. Only when we meet each other, when we look at each other and get to know each other can we gain understanding for a different culture, different ways of life and the life stories of other people. This is a condition for living together peacefully and respectfully.

Festivals and encounters as well as plays, film screenings, and readings by foreign authors are supposed to engender and foster such mutual understanding. In parishes and congregations, the commitment for immigrants and refugees has grown. Many parishes invite immigrants to meetings and liturgies. Many ethnic parishes (parishes that celebrate in a language other than German, G.G.) participate in the "Week of the Immigrant." Considering only the Catholic side, there are almost 600 such ethnic parishes in Germany that are ministered to by more than 500 foreign priests. Many of these priests are naturally working also in the local parishes. Each year there are several thousand events taking place in Germany.

The initiative that began as a church activity has long since grown into an event of the larger society: also unions, immigrant groups, local governments and action groups offer events. Each year the ecumenical preparation committee counts about 2,000 events taking place at several hundred sites throughout Germany. The week counts with several hundred thousand participants. The churches were able to launch an initiative that goes far beyond their own realm and is now well grounded in our society. Nevertheless the level of xenophobia in the population is still very high. If we compare the situation with 1975, however, we have to state that also the commitment for immigrants and refugees at the grassroot level has grown in a positive way.

The "Week of the Immigrant" is also a public demonstration. We state our solidarity, encourage open and relaxed relations with people of other cultures and hope that this will inspire as many as possible. We have to show openly that we regard also immigrants as our sisters and brothers. For us as church, there are no strangers. All human beings are created, accepted, and loved by God in the same way.

Acts of violence and discrimination against immigrants, but also against homeless and handicapped people sadden us very much. They cannot be countered only with police activity—as important as this is. We have to ask for the causes. We have to ask why especially young people lend themselves to such acts of violence. But this is not only a youth problem. Many young people feel encouraged and supported by adults in their hatred against anything different.

For a long time there was much placation and empty promise, but also extenuation and looking away. Those who began early on to fight against violence and xenophobia were often not taken seriously enough, sometimes laughed at as "good guys" and discredited. Also church personnel have had such personal experiences.

Fear, marginalization and hatred cannot be the foundation of a society in the long run. This has to be addressed. But in this dialogue, also justified worries and fears have to be articulated. Fear of strangers may not lead automatically to the reproach of xenophobia. Therefore, also difficulties and problems have to be addressed openly. If this does not happen, reservations and fear express themselves uncontrolled. The pub is not the right place to address these topics appropriately.

Our country needs a broader base of responsibility, and therefore more than ever a respectful, realistic and thoughtful debate that involves the whole society about the future of Germany in a time of globalization and migration. We also need a debate about the challenges of a politic of integration made necessary by this migration. Such a process of reflection that involves the whole society has to be all encompassing instead of only sporadic and fragmentary. But it also needs sensitive political leadership.

In these past years, the Christian churches have again and again made the challenges of migration and refuge public in the eye of stricter immigration policies. This has also found its expression in the fact that part of the "Week of the Immigrant" is a "Day of the Refugee" that draws attention to the special problems of refugees. In this context, see the 1997 joint declaration (of the German Protestant and Catholic churches, G.G.) "and the Stranger in Your Gates."

Christian existence in word and deed asks us to reject any discrimination against color, culture, or religion of a person as contrary to the will of God. It means to give witness to a life as sisters and brothers based on the gospel, to respect cultural differences and to be open for sincere and trusting dialogue.

The past 25 years of the "Week of the Immigrant," which for the last 10 years or so has also been held in many places in Eastern Germany, are an occasion for us to thank all those, who in the past years and decades stood on the side of people of other language and origin and worked for their rights and dignity. They were, and continue to be, willing to do this publicly.

Past Themes of the "Week of the Immigrant":

1975	"Together for Justice"
1978	"For a Future Together"
1980	"Different Cultures—Same Rights. For a Future Together."
1982/1983	"Overcoming Fear—Becoming Neighbors"
1984/1985	"Being Neighbors to Create Peace"
1986/1987/1988	"Living Together, Deciding Together"
1989/1990	"Human Dignity Is Unimpeachable"
1991/1992	"Many Cultures—One Future"
1993/1994	"Building Peace—Overcoming Violence"
1995/1996	"Together for Justice"
1997/1998	"Open for Europe—Open for Others"
1999/2000	"Human Dignity Is Unimpeachable"

23. Responding to Racism: A Challenge and a Task for the Catholic Community

IRISH COMMISSION FOR JUSTICE AND PEACE OF THE IRISH CATHOLIC BISHOPS' CONFERENCE, 2001

Full text of document available from the Irish Commission for Justice and Social Affairs: Columba Centre, Maynooth, Co. Kildare, Ireland

Abstract

The teaching of St. Paul and the Church's social teaching ground the Church's moral mandate to work against racism. Special attention is given to the Irish Travellers, immigrants, asylum seekers, and racism as an ideology. Catholics are challenged to solidarity, to genuinely welcoming all peoples, and to make their responses to all others real.

Historical Note

Instead of issuing only a pastoral letter on racism, on February 8, 2001, at Gort Muire, Dublin, responding to a mandate given them by the Irish bishops, the Irish Commission for Justice and Peace of the Irish Catholic Bishops' Conference held a conference on racial justice. This document is the proceedings of the official conference. It was promulgated as a whole to "stimulate reflection and promote a more informed and committed Catholic response to racism." The presenters were Archbishop Seán Brady, president of the Irish Catholic Bishops' Conference; Scripture scholar Kiren J. O'Mahony, OSA; and Kevin Doran, Ph.D., priest of the Dublin Diocese.

Discussion Questions

1. "Racism touches the heart of our faith." Explain.
2. Imagine what it would be like to be forced into exile. Or if this is part of your life experience, share some part of the journey you can share comfortably. What effect would or did this have on your family life, relationships, income, health, and faith in God?
3. Research "Irish Travellers." Is there a comparable group of people who live in your country?

Excerpts from the Text

Foreword

It is "inconceivable," said Pope Paul VI, in his 1978 address to the Diplomatic Corps, "for those who accept the Gospel message to deny fundamental human equality in the name of the alleged superiority of a race or ethnic group. Yet racism persists among many Christians. Few if any of us can say honestly to ourselves that we are absolutely free of it. This is why we have to keep reminding ourselves that racial discrimination is evil, no matter how it is practised, no matter who does it or why" (ib).

Racism can take many different forms. It can be blatant, but also insidious and implicit. Given the different guises it can assume, a continuing formation of conscience is needed, for example in the wake of frequent failures to respect the rights and dignity of Travellers. Today the Catholic community needs increasingly to reflect on the new situation confronting Irish society in the face of growing numbers of immigrant workers and of asylum seekers.

To stimulate such reflection and promote a more informed and committed Catholic response to racism, the Irish Commission for Justice and Peace organised a conference on "The Church and Racism" in February 2001, in Gort Muire, Dublin. This publication contains the texts of the papers given at that conference, together with questions for reflection and group discussion.

As President of the Irish *Commission* for Justice and Peace I wish to thank once more all those who participated in the conference and to offer this publication as a resource to the Irish Church at large, in the hope that *it* will contribute, however modestly, to raising awareness of the evil of racism.

☩Bishop Raymond Field, Auxiliary Bishop of Dublin

24. The Victims of Nazi Ideology

CATHOLIC BISHOPS IN POLAND, 1995

Full text of document available at: http://www.bc.edu/research/cjl/meta-el-ements/texts/cjrelations/resources/documents/catholic/poland_victims.html

Abstract

Jewish-Christian relations in Poland are commemorated and celebrated by recalling common faith and common suffering under Nazi ideology during World War II. The religious commitment of both Jews and Christians is to always uphold the inviolable dignity of the human person created in God's image and likeness.

Historical Note

The Catholic Bishops in Poland issued this statement on the fiftieth anniversary of the liberation of the Auschwitz-Birkenau concentration camp on January 27, 1945. In that camp, 1 million Jews, 70,000–75,000 Poles, 21,000 Gypsies, 15, 000 Russians, and 10,000–15,000 persons of other nationalities found an atrocious death.

Discussion Questions

1. Research the social, political, and economic conditions in Poland prior to World War II and the position of the Catholic Church concerning the "Jewish Question."
2. From a Jewish perspective, is this statement helpful? Explain.
3. What lessons can be learned from this statement about racial justice and anti-Semitism?

Excerpts from the Text

Extermination, called *Shoah*, has weighed painfully not only in relations between Germans and Jews, but also to a great extent in relations between Jews and Poles, who together, though not to the same degree, were the victims of Nazi ideology. Because they lived in close proximity, they became involuntary witnesses to the extermination of Jews. Regretfully, it has to be stated that for many years Auschwitz-Birkenau was treated by the communist regime almost entirely in terms of an antifascist struggle that did not help to convey the extent of the extermination of Jews.

Seeing the Nazi extermination of Jews, many Poles reacted with heroic courage and sacrifice, risking their lives and that of their families. The virtues of the Gospel and solidarity with the suffering and the persecuted motivated almost every convent in the general government to give Jewish children refuge. Many Poles lost their lives, in defiance of threats of the death penalty with regard to themselves and their family members, because they dared to shelter Jews. It should be mentioned that, as a consequence of giving refuge to Jews, the rule of common responsibility was applied to Poles. Often whole families, from children to grandparents, were killed for harboring Jews. In acknowledgment of this, thousands were awarded with medals "righteous among the nations of the world." Nameless others also brought help.

Unfortunately, there were also those who were capable of actions unworthy of being called Christian. There were those who not only blackmailed, but also gave away Jews in hiding into German hands. Nothing can justify such an attitude, though the inhumane time of war and the cruelty of the Nazis led to Jews, themselves tormented by the occupier, being forced to hand over their brothers into the hands of the Germans. Once again, we recall the words of the Polish bishops' pastoral letter that was read at all Catholic churches and chapels on January 20, 1991, which stated: "In spite of numerous heroic examples of Polish Christians, there were those who remained indifferent to that inconceivable tragedy. In particular, we mourn the fact that there were also those among Catholics who in some way had contributed to the death of Jews. They will forever remain a source of remorse in the social dimension."

The creators of Auschwitz were the Nazi Germans, not Poles. [...] Nazism also meant trampling on the dignity of the human being as an image of God. There existed a dramatic community of fate between Poles and Jews in constraint and ruthless extermination. However, it was the Jews who became the victims of the Nazi plan of systematic and total liquidation. "An insane ideology decided on this plan in the name of a wretched form of racism and carried it out mercilessly" (John Paul II, beatification of Edith Stein, Cologne, Germany, May 1, 1987).

The half century that has passed since the liberation of Auschwitz-Birkenau obliges us to express a clear objection to all signs of disregard for human dignity such as racism, anti-Semitism, xenophobia, and anti-Polish attitudes. Living in a country marked with the burden of a horrible event called Shoah, with Edith Stein, who died at Auschwitz because she was a Jew, with faith and total confidence in God, the Father of all humanity, we emphatically repeat: Hatred will never have the last word in this world (John Paul II's message prior to visiting the Federal Republic of Germany, April 25, 1987).

Latin America

25. **Evangelization in Latin America's Present and Future:**
Part II, Chapter 1, Section 3 and Part II, Chapter 2, Section 4

THE THIRD GENERAL CONFERENCE OF THE LATIN AMERICAN EPISCOPATE,
PUEBLA DE LOS ANGELES, MEXICO, 1979*

Full text of document available in John Eagleson and Philip Scharper, eds.,
trans. John Drury, *Puebla and Beyond: Documentation and Commentary*
(Maryknoll, NY: Orbis Books, 1979).

Abstract

These two sections of the Puebla document outline the basis for Christian
anthropology and ground Catholic social teaching in the Gospel. Among the
most significant contributions of the Puebla conference, they theologically
and pastorally militate against all forms of racial injustice.

Historical Note

The Puebla conference reaffirmed and updated the teachings of Medellín
(1968). The section "The Truth about Human Beings: Human Dignity"
followed Pope John Paul II's recommendation of a three-part framework,
addressing Christ, the Church, and human beings. The section "Evangelization, Liberation, and Human Promotion," develops the Gospel founda-

---

*The numbers used for reference to the Final Document paragraphs follow those in John
Eagleson and Philip Scharper, eds., trans. John Drury, *Puebla and Beyond: Documentation and
Commentary* (Maryknoll, NY: Orbis Books, 1979). See also the explanation for indexing given
at 347.

tions for Catholic social teaching as integral to evangelization. Gross violation of human rights and state sponsored violence had dramatically increased in the past decade. The bishops' denouncement of the effects of liberal capitalism, Marxist collectivism, and the national security state on the poor in this period frames the background for these sections.

Discussion Questions

1. In what ways do inadequate views of the human person such as determinism, economism, statism, or scientism open the door to racism and racial injustice?
2. What is "the truth about the human person" that the bishops proclaim? Is this truth effective against racism and racial injustice? Why or why not?

Excerpts from the Text

3. The Truth about Human Beings: Human Dignity

(304) Here we consider the Christian vision of the human being in the light of both faith and reason, in order to judge the human situation in Latin America and to help toward building a more Christian, and hence more human, society.

Inadequate Views of the Human Being Propagated in Latin America

3.1.1. Introduction. (305) In the mystery of Christ, God comes down to the very abyss of human beings in order to restore their dignity from within. Hence faith in Christ gives us the fundamental criteria for acquiring an integral vision of the human being. That vision complements and sheds light on the image conceived by philosophy and the contributions of the other human sciences regarding the being of humanity and its historical realization. [...]

3.2. Doctrinal Reflection

3.2.1. A basic proclamation. (316) To our brothers and sisters in Latin America we have a serious obligation to proclaim the dignity that properly belongs to all without distinction (Gen 1:26–28; 9:2–7; Sir 17:2–4; Wisd 9:2–3; Ps 8:5–9), but that we see crushed underfoot so frequently and so viciously. We are moved to reclaim and defend this dignity by the revelation contained in the message and person of Jesus Christ. He "was well aware of what was in man's heart" (John 2:25). Yet he did not hesitate to take on "the form of a slave" (Phil 2:7); nor did he refuse to live his whole life, right up to his death, alongside the most neglected people in order to make them sharers in the exaltation that he himself merited from God the Father.

(317) And so we profess that every man and every woman Gal 5:13–24), however insignificant they may seem, possesses an inviolable nobility that they themselves and others must respect, and ensure respect for, without any conditions attached; that every human life deserves to be dignified in itself in whatever circumstances; that all human life together must be grounded on the common good which lies in the ever-more fraternal realization of the common dignity of all. And this requires that none be used as instruments for the benefit of others, and that all be willing even to sacrifice private benefits.

4.2. *The Social Teaching of the Church*

(472) The contribution of the Church to liberation and human promotion has gradually been taking shape in a series of doctrinal guidelines and criteria for action that we now are accustomed to call "the social teaching of the Church." These teachings have their source in Sacred Scripture, in the teaching of the Fathers and major theologians of the Church, and in the Magisterium (particularly that of the most recent popes). As is evident from their origin, they contain permanently valid elements that are grounded in an anthropology that derives from the message of Christ and in the perennial values of Christian ethics. But they also contain changing elements that correspond to the particular conditions of each country and each epoch.

(473) Following Paul VI (OA:4), we can formulate the matter this way: attentive to the signs of the time, which are interpreted in the light of the Gospel and the Church's Magisterium, the whole Christian community is called upon to assume responsibility for concrete options and their effective implementation in order to respond to the summons presented by changing circumstances. Thus these social teachings possess a dynamic character. In their elaboration and application lay people are not to be passive executors but rather active collaborators with their pastors, contributing their experience as Christians, and their professional, scientific competence (GS:42).

(474) Clearly, then, it is the whole Christian community, in communion with its legitimate pastors and guided by them, that is the responsible subject of evangelization, liberation, and human promotion.

(475) The primary object of this social teaching is the personal dignity of the human being, who is the image of God, and the protection of all inalienable human rights (PP:14–21). As the need has arisen, the Church has proceeded to spell out its teaching with regard to other areas of life: social life, economics, politics, and cultural life. But the aim of this doctrine of the Church, which offers its own special vision of the human being and humanity (PP:13), is always the promotion and integral liberation of human beings in terms of both their earthly and their transcendent dimensions. [...]

26. The Great Jubilee and Land Rights of the Aboriginal Peoples

THE 79TH PLENARY ASSEMBLY OF THE BISHOPS OF THE REPUBLIC
OF ARGENTINA, 2000

Full text of document available at: http://www.aica.org/aica/documentos_
files/CEA/Comisiones_Episcopales/Pastoral_Aborigen/Derecho_a_la_tierrra
.htm (Spanish)

Abstract

The bishops refer to the Pontifical Council for Justice and Peace 1998
document *For a Greater Distribution of Land: The Challenge of Agrarian
Reform*. In light of that document and in view of the biblical understanding of "jubilee" they examine the situation of the indigenous of Argentina
and the need for reform.

Historical Note

The bishops promulgated this pastoral following their reflections at their
seventy-ninth Plenary Assembly in San Miguel on May 11, 2000.

Discussion Questions

1. What is the relationship between racism and rights to land?
2. Does your country have constitutional protections for indigenous peoples?
3. Discuss the emphasis placed on indigenous peoples' "right to exist" and
   racism.

Excerpts from the Text

Reality of Aboriginal Lands

5. In recent years, some Aboriginal communities have had their land returned to them, but not all. Though there remain some situations in the
northern and southern parts of the country that are contrary to the existence
of the aboriginal citizens:

   a. Land titles are coming to comply with the constitution.
   b. In some areas there isn't sufficient land to support subsistence and hu-
      man development.
   c. There are many conflicts about ownership including claims by new
      proprietors who received their land as political favors.
   d. Having titles to land is against the unified perception of the land as a
      cohesive ecosystem and this threatens the unity and the organization
      of Indigenous Peoples.

e. At times land is offered to Indigenous Peoples that is far from their traditional territory and the ecosystems are inadequate to support their culture and ways of life.

f. There are unexplained delays in political decisions.

g. Recently there was an increase in unjust appropriations of the land of small farmers and Indigenous Peoples by national, international, and government in violation of their rights.

Recommendations

6. In the spirit of the Great Jubilee:

a. We exhort the national and provincial governments and all in power to accelerate the return of the land and recognize their communities.

b. Solicit compliance by the government to "*Convenio 169 of the OIT*" and the national law No· 24.071 that safeguard aboriginal rights.

c. Instigate mechanisms to enable Indigenous Peoples to be fully informed about and participate in decisions affecting them.

d. Engage the Church agencies in the aboriginal areas to help promote solidarity.

e. Promote ways for the Creoles and the Aboriginal Peoples to share land and live together amicably.

7. The Church will engage with an ecumenical spirit in working with private, government, and other Christian groups for the good of the Aboriginal Peoples.

8. The Church asks forgiveness of the Indigenous and from God for past injustices it perpetrated against Aboriginal Peoples in infidelity to Christ. The Church also seeks the accompaniment of the Virgin of Guadalupe and of Juan Diego in its work on behalf of the Aboriginal Peoples.

27. Ministry for Afro-Brazilians

National Conference of Brazilian Bishops, 2005

Full text of document available at: http://www.cnbb.org.br/index.php?op= pagina&chaveid=209.002 (Portuguese)

Abstract

The Brazilian bishops reaffirm the Church's concern for the just treatment and inclusion of the Afro-Brazilians and call for renewed efforts for their full participation in the life of the Church and society.

Historical Note

The theme of the 43rd General Assembly the Brazilian bishops was "Evangelization and Prophecy: New Challenges to the Church's Mission." The bishops updated themselves on Afro-Brazilian needs and issues and reviewed Church efforts to attend them.

Discussion Questions

1. Research the status of Afro-Brazilians in Brazilian society.
2. The bishops state that their ministerial concern for Afro-Brazilians implies their knowledge and appreciation of God's gift present in "being black." Discuss the meaning of this gift.
3. What dimensions of the African religions practiced by Afro-Brazilians can contribute to establishing and sustaining racial justice?

Excerpts from the Text

Introduction

The central theme of the 43ª CNBB's Assembly, "Evangelization and Prophecy—New Challenges for the Church's Mission" points necessarily to the afro-descendents, the poorest among the poor.

Our prophetic actions should be for the blacks (*negros e negras*) a sacrament, icon, epiphany of the Good Shepherd, Jesus Christ, who came to serve with loving mercy.

From Christ's perspective there is meaning to living out the "new vision of charity" that manifests itself not only in the efficacy of practical assistance but in the capacity to think and be in solidarity with those who suffer in such form that our gestures of help would be not only an humiliatingly small contribution but a fraternal sharing" (NMI, 50).

Our ministerial charity to the Afro-Brazilians implies:

- The knowledge and appreciation of God's gift present in their blackness;
- The overcoming of racism and racial discrimination;
- A full-title promotion of citizenship to the blacks;
- Ecumenical and interreligious dialogue, without excluding African religions and identities;
- Enriching the process of inculturation in the evangelizing pastoral action of the Church.

In the Official Magisterium of the Catholic Church, after the Vatican Council II (1962), in the conferences of Puebla (1979) and Santo Domingo (1992), and in the General Norms for the Evangelizing Pastoral Action 2003–2007 of CNBB, the concerns of the Black Catholic Population of

Brazil are recognized and addressed, and the organized black communities are vindicated. They stress the preferential option for the poor, considering the conditions of the black as excluded from the full citizenship, and the importance of their religious and cultural values in the process of Evangelizing Pastoral Action of the Church in Brazil.

Regarding the process of conscientization of the hierarchy of the Church itself, after critically evaluating the social reality of Brazilian people, the Church's renewal opened up possible paths to work in ministry with Afro-Brazilians. According to demographic data, the poor represent 45 percent of the population, which means that 80 percent of the poor are blacks. In this context the Church understands the importance of ministering to the Afro-Brazilians.

It is true that the responsibility to fight racism, to promote equality, and to adopt affirmative political actions* is not an isolated mission for the government. All the forces of our society are extremely necessary. The church, via the National Conference of Brazilian Bishops, in the General Norms for the Evangelizing Pastoral Action 2003 and 2006, recommends: "the reality of Afro-Brazilians is another particular responsibility that imposes itself in the ecclesial community of Brazil. In this context of reality and in face of and despite the unanimity concerning an awareness of racism, the Brazilian society is still unjust to the population of African descent. The ecclesial communities could and should contribute to the overcoming of every kind of stereotype recognizing the religious values of African culture and facilitating the access of children and young people of African descent to health and education."

"We are living in the third Millennium where the Brazilian nation hopes to faithfully live out its most profound identity, and therefore hopes to be free of anything that up to now has stopped its people to manifest fully: dependence, inequality, humiliation, and discrimination" (CNBB. Doc. 65, n. 62).

The Afro-Pastoral Journey

The theme about the African Brazilian community is the topic of society and it has taken determinative actions that were private before, promoting activities that tend to valorize and characterize opportunities to the Afro Brazilians.

The Afro-Brazilian pastoral initiatives are not a movement. They are the action of the Church. It has a spirit that should penetrate the entire atmosphere; parishes and places where there are Afro-Brazilians.

In many regions of Brazil, as in many countries of Latin America and the Caribbean, the Afro-Brazilians animate the communities. In the Church the

---

*Temporary amendments adopted by society and government with the goal to overcome the inequalities and discriminations that affect specific groups who are historically marginalized due to stereotypes.

vocation promotion and also the actions of *Instituto Mariama* have fostered vocations of people of Afro-Brazilian descent. We have enthusiastic priests and lay ministers that have found their identity and specific vocation in God's people.

Therefore it is necessary that our ministry becomes broader in order to reach the areas populated by Afro-Brazilians and involve them in all other ministries. However there is still a lot to be done. The incentive, the participation, and the commitment of Dioceses, Regions, Parishes, Communities, Pastors, and Pastoral Agents, are crucial to establish and spread the Ministry with the Afro-Brazilians.

The Church, regarding national questions, also walks together with society and serves with zeal. It has been seventeen years since, in 1988, the topic of blackness has been raised up in the Fraternity Campaign "I have heard my people."

Currently the themes of diversity, multiculturalism, interethnicity, inculturation, and others are being suggested in a new Fraternity Campaign stressing dialogue on racial inequality, the human rights, the evangelical option for the poor and the excluded, in light of a mystical spirituality.

May all be committed to the Ministry with the Afro-Brazilians in this continual journey with hope and joy; indeed, it is esteem and love that moves us to prophetic and generous service. The prophetic mission of the Church in Brazil is to give witness by accomplishing its task in this multicultural world.

With esteem we continue in the hope of counting on the support of all in this journey.

✝Dom Gílio Felício, Bispo de Bagé e Referencial da Pastoral Afro-brasileira

28. We Will Have Peace in Our Land When We Discover We Are One Family

THE 69TH ORDINARY PLENARY ASSEMBLY OF THE EPISCOPAL CONFERENCE OF COLOMBIA, 2000

Full text of document available at: http://www.cec.org.co/menu2/asambleas .htm?AA_SL_Session=51f4e46f8dfc52670d2f7d19eea02a6a&scrl=1&scr_ scr_Go=2 (Spanish)

Abstract

The bishops reviewed the present situation, raising both the signs of hope and their urgent concerns. They sought to give their support to finding new avenues for peace, applying Gospel and the Church's social thought to bring Christian demands for justice to reality.

Historical Note

This pastoral was the product of the Colombian bishops' reflection at their 69th Ordinary Plenary Assembly in Santafé de Bogotá, D.C., July 3 to 8, 2000. At this time, there were new initiatives for negotiating peace between the various warring factions. Among the people most affected by the violence were numerous Afro-Colombians who lived in the rural, coastal, and mountain regions of Colombia. The document was released July 7, 2000.

Discussion Questions

1. What is the relationship between peace and racial justice?
2. Research the living conditions of Afro-Colombians.
3. Choose one group of indigenous people in Colombia and research their living conditions.

Excerpts from the Text

[...] We are inspired to reflect on our country's situation by Pope John Paul II's *World Day of Peace Message*, January 1, 2000, no. 5: "But we can set forth one certain principle: *there will be peace only to the extent that humanity as a whole rediscovers its fundamental calling to be one family*, a family in which the dignity and rights of individuals—whatever their status, race or religion—are accepted as prior and superior to any kind of difference or distinction."

The current situation is full of signs of both hope and of death. We want to support finding new avenues for peace, applying Gospel and the Church's social thought toward bringing the Christian demand for justice to reality.

1. A LOOK AT COLOMBIA

1.1 Dimensions of Human Dignity

Signs of Hope

a. There is an increase in the consciousness of our people of the need to promote, defend, and comply with standards of human rights.
b. Both NGOs and governments are trying to act in favor of human rights.
c. The state is reinforcing the administration of justice and activities in favor of human rights.
d. The Bishops' Conference has initiated a "Law Project" that is working to seek reforms in the prison and judicial systems to find better ways to rehabilitate prisoners and restore their human dignity.

e. The Church is working with displaced persons, Afro-Colombians, and Indigenous communities, and marginalized persons to defend their collective rights.

Signs that Concern Us

a. In Colombia there is a crisis of grave violations of human rights—torture, disappearances, and armed imposition of interests—rather than reason and dialogue.
b. Massacres, assassinations, genocide, and ethnic cleansing have taken place with impunity.
c. The situation is spiraling downward due to the increase in numbers of vigilante groups and new levels of cruelty.
d. Many needed to abandon their homes; there is extortion, and the especially egregious kidnapping and recruiting of children for war.

3. PROPHETIC CALL

One more time we reject:

1. All forms of violence by the state and the insurgency
2. Narcotrafficking with all of the links in its chain of death
3. All public and private manifestations of corruption and unjust appropriation
4. All arms trafficking as an enemy of peace

We demand:

1. That government enforces all guarantees to victim families and their right to truth throughout the juridical process, and holds persons responsible for their violations of human and personal rights.
2. Negotiations for peace and a response to the expectations of the society.
3. That all actions in the conflict are held against the norms of international justice and that those kidnapped be safely returned.

Our convictions:

1. All People of God and all people of good will should join in a "Common Front for Life, Justice and Peace" [cf. John Paul II, *Centesimus Annus*, no. 46).
2. All Colombians should pray for peace in our homes, churches, or parishes.

We invite:

1. Organizations to seek all the reforms (above).
2. The solidarity of the international community to help provide the solutions to the armed conflict.
3. War against drug traffickers by controlling their supplies for production and their money.
4. Control of the arms trade with Colombians.

What we commit to do:

1. To continue the integral evangelization of Jesus Christ proclaiming the human dignity of all people.
2. To continue to work for a negotiated solution to the armed conflict [by activities such as:] [...] supporting communities of peace fleeing the armed conflict; [...] strengthening the Church's efforts at all levels of dialogue and humanitarian work with those affected by the conflict; [...] supporting international verification and mediation necessary for an effective and just peace.

29. A Message from the Bishops of Perú to the Migrants Who Find Themselves Far from Their Country and Their Homes

THE EPISCOPAL CONFERENCE OF PERÚ, 2003

Full text of document available at: http://www.iglesiacatolica.org.pe/cep/cep_documentos/archivo_2003/mensaje_180803.htm (Spanish)

Abstract

The bishops acknowledge the increased numbers of migrants in their country, and they seek to welcome them, advocate for their just treatment, and provide necessary supportive services for them.

Historical Note

On the Day for Migrants, the first Sunday of September 2003, the bishops launched their program, COMPARTIR, 2003. They used the occasion to issue a short pastoral letter to educate the people about the plight of migrants.

Discussion Questions

1. What is the relationship between migrants and racial discrimination?

2. What is it about Christianity that requires Christians to be the primary teachers of solidarity?
3. Research the COMPARTIR, 2003 program. Are there similar programs in your country?

Excerpts from the Text

Dear Brothers and Sisters:

As we initiate the solidarity campaign COMPARTIR, 2003, which is called "Global Solidarity with the Migrants," and on the occasion of the Day for Migrants, the first Sunday of September, we Peruvian bishops stand in solidarity with all migrants who are far from their countries and their homes. Through the COMPARTIR, 2003 program the Episcopal Conference of Peru wants to recognize the migrant's pain, loneliness, and anxiety and to extend hope to them.

The COMPARTIR, 2003 program is a powerful moment in which to evangelize and conscientize all Peruvians about the reality of migrant families and the causes and consequences of migration. The purpose of the COMPARTIR, 2003 campaign is to form institutions and projects as part of all dioceses in Peru in order to support and offer solidarity to migrants.

It is also to initiate a change that is needed from a mentality of discrimination against migrants to a mentality of dialogue with those who suffer. We Christians should be the primary teachers of solidarity with the migrants.

We bishops affirm the migrants' generosity in sending money home to support their families and we hope for a better tomorrow for them. With John Paul II we ask migrants to respect the laws, culture, and traditions of their host nation as a way of creating social harmony.

We Peruvian bishops express gratitude to the Church and to all pastoral workers who support and accompany migrants in their communities.

May our faith in the Lord of the miracles, the first among migrants, and our devotion to St. Martin de Porres, Saint Rose of Lima ... our traditional patroness, give us strength and hope for all moments of life. We also ask the intercession and blessing of Mary the migrant mother (Lk 1:39), for all migrants.

North America

30. Aboriginal Land Rights: A Jubilee Challenge Facing Canada

LEADERS OF CHRISTIAN CHURCHES ON ABORIGINAL LAND CLAIMS, 2000*

Full text of document available at: http://www.cccb.ca/site/content/view/153/1063/lang,eng/

Abstract

The Jubilee Year 2000 was the occasion for repentance, reconciliation, restitution, and restoration for the many injustices (often well-intended) Christians committed against Aboriginal peoples of Canada.

Historical Note

Recent legislative and legal efforts by native peoples to regain their traditional land rights and the accompanying tense debates, including the major Royal Commission report (1996) on conditions among the Aboriginals, and the Canadian government's response (1997) offering numerous proposals for rectifying past injustices, raised new awareness of atrocities Christians had

---

*This document was signed by the following: Archbishop Michael Peers, Primate, Anglican Church of Canada; Most Reverend Gerald Wiesner, OMI, President of the Canadian Conference of Catholic Bishops; Anne-Marie Savoie, rhsj, President of the Canadian Religious Conference; Kim Foster, President, Canadian Unitarian Church; Gordon Pols, Chair, Canadian Board of Trustees, Council of Christian Reformed Churches in Canada; Bishop Telmor Sartison, Evangelical Lutheran Church of Canada; Claude Champagne, OMI, President, Oblate Conference of Canada; Glen Davis, Moderator, United Presbyterian Church in Canada; Gordon McClure, Clerk, Canadian Yearly Meeting of the Religious Society of Friends (Quakers); Marion Pardy, Moderator, United Church of Canada.

perpetrated on the Aboriginals. The proposed land claims process for the Aboriginal peoples had met with only limited success and was near breakdown. The Ecumenical Christian community issued this statement on September 25, 2000.

Discussion Questions

1. Research the history of one group of Canadian Aboriginal peoples.
2. What dimensions of the biblical jubilee can assist in establishing and sustaining racial justice for the Aboriginal peoples?
3. What would just restitution of Native lands include? Explain.

Excerpts from the Text

15. Today, in 2000, guided by advice coming from Aboriginal communities, we repeat our call for a new covenant. The focus of our joint message at this new moment is to invite the people of our churches, and indeed all Canadians who care about the common good, to support a fundamental goal of the Royal Commission on Aboriginal Peoples: the provision of an adequate land base for First Nations, with sufficient resources for sustaining viable economies.

16. Our analysis of the status of land negotiations in Canada today leads us to conclude, sadly, that the present system works for no one. [...]

17. The primary responsibility for the liberation and healing of Aboriginal communities rests, of course, on Aboriginal shoulders. Nevertheless, every citizen of Canada inherits a share of responsibility in this great matter. One aspect of the work to be done is the construction of a just and solid public-policy platform on which Aboriginal peoples can stand as they build a dramatically better future for their communities.

A new beginning for land and treaty rights negotiations is needed in Canada. [...]

21. The recognition and just implementation of Aboriginal land rights in Canada will be a difficult achievement. Nevertheless, it is a goal overflowing with promise. The struggle to achieve it has the potential to correct old, unjust distortions in the very structure of our country. It has the potential to rebuild confidence, responsibility, vision and zeal among Aboriginal peoples, transforming for young Aboriginals their sense of what the future holds for them. The diversity among Aboriginal peoples, and the variety of situations they will inherit, could stimulate new, innovative patterns of economic and human development perhaps far more sustainable, far more attentive to the earth and to human community than are the currently dominant economic and technological patterns that have all of us in their grip.

22. To share in such a great effort, all Canadians will have to banish from their hearts racism, indifference, hopelessness and self-absorption. In summoning Canada's Christians to embrace the cause of Aboriginal land rights, we are at the same time calling on God to convert our hearts, and to plant in our soil that justice, love and neighborliness that will redeem the human future.

23. The Canadian Ecumenical Jubilee Initiative [...] is promoting a petition to the Prime Minister [...] As church leaders, we fully support that petition.

- We call upon congregations, schools and other church bodies to study this cause and take it up.
- We invite everyone to take advantage of Jubilee Initiative resource materials in examining the issues involved.
- We encourage church members, when studying the issues, to engage others, especially Aboriginal people, in dialogue.

24. Finally, we invite everyone to pray with us that the One who dwells with humankind, the One who "will wipe every tear from their eyes", will bless the efforts of everyone who contributes to this great and many-leveled search for a just reconciliation of the rights of all who live in this land. [...]

31. Eliminate Racial and Religious Discrimination: See Every Person as My Sister or Brother

EPISCOPAL COMMISSION FOR SOCIAL AFFAIRS AND THE EPISCOPAL COMMISSION FOR INTERFAITH DIALOGUE, CANADIAN CONFERENCE OF CATHOLIC BISHOPS, 2004

Full text of document available at: http://www.cccb.ca/site/Files/March21-2004Racism.html

Abstract

In light of renewed racial and religious discrimination arising from the war on terrorism and the recovery of the Church's atrociously racist role in Canada's Residential Schools, the bishops apologize for past injustices, seek reconciliation, and commit to promoting harmony, respect, and dialogue with peoples of all races and religions.

Historical Note

March 21, 2004, was International Day for the Elimination of Racial Discrimination. Its purpose was to acknowledge the existence of racism and to deepen understanding about how racism and religious discrimination militates against the quality of life of all people. The war on terrorism had exposed discrimination especially against Muslim people. Canada signed the

Safe Third Country Agreement with the United States in 2002 to more effectively manage the flow of refugee claimants in both countries.

Discussion Questions

1. Research the "Safe Third Country Agreement" between Canada and the United States.
2. What are some specific ways Catholics can become more aware of and recognize discrimination?
3. In what ways is racism a threat to peace?

Excerpts from the Text

3. As Canadian bishops we reject all forms of racism and all discrimination on the basis of race or religion. From police and media reports and from our friends in the Aboriginal, Black, Jewish, Muslim, and other communities we have been made aware of incidents of racism, racial profiling and discrimination of various kinds. Some of these situations have occurred as a result of new tensions arising from "the war on terrorism." Other situations are not new, but may arise from entrenched inequalities from Canada's past.

7. **In the Church:** [...] the Church wants first and foremost to change racist attitudes, including those within Christian communities. The Church appeals first of all to the moral and religious sense of people, asking God to change hearts. The Church offers a place for reconciliation, and promotes initiatives of welcome, exchange, and mutual assistance for men and women belonging to other ethnic and religious groups. Despite the sinful limitations of its members in every age, the Church is to be a sign and instrument of the unity of humankind. The message the Church proposes to everyone, and which Catholics have to live is "Every person is my brother or sister."

8. In this spirit, leaders within the Catholic Church have apologized for individual and collective actions that contributed to the injustice that Aboriginal people continue to bear. Much of the activity of our Conference of Bishops (often in tandem with our ecumenical colleagues) is currently directed towards speaking out on issues of Aboriginal justice and developing Aboriginal catechesis and formation programs that respect their profound spiritual, moral and cultural heritage. [...]

9. Interfaith dialogue and respectful contact with people of other religions are privileged ways for Catholics to promote more just relationships. [...]

13. **In the policies of our governments:** In Canada today, governments should renew their efforts to defend and welcome refugees and migrants. Church communities can then enhance settlement activities. Under the new Citizenship and Immigration law, it should not become more difficult for migrants to be accepted into our country. Refugees applying from U.S. ports

of entry should not be prohibited from entering Canada due to the new Safe Third Country agreement. Even more dramatic realities are encountered in the squalid situations which millions of persons, our sisters and brothers, are forced to endure in refugee camps throughout the world. Increased Canadian financial assistance needs to be directed to the United Nations High Commission for Refugees and non-governmental groups such as the International Catholic Migration Commission.

14. In the search for peace: "Racism is a challenge to peace. Peace can only be constructed in a climate of mutual respect and understanding." Thus the call to each of us to work for peace (Matt 5:9) should find a greater echo in our attitudes and actions to promote harmony, respect, acceptance and justice. As Pope John Paul II said in his 2003 Message for the World Day of Peace, "Gestures of peace spring from the lives of people who foster peace first of all in their own hearts." Praying and acting for peace throughout this troubled world is the vocation of every individual Christian, every family and every community. Efforts to end racial prejudice and religious discrimination are urgently required for peace to grow in our hearts, in our Church, in our communities and in our world. By the grace of Christ, may we all come to more deeply understand and love every person as our sister or our brother.

32. In You Also, I Place My Full Confidence

MEXICAN EPISCOPAL COMMISSION FOR MINISTRY TO INDIGENOUS PEOPLES AND THE MEXICAN EPISCOPAL COMMISSION FOR SOCIAL MINISTRY, 2002

Full text of document available at: http://www.cem.org.mx/doctos/cem/colectivos/trienio0103/mensaje6.htm (Spanish)

Abstract

The message of Our Lady of Guadalupe and the model of Juan Diego serve as indications of justice and the value of indigenous peoples in the vision of the Church. The Church asks for forgiveness in its complicity in harm done to the indigenous peoples and seeks to support efforts to bring justice, defend the existence, and preserve the culture and rights of the indigenous peoples of Mexico.

Historical Note

This document was released on the fifth day of the visit of John Paul II for the canonization of Juan Diego Cuauhtlatoatzin on July 31, 2002, in Mexico City and the beatification of Juan Bautista y Jacinto de los Ángeles on August 1, 2002. The bishops reference their pastoral, *Carta Pastoral del Encuentro con Jesucristo a al Solidarida con todos, México 2000.*

Discussion Questions

1. Research the speeches of Pope John Paul II in Mexico. How does this document develop his messages?
2. In what ways is the Virgin of Guadalupe important for the understanding of racial justice?
3. Why is appropriation of the land of indigenous people a manifestation of racism?

Excerpts from the Text

15. So, we believe that our call for "recognition and protection of the diverse cultures that form our nation is pertinent; that they are preserved from the power of the state or market forces that damage them without regard for their legitimate sovereignty. The cultures that make up our nation act in the capacity of subsoil upon which we cultivate and construct our future as a community, and they school our nation and the world in integrating social, economic, and political dynamics."

16. We also called for a major effort to advance the indigenous cultures and communities in the context of our nation in a way that does not diminish their legitimate autonomy, but that adequately respects their particular contributions and valuable participation, making the necessary juridical changes so this can happen. This includes all dynamics of the cultural and ethnic realities that unfold their fidelity and identity and opens the context in which they live. The danger for the indigenous communities is the arbitrary and indiscriminant process of destruction by and the gradual changes in response to other causes of the world around them.

17. That the constitutional recognition of the legal rights and the indigenous cultural identity must be safeguarded as a subject of the national culture—protecting their voice, history and culture, the expression of their diverse traditions and beliefs. All of this is assumed and included in the *Convento 169de la OIT* which must be ratified and affirmed in our country.

19. To guarantee the reestablishment of peace in our country, a precise response to the basic demands of the indigenous peoples is needed. They do not want continued bloodshed. We hope for a response to the dialogue of the peace process. We call on all Mexicans to work to:

1. Recognize Indigenous rights and culture
2. See their story as a mediation congruent with the universal truth of Christ
3. Support the education of children in their indigenous languages
4. Promote mechanisms for the production and marketing of Indigenous products
5. Support justice for the Indigenous at all levels and the use of their languages

6. Form the conscience of the nation concerning the history of Indigenous Peoples
7. Protect their knowledge of and right to the natural world against development by transnational corporations
8. Support indigenous organizations that use their knowledge for economic development
9. Support programs for Indigenous youth to help them represent their community's cultural, social, and economic development
10. Protect their habitat and preserve cultural values against agribusiness, the destruction of forests, and contamination of their living environment.

33. Strangers No Longer: Together on the Journey of Hope

CATHOLIC BISHOPS OF MEXICO AND THE UNITED STATES, 2003*

Full text of document available at: http://www.usccb.org/mrs/stranger.shtml

Abstract

Factors contributing to injustices resulting from migration from Mexico to the United States are enumerated. Between the United States and Mexico there is common history of immigration and faith in Jesus Christ. The pastoral letter lists five principles of Catholic social teaching that guide the Bishops' views on migration issues. The concluding discussion explores pastoral and public policy challenges facing Mexico and the United States concerning migration.

Historical Note

This document resulted from a two-year collaborative process of the Mexican and U.S. bishops. It was inspired by Pope John Paul II's apostolic exhortation *Ecclesia in America* following the Synod of Bishops of America. The bishops express gratitude for the dialogue begun by the presidents of Mexico and the United States concerning migration issues, and they hope policy changes will result.

---

*See Edward DeBerri, et al., eds., *Catholic Social Teaching: Our Best Kept Secret*, Fourth Revised and Expanded Edition (Maryknoll, NY: Orbis Books, 2003), 162–167, 229.

Discussion Questions

1. Why are the bishops from both countries concerned about Mexican migration to the United States?
2. How does the image of Jesus, Mary, and Joseph as refugees speak to Christians today?
3. What are rights that the bishops call to our attention? How can these rights be balanced?

Excerpts from the Text

2. We speak as two episcopal conferences but as one Church, united in the view that migration between our two nations is necessary and beneficial. At the same time, some aspects of the migrant experience are far from the vision of the Kingdom of God that Jesus proclaimed: many persons who seek to migrate are suffering, and, in some cases, tragically dying; human rights are abused; families are kept apart; and racist and xenophobic attitudes remain.

Migration in the Light of Catholic Social Teaching

28. Catholic teaching has a long and rich tradition in defending the right to migrate. Based on the life and teachings of Jesus, the Church's teaching has provided the basis for the development of basic principles regarding the right to migrate for those attempting to exercise their God-given human rights. Catholic teaching also states that the root causes of migration—poverty, injustice, religious intolerance, armed conflicts—must be addressed so that migrants can remain in their homeland and support their families.

33. Both of our episcopal conferences have echoed the rich tradition of church teachings with regard to migration. Five principles emerge from such teachings, which guide the Church's view on migration issues.

I. Persons have the right to find opportunities in their homeland.

34. All persons have the right to find in their own countries the economic, political, and social opportunities to live in dignity and achieve a full life through the use of their God-given gifts. [...]

II. Persons have the right to migrate to support themselves and their families.

35. The Church recognizes that all the goods of the earth belong to all people. [...]

III. Sovereign nations have the right to control their borders.

36. The Church recognizes the right of sovereign nations to control their territories but rejects such control when it is exerted merely for the purpose of acquiring additional wealth. [...]

IV. Refugees and asylum seekers should be afforded protection.

37. Those who flee wars and persecution should be protected by the global community. [...]

V. The human dignity and human rights of undocumented migrants should be respected.

38. Regardless of their legal status, migrants, like all persons, possess inherent human dignity that should be respected. [...]

39. The Church recognizes the right of a sovereign state to control its borders in furtherance of the common good. It also recognizes the right of human persons to migrate so that they can realize their God-given rights. These teachings complement each other. While the sovereign state may impose reasonable limits on immigration, the common good is not served when the basic human rights of the individual are violated. In the current condition of the world, in which global poverty and persecution are rampant, the presumption is that persons must migrate in order to support and protect themselves and that nations who are able to receive them should do so whenever possible. It is through this lens that we assess the current migration reality between the United States and Mexico.

34. Statement of the U.S. Catholic Bishops on American Indians

UNITED STATES CATHOLIC CONFERENCE, 1977

Document is out of print. A summary of the document available at: http://www.shc.edu/theolibrary/resources/ind1977.htm

Abstract

The bishops recognize the need to engage in dialogue with Native American Catholics to rectify past injustices and renew efforts for the just participation of American Indians in the life of the Church.

Historical Note

Amid the burgeoning civil rights movements in the United States, there was a reawakening to the profound injustices perpetrated on Native Americans throughout U.S. history from the "discovery" of America to the present day. The Church was often well-intended, yet highly complicit, in the injustices of striping indigenous peoples of their languages, traditions, and ways of life. Key events included the founding of the American Indian Movement in 1968 in Minneapolis to protect Native Americans from police brutality and the massacre at Wounded Knee, South Dakota, in 1973.

Discussion Questions

1. In light of the checkered past of mission activity, explain why bishops stress "dialogue" with Native Americans.
2. What has been done to incorporate Native American languages, symbols, or rituals into the liturgy of the Catholic Church?
3. How are Native American views of history taught in the schools of your community? How do these views contribute to racial justice?

Excerpts from the Text

The Church and Justice

9. The Church is also required by the Gospel and by its tradition to promote and defend human rights and human dignity. Pope Paul VI has underscored the fact that "between evangelization and human advancement—development and liberation—there are in fact profound links.... The necessity of ensuring fundamental human rights cannot be separated from this just liberation which is bound up with evangelization and which endeavors to secure structures safeguarding human freedoms." The Church, Pope Paul continued, "has the duty to proclaim the liberation of millions of human beings—the duty of assisting the birth of this liberation, of giving witness to it, of ensuring that it is complete. This is not foreign to evangelization."

10. In all its activities the Church must seek to preach and act in ways that lead to greater justice for all people. Its ministry cannot neglect the violations of human rights resulting from racism, poverty, poor housing, inadequate education and health care, widespread apathy and indifference, and a lack of freedom. These realities are fundamentally incompatible with our faith and the Church is required to oppose them. Pope Paul VI stressed the profound link between the Church's mission to preach the Gospel and action on behalf of justice: "How in fact can one proclaim the new commandment without promoting justice?" (LG41)

14. But the arrival of later immigrants created conflicts not yet resolved. Indian ways of life were challenged; their very existence continually threat-

ened by newcomers who were their superiors in the arts of war. For the Indians, the saga of nation building in America has been a story filled with sorrow and death.

17. During recent decades, increasing numbers of American Indians, especially the young people, have migrated to cities in search of jobs, shelter and social services which are sorely lacking on many reservations. Those who have chosen or been forced to migrate to cities in response to promises of employment and a better life have too often found only new frustrations and broken dreams. Many contend with a deep sense of uprootedness, trying to maintain ties with their families and tribes while coping with the economic hardships and social prejudices, even racism, of urban society.

35. Brothers and Sisters to Us

UNITED STATES BISHOPS, 1979*

Full text of document available at: http://www.nccbuscc.org/saac/bishops pastoral.shtml

Abstract

The bishops call racism a sin and an evil. They discuss various manifestations of racism—past and at present—in the Church and society. The Bishops affirm that all people are created in the image of God and should be treated with corresponding dignity. The pastoral concludes with a plan for combating racism on the individual, Church, national, and international levels.

Historical Note

This pastoral statement denouncing racism followed upon the U.S. bishops' previous 1958 and 1968 pastorals. This letter responded to the consultation on social justice which formed the "Call to Action," a vehicle for Catholic participation in the U.S. bicentennial.

Discussion Questions

1. What are some ways your parish or school can assist in the process of conversion and renewal to change unjust systems and structures that support racism?
2. What are some goals of racial justice that we should work for?

---

*See Edward P. DeBerri, et al. eds., *Catholic Social Teaching: Our Best Kept Secret*, Fourth Revised and Expanded Edition (Maryknoll, NY: Orbis, 2003), 133–135, 227.

Excerpts from the Text

The Sin of Racism

Racism is a sin: a sin that divides the human family, blots out the image of God among specific members of that family, and violates the fundamental human dignity of those called to be children of the same Father. Racism is the sin that says some human beings are inherently superior and others essentially inferior because of races. It is the sin that makes racial characteristics the determining factor for the exercise of human rights. It mocks the words of Jesus: "Treat others the way you would have them treat you" (Mt 7:12). Indeed, racism is more than a disregard for the words of Jesus; it is a denial of the truth of the dignity of each human being revealed by the mystery of the Incarnation.

In order to find the strength to overcome the evil of racism, we must look to Christ. In Christ Jesus "there does not exist among you Jew or Greek, slave or freedom, male or female. All are one in Christ Jesus" (Gal 3:28). As Pope John Paul II has said so clearly, "Our spirit is set in one direction, the only direction for our intellect, will and heart is—toward Christ our Redeemer, toward Christ the Redeemer of [humanity.]" It is in Christ, then, that the Church finds the central cause for its commitment to justice, and to the struggle for the human rights and dignity of all persons.

When we give in to our fears of the other because he or she is of a race different from ourselves, when we prejudge the motives of others precisely because they are of a different color, when we stereotype or ridicule the other because of racial characteristics and heritage, we fail to heed the command of the Prophet Amos: "Seek good and not evil, that you may live; then truly will the Lord ... be with you as you claim! ... Then let justice surge like water, and goodness like an unfailing stream" (Amos 5:14, 24).

Today in our country men, women, and children are being denied opportunities for full participation and advancement in our society because of their race. The educational, legal, and financial systems, along with other structures and sectors of our society, impede people's progress and narrow their access because they are black, Hispanic, Native American or Asian.

The structures of our society are subtly racist, for these structures reflect the values which society upholds. They are geared to the success of the majority and the failure of the minority. Members of both groups give unwitting approval by accepting things as they are. Perhaps no single individual is to blame. The sinfulness is often anonymous but nonetheless real. The sin is social in nature in that each of us, in varying degrees, is responsible. All of us in some measure are accomplices. As our recent pastoral letter on moral values states: "The absence of personal fault for an evil does not absolve one of all responsibility. We must seek to resist and undo injustices we have not ceased, least we become bystanders who tacitly endorse evil and so share in guilt in it."

Racism Is a Fact

Because the Courts have eliminated statutory racial discrimination and Congress has enacted civil rights legislation, and because some minority people have achieved some measure of success, many people believe that racism is no longer a problem in American life. The continuing existence of racism becomes apparent, however, when we look beneath the surface of our national life: as, for example, in the case of unemployment figures. [...] Quite simply, this means that an alarming proportion of tomorrow's adults are cut off from gainful employment—an essential prerequisite of responsible adulthood. These same youths presently suffer the crippling effects of a segregated educational system which in many cases fails to enlighten the mind and free the spirit, which too often inculcates a conviction of inferiority and which frequently graduates persons who are ill-prepared and inadequately trained. In addition, racism raises its ugly head in the violence that frequently surrounds attempts to achieve racial balance in education and housing. [...]

Our Response

Racism is not merely one sin among many; it is a radical evil that divides the human family and denies the new creation of a redeemed world. To struggle against it demands an equally radical transformation, in our own minds and hearts as well as in the structure of our society. [...]

36. The Hispanic Presence: Challenge and Commitment

THE UNITED STATES CATHOLIC BISHOPS, 1984*

Full text of document available at: http://www.usccbpublishing.org/

Abstract

The pastoral focuses on the reality of Hispanics in the United States. The increase in the number of Hispanics is a "pastoral opportunity" with many pastoral implications. The bishops call for a wide range of responses involving all Catholics. The bishops conclude by articulating their commitment to Hispanic ministry.

---

*See Edward DeBerri, et al., eds., *Catholic Social Teaching: Our Best Kept Secret*, Fourth Revised Edition (Maryknoll, NY: Orbis Books, 2003), 142–144.

Historical Note

This is the first pastoral letter by the U.S. Bishops exclusively on Hispanic ministry. The Bishops sought to respond to the needs of the then twenty million U.S. Hispanics. They followed this pastoral letter with a pastoral plan published in 1987. Earlier pastorals on Hispanic ministry came from the U.S. Hispanic bishops and the Santa Fe province bishops (1982). The U.S. Hispanic population continues to increase significantly.

Discussion Questions

1. What are some of the conditions that create situations of "pervasive poverty" for so many Hispanics in the United States? What must be challenged in order to help them?
2. What are a few concrete things the U.S. Church can do to assist the Latin American Church?

Excerpts from the Text

12.m. Prejudice and Racism

Within our memory, Hispanics in this country have experienced cruel prejudice. So extensive has it been in some areas that they have been denied basic human and civil rights. Even today Hispanics, blacks, the recent Southeast Asian refugees, and Native Americans continue to suffer from such dehumanizing treatment, treatment which makes us aware that the sin of racism lingers in our society. Despite great strides in eliminating racial prejudice, both in our country and in our Church, there remains an urgent need for continued purification and reconciliation. It is particularly disheartening to know that some Catholics hold strong prejudices against Hispanics and others and deny them the respect and love due their God-given human dignity.

This is evident even in some parish communities where one finds a reluctance among some non-Hispanics to serve with Hispanics or to socialize with them at parochial events. We appeal to those with this unchristian attitude to examine their behavior in the light of Jesus' commandment of love and to accept their Hispanic brothers and sisters as full partners in the work and life of their parishes. Our words in our pastoral letter on racism deserve repeating: "Racism is not merely one sin among many, it is a radical evil dividing the human family and denying the new creation of a redeemed world. To struggle against it demands an equally radical transformation in our own minds and hearts as well as the structure of our society" (BSU, p. 10).

We urge those who employ Hispanics to provide them with safe and decent working conditions and to pay them salaries which enable them to provide adequately for their families. The inhuman condition of pervasive poverty forced on many Hispanics is at the root of many social problems in their lives. Decent working conditions and adequate salaries are required by justice and basic fairness.

Commitment to Catholicity

14. The universal character of the Church involves both pluralism and unity. Humanity, in its cultures and peoples, is so various that it could only have been crafted by the hand of God. The Church recognizes this in saying that "each individual part contributes through its special gifts" (LG, 13). Yet the Church transcends all limits of time and race; humanity as a whole is called to become a People of God in peace and unity.

The Gospel teaching that no one is a stranger in the Church is timeless. As the Apostle Paul says, "there does not exist among you Jew or Greek, slave or freeman, male or female. All are one in Christ Jesus" (Gal 3:28).

Our commitment to Hispanic ministry therefore leads us, as teachers, to invite *all* Catholics to adopt a more welcoming attitude toward others. Hispanics, whose presence in this land is antedated only by that of Native Americans, are called to welcome their brothers and sisters, the descendants of other European immigrants. Similarly, the latter are called to embrace Hispanic newcomers from Latin America. Where all are freed from attitudes of cultural or ethnic dominance, the gifts of all will enrich the Church and give witness to the Gospel of Jesus Christ.

37. Asian and Pacific Presence: Harmony in Faith

UNITED STATES CONFERENCE OF CATHOLIC BISHOPS, 2001

Full text of document available at: http://www.usccb.org/mrs/harmony.shtml

Abstract

Building on *Welcoming the Stranger Among Us: Unity in Diversity* (2000), the bishops recognized and affirmed the presence of Asian and Pacific Catholics. They noted the challenges facing this vastly diverse group of peoples and they responded with recommendations.

Historical Note

This was the U.S. bishops' follow-up to John Paul II's Apostolic Exhortation *Ecclesia in Asia* (1999). In 2001, Pacific and Asian Catholics in the United States were 2.6% of the Catholic population and growing.

Discussion Questions

1. What are some ways you can engage the threefold dialogue with other religions, cultures, and the poor?
2. Research the Chinese Exclusion Act, Executive Order 9066, and the Johnson-Reed Act of 1924.
3. What are some of the racialized stereotypes of Asian and Pacific people? What can you do to help eradicate these images?
4. Why do Asian and Pacific peoples sometimes seek their own worshiping communities? How can you welcome them?

Excerpts from the Text

Experiencing Racial Discrimination

Part of the sad reality for minorities and many immigrants—among them Asian and Pacific Islanders—to the United States is racial discrimination and prejudice. Racially restrictive laws have ranged from those that affect all non-white populations, including Asian and Pacific groups, to those that target specific Asian groups. Prior to the 1950s, Asian immigrants were denied the right to become naturalized citizens—a right granted to all other immigrants to the United States. Laws in many states forbade marriages between non-whites (including Asians) and whites, although social pressures were probably the major impediment to interracial marriages. The Chinese Exclusion Law of 1882, which remained in effect until 1943, barred additional Chinese laborers from entering the United States and prevented Chinese aliens from obtaining American citizenship. A 1909 law denied citizenship to 50,000 persons from Arabia because they were considered Asians. Japanese laborers were brought to the United States in lieu of Chinese laborers until 1907, when the Gentlemen's Agreement with Japan curtailed Japanese immigration temporarily; and the Johnson-Reed Act of 1924, known as the "Japanese Exclusion Act," banned immigration of Japanese laborers. Perhaps the most tragic instance of racial discrimination was Executive Order 9066 of 1942, which forced Japanese immigrants, including two-thirds who were American citizens mainly from the west coast, into internment camps under the guise of military necessity. This experience cannot be described without noting the heroic efforts of many religious, such as the Maryknoll fathers, brothers, and sisters, who accompanied the Japanese internees to the camps and stayed with them. Without such loving ministry, many Japanese American Catholics might have felt abandoned and left their Catholic faith.

While legal provisions have changed, discriminatory actions by individuals and groups sadly perdure. Throughout history, Asians in the United

States, native-born and immigrant, have been characterized as "permanent aliens," a race of foreigners given externally imposed labels and racial identities and only referred to in passing or even omitted altogether in classic immigration history. Asian and Pacific contributions in building the nation have been mostly unrecognized and ignored. The recent episodes of racial attacks against Asian persons and businesses in Los Angeles and Detroit are tragic reminders of the ongoing need for conversion against any form of racial discrimination.

Some Asian immigrant groups are still relegated to jobs that pay low wages, require them to work long hours, and provide substandard working conditions and unfair labor practices. To escape from such exploitative conditions, some Asian entrepreneurs resort to establishing small businesses in their own communities, sometimes with the help of affirmative action programs, through which Asian and Pacific Americans also have obtained college and advanced degrees.

A Threefold Dialogue with Religions, Cultures, and the Poor

Since the Second Vatican Council, our brother bishops in Asia, who gather regularly as the Federation of Asian Bishops' Conferences, have developed a pastoral approach that emphasizes a threefold dialogue: with other religions, with cultures, and with the poor. Such dialogue can also be explored for its enriching fruitfulness at all levels of the Church in the United States.

Dialogue with Other Religions. Like other immigrants before them, those from Asian and Pacific communities want to be companions on the faith journey with the American people. Essential to an understanding of Asian and Pacific communities is the dialogue with other religions. This means recognizing key themes of the spirituality and theology of religions, especially Buddhism, Confucianism, Islam, Taoism, and some indigenous religions. In beginning the dialogue, as the Holy Father points out, several religious values exist that are of the highest significance: for example, in Islam, the centrality of the will of God; in Hinduism, the practice of meditation, contemplation, renunciation of one's will, and the spirit of nonviolence; in Buddhism, detachment and compassion; in Confucianism, filial piety and humanitarianism; in Taoism, simplicity and humility; in other traditional religions, reverence and respect for patience. Interreligious dialogue at its deepest level is always a dialogue of salvation, because it seeks to discover, classify, and understand better the signs of the age-long dialogue that God maintains with humanity. This dialogue will bring about truly inculturated theology, liturgy, and spirituality among Asian and Pacific Americans in order to live and announce the message of Christ.

38. Dwell in My Love

FRANCIS CARDINAL GEORGE, O.M.I., ARCHBISHOP OF CHICAGO, 2001

Full text of document available at: http://www.archchicago.org/cardinal/dwellinmylove/dwellinmylove.shtm

Abstract

The cardinal speaks from experience, addressing various dimensions of racial justice. He addresses racial justice in the Archdiocese of Chicago because it is integral to our faith and racism is a sin that cannot be ignored.

Historical Note

The cardinal responded to John Paul II's Jubilee call to welcome all peoples in our midst. Historically, Chicago was a "Catholic city" known for having a different "national Church" on nearly every city block. Diversity in the Church of Chicago has occasioned blessing and deep pain. Published in spring 2001, it took on increased relevance on September 11, 2001. Indeed, on September 11, 2001, reports were that Chicago's Sears Tower had also been threatened.

Discussion Questions

1. Explain the four types of racism the cardinal defines. Give some examples from your experience of each type.
2. What role can you play in the pastoral plan the cardinal outlines for eliminating racism?

Excerpts from the Text

Four Types of Racism: Spatial, Institutional, Internalized, and Individual

The face of racism looks different today than it did thirty years ago. Overt racism is easily condemned, but the sin is often with us in more subtle forms. In examining patterns of racism today, four forms of racism merit particular attention: spatial racism, institutional racism, internalized racism and individual racism.

Spatial Racism

Spatial racism refers to patterns of metropolitan development in which some affluent whites create racially and economically segregated suburbs or gentrified areas of cities, leaving the poor—mainly African Americans, Hispanics and some newly arrived immigrants—isolated in deteriorating areas of the cities and older suburbs. [...]

The spatial racism of our society creates a similar pattern in the Church. Geographically based parishes reflect the racial and cultural segregation patterns of neighborhoods and towns.

Institutional Racism

Racism also finds institutional form. Patterns of social and racial superiority continue as long as no one asks why they should be taken for granted. People who assume, consciously or unconsciously, that white people are superior create and sustain institutions that privilege people like themselves and habitually ignore the contributions of other peoples and cultures. This "white privilege" often goes undetected because it has become internalized and integrated as part of one's outlook on the world by custom, habit and tradition. It can be seen in most of our institutions: judicial and political systems, social clubs, associations, hospitals, universities, labor unions, small and large businesses, major corporations, the professions, sports teams and in the arts. In the Church as well, "... all too often in the very places where blacks, Hispanics, Native Americans and Asians are numerous, the Church's officials and representatives, both clerical and laity, are predominantly white." [...]

Indifference to rates of violence against the lives of blacks, Hispanics, Asians and Native peoples is another sign of institutional racism. "Abortion rates are much higher among the poor and people of color than among the middle class. As a result of abortion, the United States is a far less diverse place." Racism is also visible in imprisonment and in the administration of the death penalty. There are a disproportionate number of blacks, Hispanics, Asians and Native Americans and low-income persons from all ethnic and racial groups on death row. "[Such] defendants are more likely to be sentenced to death than white defendants, for the same crimes." Other areas where institutional racism finds a home are in health care, education and housing.

Internalized Racism

Many blacks, Hispanics, Asians and Native Americans are socialized and educated in institutions which devalue the presence and contributions of people of color and celebrate only the contributions of whites. Because of their socialization within the dominant racial and cultural system, people of color can come to see themselves and their communities primarily through the eyes of that dominant culture. They receive little or no information about their own history and culture and perceive themselves and their communities as "culturally deprived." Seeing few men and women from their own culture or class in leadership roles, they begin to apply to themselves the negative stereotypes about their group that the dominant culture chooses to believe.

Individual Racism

Unlike spatial and institutionalized racism, which are more public in nature, individual racism perpetuates itself quietly when people grow up with a sense of white racial superiority, whether conscious or unconscious. Racist attitudes find expression in racial slurs, in crimes born of racial hatred and in many other subtle and not so subtle ways. People that are horrified by the Ku Klux Klan might quite readily subscribe to racial stereotypes about people of color. [...]

39. Made in the Image of God

ALFRED HUGHES, ARCHBISHOP OF NEW ORLEANS, 2006

Full text of document available at: http://www.archdiocese-no.org/121506.pdf

Abstract

Using the image of New Orleans jazz, the archbishop declares that the Gospel impels Christ's followers to work for racial and cultural harmony. Hurricane Katrina exposed once again that people of color disproportionately receive substandard education, employment, housing, and health care. Recovery from Katrina (which means "cleansing") is an opportunity to start afresh to create justice and harmony among the diverse peoples of New Orleans. Hughes apologized for the racist complicity of the Church and its members and pledged action according to the plan concluding the document.

Historical Note

This document commemorated the fiftieth anniversary of "The Morality of Racial Segregation," by Archbishop Joseph Rummel. On August 29, 2005, hurricane Katrina killed hundreds and destroyed 80 percent of New Orleans; the levees broke flooding the city and surrounding areas. Hughes' pastoral originally slated for September 2005, was revised to include the hurricane's blatant revelations of the longstanding and deep effects of racism. In all areas of life, the historic racial divide disproportionately placed people of color at severe, often life-threatening disadvantage. For example, one of every three people who lived in the areas hit hardest by the hurricane was African American. (Nationally, one of every eight people is African American.) In New Orleans 35 percent of black households and 59 percent of poor black households lacked a vehicle before the hurricane struck (compared to 15 percent among whites).

Discussion Questions

1. Research one of the heroines or heroes listed by the archbishop as people who stood for racial justice. What lessons can we learn from this person?
2. In what ways do you benefit from "white privilege?" How are you harmed by "white privilege?"
3. In what ways are fear of the stranger and racism alike? How are they different?
4. What do many immigrants and the victims of Katrina have in common concerning racial justice?

Excerpts from the Text

Continuing Disharmony

Unfortunately, today as in the past, we in the Church have been slow to appreciate the full depth and breadth of the meaning of Divine Revelation that each human person is made in the image and likeness of God. Christ, through His cross, has granted us the grace to live a new life in Him. Racial and cultural differences are no longer to be causes of division (Gal 3:26–28). [...]

As we continue to work toward racial justice today, it is important to understand what is recognized as "white privilege." Those with lighter skin color have certain advantages, privileges and benefits that persons of darker color do not enjoy. (In Louisiana, 36 percent of African American families live in poverty, compared to 11 percent of whites.) People of color have certain systemic disadvantages, burdens and stigmas that they have to overcome. From a white perspective, everything is normal because white people often do not see the advantages that are inherent simply in being born into society with physical characteristics valued by that society. Such privilege shows up, however, in current everyday occurrences. In stores and restaurants, preferred treatment is at times given to some, while others are delayed or denied the same equal service.

As members of a privileged race, we may not have espoused a conviction that our race was better than other races, but we probably have accepted uncritically the privileges attached to our race no matter how this has impacted others. Anyone who has accepted social privilege at the expense of people of another race is complicit in the fostering of attitudes and behavior that unfortunately can feed racial disharmony.

The Need of the Church—and of Us as Members—
To Respond in This Twenty-First Century

> *"Once you know all these things, blest will you be if you put them into practice." (Jn 13:17)*

The action plan proposed later in this pastoral outlines a strategy for moving forward as Church and as a post-Katrina community. It is important for us to take concrete initiatives in order to make up for abuses or disadvantages in the past. [...]

Oceania

40. A Generous Heart in the Love of Christ: Challenging Racism in Australia Today

AUSTRALIAN CATHOLIC BISHOPS' CONFERENCE, 2003

Full text of document available at: http://www.socialjustice.catholic.org.au/
CONTENT/publications/documentation/A%20Generous%20Heart%20in
%20the%20Love%20of%20Christ.pdf

Abstract

This document was published for Social Justice Sunday, September 22, 2003. It traces Australia's story of welcome and exclusion from the time white settlers arrived and confronted the indigenous peoples, to the development of a multicultural nation. Disturbing and recurring racial hostility and rejection is expressed most clearly today in Australians' attitudes toward immigrants and asylum seekers, especially against those from the Middle East.

Historical Note

This document was written after September 11, 2001, military action in Afghanistan, the bombing in Bali, and the war in Iraq, and subsequent terrorist attacks. Worldwide, there was a noticeable rise in xenophobia.

Discussion Questions

1. Research the "white Australia Policy."

2. Compare and contrast the "times of welcome" with the "times of exclusion" in Australian history. What were the critical differences in the conditions in each period concerning racial justice?
3. How can you help make the media more responsible in "welcoming the stranger?"

Excerpts from the Text

Human Dignity and Discrimination

The Gospel urges us to welcome strangers because we are all precious in God's sight. Our worth does not depend on the colour of our skin, our customs, or our religion. We are made in God's image, each deeply loved by God, and that is finally the source of our human dignity. Because each of us is infinitely precious, no one may be treated as a thing or used to achieve some grand goal. When we welcome the stranger, we welcome Christ. *How can the baptised claim to welcome Christ if they close the door to the foreigner who comes knocking? "If anyone has the world's goods and sees his brothers or sisters in need, yet closes his heart against them, how does God's love abide in him?"* (1.Jn.3.17. Pope John Paul II, Message for World Migration Day 2000, no. 5)

The Gift of Diversity

Culture, language, religion and nationality are important to us because they are the building blocks of our identity and self-confidence. They shape our relationships to one another and our world. Our language and culture give us eyes with which to see our world, words and silences with which to celebrate it with other people, and the words and rituals that open a path to God. Our culture, language and religion are not like clothes that we can change when we travel. They are like the skin that enables us to go confidently into our world; they are not possessions, but part of our self. To expect people to give up their own culture when they enter ours is like asking them to amputate a limb.

Respect for persons demands respect for their cultures. What makes us different from one another is what most enriches us as human beings and makes possible deep relationships between us. Our differences reflect the variety and inexhaustible beauty of God. If multiculturalism implies that we should not only support immigrants as individuals but should also regard their culture as an enrichment, it simply states what ought to be obvious.

Churches nourish the spiritual and cultural life of immigrants and help them feel at home in their adopted land. Because our relationship to God lies at the heart of who we are as persons, it is vital for us to be able to pray in our own ways and to hear the Word of God in our own language. The churches that receive immigrants make a cultural space where people can pray together out of the richness of their own culture.

41. The Heart of Our Country: Dignity and Justice for Our Indigenous Brothers and Sisters

AUSTRALIAN CATHOLIC BISHOPS' CONFERENCE, 2006

Full text of document available at: http://www.acbc.catholic.org.au/pdf/ Social%20Justice%20Sunday%20Statement%202006.pdf

Abstract

This statement was prepared for Social Justice Sunday, September 24, 2006. The bishops invite Australians to examine how they have supported Aboriginal and Torres Strait Islanders in preserving strong the elements of their culture. The bishops challenge Australians to joyfully receive the contributions of the indigenous peoples' cultures and traditions into their life.

Historical Note

In 1986, in Alice Springs, Pope John Paul II addressed the Aboriginal and Torres Strait Islander peoples of Australia, offering the Church's assistance in their spiritual and material needs. While much has been achieved toward that end, much is left to be done. However, the pope's challenges are still being taken up by the Australian Church.

Discussion Questions

1. In what ways can you welcome Aboriginal people and assist them in the preservation of their culture?
2. How can the spiritual practice of *dadirri* contribute to establishing and sustaining racial justice?

Excerpts from the Text

The Message Stick

A significant way for Aboriginal Australians to maintain and pass on their ancient culture was through *Message Sticks*. These wooden sticks were marked with symbols and were shown to the Elders of each group that the carriers, young males, met on their journey. The bearer was then allowed to pass. From ancient times, the Message Stick has been used to call people from different tribes together. Now, as the Aboriginal Catholic Ministry in

Melbourne tells us, 'The call to embrace Australia's Indigenous peoples is issued to the whole Church and the whole nation in nine "Pass It On" Message Sticks bearing symbolically the messages of the Pope's 1986 statement.' The sticks are similar in size and bear symbols of Christ, of the Pope's 1986 message and of Aboriginal and Torres Strait Islander peoples. The Message Sticks involve the interpretation of the Pope's message in liturgy, song, dance, story, activities and other ceremonies. They are calling us to commemorate in October 2006 the 20th anniversary of Pope John Paul II's historic speech at Alice Springs. The Message Sticks carry an invitation to all of us to celebrate the message of hope and reconciliation in our local communities. They also carry with them the call to reflect on the message delivered by Pope John Paul II and to evaluate the extent to which we have responded to that message over the past 20 years.

What Was the Message in 1986?

Dear Brothers and Sisters, it is a great joy for me to be here today in Alice Springs and to meet so many of you, the Aborigines and Torres Strait Islanders of Australia. I want to tell you right away how much the Church esteems and loves you, and how much she wishes to assist you in your spiritual and material needs. The full impact of these words spoken 20 years ago is still being realised, as the nation and the Catholic Church continue to explore the path to reconciliation with the Aboriginal and Torres Strait Islander peoples of Australia.

Pope John Paul II identified four very important issues when he spoke to the Aboriginal people in Blatherskite Park at Alice Springs:

- He challenged all Australians to ensure the preservation of Indigenous cultures and to keep working for an inclusive multicultural Australia.
- He called us to seek and explore the points of agreement between Indigenous traditions and those of Jesus and all his people.
- He praised the way the Indigenous peoples had cared for the land and then challenged us to learn together how to preserve our fragile environment.
- Finally, by naming past hurts and continuing injustices, John Paul II confronted us as a nation with the need to move towards true reconciliation.

Reclaiming the Message

Part of the message delivered by Pope John Paul II to the Bishops gathered in Rome in 2001 included an apology for the part played by the Catholic Church in past injustices suffered by Aboriginal and Torres Strait Islander peoples: *The Church expresses deep regret and asks forgiveness where her children have been or still are party to these wrongs. Aware of the shameful injustices done to the indigenous peoples in Oceania, the*

Synod Fathers apologised unreservedly for the part played in these by mem-
bers of the Church, especially where children were forcibly separated from
their families... The challenge is now ours to move closer to achieving a new
reconciliation.

In celebrating the 20th anniversary of the late Holy Father's address at
Blatherskite Park in Alice Springs, we Catholic Bishops of Australia echo his
words. We reclaim the message and pass it on!

42. *He Tau Whakamaharatanga Mo Aotearoa-Nui Tireni:* A Commemoration Year for Aotearoa-New Zealand

NEW ZEALAND CATHOLIC BISHOPS' CONFERENCE, 1990

Full text of document available at: http://catholic.org.nz/statements/90_com
memoration.php

Abstract

The bishops seek reconciliation with the Maori and to actively work for
racial harmony and justice between the different peoples of New Zealand.

Historical Note

The year 1988 marked the one hundred fiftieth anniversary of the
Catholic Church's ministry in Aotearoa-New Zealand. The year 1990 was
the one hundred fiftieth year since the signing of *Te Tiriti o Waitangi*/The
Treaty of *Waitangi*, the document that established New Zealand as a nation.

Discussion Questions

1. The bishops state that reconciliation requires both internal and external
   renewal. What might such renewal look like? Name some of its elements.
2. Research the Maori people. What is one dimension of their culture or
   spirituality that can assist in reconciliation with the non-Maori population of New Zealand?

Excerpts from the Text

The review of our history clearly indicates that the promises and guarantees made in 1840 have not been consistently upheld and that the Maori
partner has suffered grave injustices. The Maori have not always been given
the protection of the State as promised under the Treaty. Worse still, the
State has often deprived them by law of many of the promised guarantees.

The State reflects the attitudes and behaviour of its people. In New Zealand racial prejudice still exists and is practiced, particularly against the Maori. Racist thoughts, attitudes and behaviour are sinful because they are clearly against the specific message of Christ, for whom neighbour is not only a person from my tribe, my milieu, my religion or my nation: it is every person that I meet along the way.

Renewal and reconciliation concern not only the interior life of each individual, but the whole Church, and also the whole of human society. The "all-consuming desire for profit" and "the thirst for power with the intention of imposing one's will on others…at any price" are sinful attitudes contributing to the creation of "structures of sin."

These powerful attitudes are reflected in the pain and suffering that Maori people constantly refer to when they talk of the principles of the Treaty of Waitangi being broken. Like a Jubilee Year, 1990 gives us an opportunity to recognise past and present injustices and to work to resolve them and effect reconciliation based on justice. With the tradition and teaching of the Church, we affirm: that the right of the first occupants to land, and a social and political organization which would allow them to preserve their cultural identity, while remaining open to others, must be guaranteed.

We believe and proclaim the importance of recognising the diversity and complementarity of one another's cultural riches and moral qualities as well as the need for building community and solidarity.

In order to achieve the necessary respect, community and solidarity which our faith requires of us, our two national bodies, Te Runanga o te Hahi Katorika ki Aotearoa (Catholic Maori body) and the Catholic Commission for Justice, Peace and Development, have proposed that we all work to promote and create "structures of grace" for Aotearoa. As Bishops, we support this call on all Catholic people and on all people of goodwill to take the creating of new structures of grace as the challenge of the present generation and of this 1990 year.

43. 1993 United Nations Year of Indigenous Peoples

NEW ZEALAND CATHOLIC BISHOPS' CONFERENCE, 1993

Full text of document available at: http://www.catholic.org.nz/statements/0493indigenous.php

Abstract

The bishops recognize the Maori people as a national treasure and the responsibility of the Church to work to ensure their rights and promote remedies to reconcile past injustices.

Historical Note

The year 1993, the UN International Year of Indigenous Peoples, provided the Church of New Zealand an opportunity to address the needs of the Maori people including employment, health care, education, and the fundamental right to exist.

Discussion Questions

1. What has the Church done since 1993 to improve the status of the Maori concerning employment, education, and health care?
2. The bishops briefly address the right of members of the Maori who wish to choose the ways of the dominant culture to do so without penalty. Research this issue. Do you think the Church has given this adequate attention?

Excerpts from the Text

The problems faced by Maori, the indigenous people of Aotearoa New Zealand, are many. They can be seen in three areas—employment, health, education—where here are immediate needs to be addressed. In September 1992, the unemployment rate for young people aged 15 to 19 years was 21.8 percent, compared with 16.7 percent in September 1990. The unemployment rate for Maori aged 15 to 19 was 45.5 percent (36.7% in September 1990). In Maori health developments the picture is still not as good as could be expected where numerous studies confirm that Maori continue to experience ill-health and thus a lower life expectancy.

The Church has clarified some fundamental principles that are relevant to indigenous peoples' needs (and those of other minorities) in any society. These principles can be a guide for our country as we make greater endeavors to move towards equality and justice. Pope John Paul II has said: The first right of minorities is the right to exist. This right can be ignored in any ways, including such extreme cases as its denial through overt or indirect forms of genocide. The right to life as such is inalienable, and the state which perpetrates or tolerates acts aimed at endangering the lives of its citizens belonging to minority groups violates the fundamental law governing the social order.

The right to exist can be undermined in more subtle ways. Certain peoples, especially those identified as native or indigenous, have always maintained a relationship to their land, a relationship connected with the group's very identity as a people having their own tribal, cultural and religious tradition. When such indigenous peoples are deprived of their land they lose a vital element of their way of life and actually run the risk of disappearing as a people.

Another right which must be safeguarded is the right of minorities to preserve and develop their culture. It is not unheard of that minority groups are threatened with cultural extinction. In some places, in fact, laws have been enacted which do not recognize their right to use their own language. At times people are forced to change their family and place names. Some minorities see their artistic and literary expressions ignored, with their festivals and celebrations given no place in public life. All this can lead to the loss of a notable cultural heritage. Closely connected with this right is the right to have contact with groups having a common cultural and historical heritage, but living in the territory of another state.

In order to establish and nurture the virtues of solidarity and peace which we deem essential in building a more just society, we must overcome all forms of ethnic inequality.

At the same time we remind all peoples that rights carry with them corresponding duties. Members of indigenous and other minority groups also have their own duties toward society and the state in which they live. Indigenous peoples and minorities can offer their own specific contribution to the building of a peaceful world that will reflect the rich diversity of all its inhabitants. Furthermore, an indigenous or minority group has the duty to promote the freedom and dignity of each one of its members and to respect the decisions of each member. This is so even if someone decides to adopt the majority culture.

Indigenous peoples have cultural heritages that contain much wisdom. This is part of a nation's wealth which all citizens need to be open to. Indigenous peoples and their cultures, including Maori, offer their treasures to all while opening themselves to the world's treasures.

44. A Consistent Ethic of Life—Te Kahu-O-Te-Ora

NEW ZEALAND CATHOLIC BISHOPS' CONFERENCE, 1997

Full text of document available at: http://www.catholic.org.nz/statements/9704_consistent.php

Abstract

The bishops acknowledge the complexity of moral decision making in today's world. They discuss eight ethical issues including racism, stressing the links between them, in light of the biblical mandate to "Choose life."

Historical Note

The document is dedicated to the late Cardinal Joseph Bernardin (1928–1996) Archbishop of Chicago (1982–1996), who developed a consistent ethic of life. The term *Te Kahu-O-Te-Ora* refers to the Maori *Kahu* which is a cape or garment of various types, the membrane enveloping the foetus, or the veil that at times covered the head of newborns. The Maori tradition was that the person with a Kahu would never drown. So *Te Kahu-O-Te-Ora,* is "The Garment of Life."

Discussion Questions

1. Discuss how issues of racial justice fit within the framework of the consistent ethic of life.
2. Research the Treaty of Waitangi. In what ways does this treaty exemplify racial justice?

Excerpts from the Text

Introduction

We live in a world of extraordinary beauty, blessed with wonderful gifts by our Creator, and containing life, love and diversity in abundance. We acknowledge that in every culture and community wonderfully mature and committed people serve the needs of their neighbour with selflessness and generosity, and we thank them for that. All these we celebrate for the great hope they offer. And yet we find that the world we live in is also a violent world. The modern consumer culture, itself imbued with an ethos of competition, can do violence to the weak, the vulnerable, the feeble, the poor, and the powerless, while rewarding the strong, the beautiful, the powerful and the rich.

The very life and ecology of the planet faces severe threats from pollution, exploitation and mismanagement of its resources. Too often the driving forces for social change are greed and the desire for power, rather than the common good and solidarity of humanity.

People continue to aspire to a life of respect for moral values. They yearn for what poet Gerard Manley Hopkins and has called "the freshness deep down things." But successive generations have perceived that guiding principles have become less clear and the moral signposts of previous generations have become blurred.

Any form of injustice built into national and international structures does violence to fundamental human rights and dignity and is sinful. Such sinfulness needs to be confronted.

Discrimination

Discrimination on any grounds is rejected by the church which states that "no inequality arising because of race, nationality, social condition or sex" should exist. A Consistent Ethic of life proclaims the dignity of every person. We are united by our common humanity, created in the image of God, and called to live in active love and tolerance of all who are different from ourselves.

The evils of racism and sexism are an affront to the dignity of the human person. They are built on the premise that one person, sex, group, culture or race is inherently superior to another. Often they take the form of petty prejudice in a community. Too often they form the basis of social structures that preclude full participation and membership.

The founding covenant for our nation of Aotearoa-New Zealand is the Treaty of Waitangi which was intended to safeguard the rights and dignity of two different races. The dignity and equality of all was won through the death and resurrection of Jesus. Racial equality will be achieved only when Christ's victory is reflected in our personal and structured relationships.

An economy based on principles of co-operation, just reward for labour and a recognition of the common good, form an essential element of the Consistent Ethic of Life. Why do we promote life's sanctity if we do not defend the right of all people to live in dignity? This has been a constant call of the Church's social teaching throughout this past century. It is a call we cannot afford to ignore.

Notes

1. Construction and Definition of "Race" and Racism

[1]Since the notion of race has been debunked as a scientific basis upon which to distinguish human beings, I use the term "race" with quotation marks unless it appears as part of a discussion that makes this point obvious, or it is used in the citation of another author's words. It is a daunting task to find a single definition for the concept of "race." As a working definition here I use the following: "Race" is a social construction arising out of racism. It is an arbitrary set of ideologies and practices imposed on less powerful people by the more powerful, in which various inequalities and differences are related to physical and cultural criteria of an ascriptive kind, and are rationalized in terms of deterministic belief systems and held to be immutable.

I use "ethnicity" to distinguish the characteristics of people of group consciousness and collective action; common ancestry, memories of a shared past, kinship, religion, language, and a shared history See Peter Ratcliffe, "Conceptualizing 'Race,' Ethnicity, and Nation: Toward a Comparative Perspective" in Peter Ratcliffe, ed., 'Race,' Ethnicity and Nation: International Perspectives on Social Conflict (London: University College of London Press, 1994), 4–5.

The term *nation* used here is understood as "an *imagined* political community ... and imagined as both inherently limited and sovereign ... It is imagined because the membership of even the smallest nation will never know most of their fellow members, meet them, or even hear of them, yet in the mind of each lives the image of their communion." See Ratcliffe, ibid. 7.

The following are the more cogent efforts at defining the term, and from which my definition is drawn: Albert Memmi, *Racism* (Minneapolis: University of Minnesota Press, 2000); Michael Omi and Howard Winant, *Racial Formation in the U.S. from the 1960s to the 1990s*, 2nd ed. (New York: Routledge, 1994), 54–55; Stephen Castles, "The Racisms of Globalization," in *Ethnicity and Globalization* (London: Sage, 2000), 165–175; Sandra Harding, "Introduction," in Sandra Harding, ed., *The "Racial" Economy of Science: Toward a Democratic Future* (Bloomington: University of Indiana Press, 1993), 8, 11; Dwight N. Hopkins, *Being Human: Race, Culture and Religion* (Minneapolis, MN: Fortress Press, 2005), 128–129; George M. Fredrickson, *Race: A Short History* (Princeton, NJ: Princeton University Press, 2002), 8–9; Peter Ratcliffe, "Conceptualizing 'Race,' Ethnicity and

Nation: Towards A Comparative Perspective," 3–6; and Gargi Bhattacharyya, John Gabriel, and Stephen Small, *Race and Power: Global Racism in the Twenty-First Century* (London: Routledge, 2002), 1–6 and 60–87.

[2]Margo Monteith and Jeffery Winters, "Why We Hate," *Psychology Today* (May/June 2002): 44–49, 87.

[3]See Jeremy Manier, "Recesses of the Mind," Perspective Section, 1, *Chicago Tribune*, October 13, 1996. See also the work of David Balots of Washington University—St. Louis, Russel Fazio of Ohio State University—Columbus, and John Bargh of New York University on unconscious cognition.

[4]A vast literature exists in support of this point. One of the best sources is Sandra Harding, ed., *The "Racial" Economy of Science: Toward a Democratic Future.* Four groundbreaking international conventions that establish this notion for the world are: the 1950 United Nations Educational, Scientific, and Cultural Organization (UNESCO) *Statement on Race*; the UNESCO 1951 *Statement on the Nature of Race and Race Differences*; UNESCO 1964 *Statement on the Biological Aspects of Race*; and the UNESCO 1967 *Statement on Race and Racial Prejudice.*

[5]See Hopkins, *Being Human*, 131. He cites Robert E. Hood, *Begrimed and Black: Christian Traditions on Blacks and Blackness* (Minneapolis, MN: Fortress, 1994), especially at 26–37.

[6]See Fredrickson, *Race: A Short History*, 53: "In 1611 a Spanish dictionary included among its definitions of *raza* an honorific use—'a caste or quality of authentic horses'—and a pejorative one, as referring to a lineage that included Jewish or Moorish ancestors."

[7]See David Brion Davis, "Constructing Race: A Reflection," in *In God's Image: Moral Values and Our Heritage of Slavery* (New Haven, CT: Yale University Press, 2001), 307–342.

[8]See ibid. 66–67. Monogenesis is the theory that all humans are "of one blood" and that all humans are descendents of Adam as proclaimed in the New Testament and in Genesis. Polygenesis is the theory that three to five separate human species were created separately with vastly different aptitudes and capabilities. British ethnologists such as James Crowles tended to support monogenesis, while the French and American ethnologists supported the polygenesis theories. See also Linda Vigilant, "Race and Biology," in Winston A. Van Horne, ed., *Global Convulsions: Race, Ethnicity and Nationalism at the End of the Twentieth Century* (Albany: State University of New York Press, 1997), 49–62, especially 53–54.

[9]See Fredrickson, *Race: A Short History*, 1–6 and at 6: The notion of "racial order" sets "a permanent group hierarchy that is believed to reflect the laws of nature or the decrees of God." The Nuremburg Laws of 1935, the Jim Crow Laws of the United States and the 1948 South African laws establishing Apartheid are cases in point.

[10]See for example Sudhir Alladi Venkatesh, *Off the Books: The Underground Economy of the Urban Poor* (Boston: Harvard University Press, 2006) in which he examines the underground economy of a south side Chicago ghetto, and attributes the causes of poverty to outside neglect and racism.

[11]See http://action.savedarfur.org/campaign.jsp?campaign_KEY=5191&track =google_ads, Accessed November 28, 2006.

[12]See http://www.twincities.com/mld/twincities/news/local/16071831.htm? template=contentModules/printstory.jsp, Accessed on November 28, 2006.

[13]Memmi, *Racism*, 100.

[14]See Neil MacMaster, *Racism in Europe: 1870–2000* (New York: Palgrave, 2001), 2.

[15]See D.W. Waruta, "Tribalism as a Moral Problem in Contemporary Africa," in J.N.K. Mugambi and Anne Nasimiyu-Wasike, eds., *Moral and Ethical Issues in African Christianity: Exploratory Essays in Moral Theology* (Nairobi: Initiatives Publishers, 1992), 120.

[16]See E. Cashmore, "Xenophobia," in E. Cashmore, et al., *Dictionary of Race and Ethnic Relations* (London: Routledge, 1994), 346. Also see "Xenophobia Won't Go Away." *The Economist* 324/7775 (1992): 27.

[17]See MacMaster, *Racism in Europe: 1870–2000*, 190–191.

[18]See J.M. Voster, "Racism, Xenophobia and Human Rights," *The Ecumenical Review* 54/3 (July 2002): 7. Note that in 1989, Ku Klux Klansman David Duke ran as a Republican for U.S. House of Representatives and won, see http://www.david duke.com/index.php?p=350.

[19]MacMaster, *Racism in Europe: 1870–2000*, 192.

[20]Jean-Marie Le Pen, cited in MacMaster, *Racism in Europe: 1870–2000*, 194.

[21]MacMaster, *Racism in Europe: 1870–2000*, 196.

[22]Ibid. 195.

[23]Ibid. 195–196.

[24]Ibid. 197–198.

[25]Ibid. 198–199.

[26]Ibid. 200–205.

[27]Ibid. 200–208.

[28]Space here does not allow a full discussion of the moral lapses of the Church, but there is an ample literature readily available that well illustrates this point. For a sample of this vast literature see John Tracy Ellis, *Catholics in Colonial America* (St. Paul, MN: North Central Publishing Company, 1965); Richard F. Greenleaf, ed., *The Roman Catholic Church in Colonial Latin America* (New York: Alfred A. Knopf, 1971); John F. Maxwell, *Slavery and the Catholic Church* (London: Barry Rose Publishers and the Anti-Slavery Society for the Protection of Human Rights, 1975); Hugo Latorre Cabal, *The Revolution of the Latin American Church*, trans. Frances K. Hendrickson and Beatrice Berler (Norman: University of Oklahoma Press, 1978); Donald W. Shriver, "The Churches and the Future of Racism," *Theology Today* 38/2 (July 1981): 152–159; Joseph Brandt, *Dismantling Racism* (Minneapolis, MN: Fortress Press, 1991), 123–154; Leannec Hurbon, "The Church and Afro-American Slavery," in Enrique Dussel, ed., *The Church in Latin America 1492–1992* (Maryknoll, NY: Orbis Books, 1992), 372; John T. Noonan, Jr., "Development in Moral Doctrine," *Theological Studies* 54 (December 1993); John T. McGreevey, *Parish Boundaries: The Catholic Encounter with Race in the Twentieth-Century Urban North* (Chicago: University of Chicago, 1996); Susan E. Davies and Sr. Paul Therese Hennessee, eds., *Ending Racism in the Church* (Cleveland, OH: United Church Press, 1998); Bradford E. Hinze, "Ethnic and Racial Diversity and the Catholicity of the Church," in Maria Pilar Aquino and Roberto S. Goizueta, eds., *Theology: Expanding the Borders*, The Annual Publication of the College Theology Society, Vol. 43 (Mystic, CT: Twenty-Third Publications, 1998), 162–199; Dennis M. Doyle, "Communion Ecclesiology on the Borders: Elizabeth E. Johnson and Roberto S. Goizueta," in *Theology: Expanding the Borders*, 200–217; Jamie T. Phelps, "Racism and the Church: An Inquiry Into the Contradictions Between Experience, Doctrine and Theological Theory," in Dwight N. Hopkins, ed., *Black Faith*

and Public Talk (Maryknoll, NY: Orbis Books, 1999), 53–76; and see also Tim Unsworth, "Racism and Religion: Partners in Crime?" at http://www.salt.claretian-pubs.org/
issues/racism/unsworth.html, Accessed August 6, 2003.

[29]See for example the compilation of papal antislavery texts in Joel S. Panzer, *The Popes and Slavery* (New York: Alba House, 1996). See next chapter for more on this discussion.

[30]See Timothy E. O'Connell, *Making Disciples: A Handbook of Christian Moral Formation* (New York: Crossroad, 1998), 116–127. See also Stephen Crites, "The Narrative Quality of Experience," in Stanley Hauerwas and L. Gregory Jones, eds., *Why Narrative?* (Grand Rapids, MI: Eerdmans, 1989), 65–88. Also, Mark B. Tappen, "Narrative, Authorship, and the Development of Moral Authority," in Mark B. Tappen and Martin J. Packer, eds., *Narrative and Storytelling: Implications for Understanding Moral Development New Directions in Child Development*, 54 (San Francisco: Jossey-Bass, 1991). Also see Paul Vitz, "The Use of Stories in Moral Development," *American Psychologist* 45 (June 1990): 709–720. In addition see Terrence Tilley, *Story Theology* (Collegeville, MN: Liturgical Press, 1985).

[31]See O'Connell, *Making Disciples*, especially chapters 5–8 in which he explains the insights from the social sciences concerning "The Values People Live," "The Place of Feeling," "The Dynamics of Group Experience," and "The Chemistry of Relationships." These sections include other valuable supporting bibliography for this point.

[32]The book of Philemon was frequently used as a case in point. For current exegesis of this text see Christopher A. Frillingos, "'For my child, Onesimus': Paul and Domestic Power in Philemon," *Journal of Biblical Literature* 119/1 (Spring 2000): 91–104; Perry V. Kea, "Paul's Letter to Philemon: A Short Analysis of its Values," *Perspectives in Religious Studies* 23 (Summer 1996): 223–232; John G. Nording, "*Onesimus Fugitives*: A Defense of the Runaway Slave Hypothesis in Philemon," *Journal of the Study of the New Testament* 41 (Fall 1991): 91–119; and William J. Richardson, "Principle and Context in the Ethics of the Epistle to Philemon," *Interpretation* 22 (July 1968): 301–316.

[33]See Ivan Hannaford, *Race: The History of and Idea in the West* (Baltimore: John Hopkins University Press, 1996) 17–57. See also Lloyd Thompson, *Romans and Blacks* (London: 1989). Also see Frank M. Snowdon, Jr., *Before Color and Prejudice: The Ancient View of Blacks* (Cambridge, MA: Harvard University Press, 1983). In addition see Frank M. Snowdon, Jr., *Blacks in Antiquity: Ethiopians in the Greco-Roman Experience* (Cambridge, MA: Harvard University Press, 1970).

[34]It is commonly argued that this stance is true in the wider Western world until the twelfth century. See Fredrickson, *Race: A Short History*, especially Chapter 1. Also see Hopkins, *Being Human*, 131.

[35]See Hood, *Begrimed and Black*, especially at 26–37.

[36]See Hopkins, *Being Human*, 132. In Hopkin's Chapter 4, he traces the well-known history of ideas concerning racism. We follow that discussion here.

[37]See Martin Bernal, "Race in History," in Van Horne, ed., *Global Convulsions*, 79.

[38]Ibid. 79–80.

[39]Ibid. 81.

[40]See Hopkins, *Being Human*, 133.

[41]Ibid.

[42]Ibid. 134.

⁴³See his theory of slavery found in Book I, Chapters iii through vii of the *Politics* and in Book VII of the *Nicomachean Ethics*.

⁴⁴See Hopkins, *Being Human*, 133. See also Frank M. Snowden, Jr., "The Negro in Ancient Greece," *American Anthropologist* 50 (1948): 31–44. Interestingly, Ptolemy was an upper Egyptian and was known to Arab writers as a black. See Bernal, "Race in History," 81.

⁴⁵Hopkins, *Being Human*, 135.

⁴⁶See Bernal, "Race in History," 80–81.

⁴⁷Guy L. Byron, *Symbolic Blackness and Ethnic Differences in Early Christian Literature* (New York: Routledge, 2002), 33–35 as cited in Hopkins, 135. For more on ancient cultures and values connoted by colors, see Bernal, "Race in History," 76–81.

⁴⁸Hopkins, *Being Human*, 135.

⁴⁹See Léon Poliakov, *The History of Anti-Semitism*, Vol. 1, *From the Time of Christ to the Court Jews*, trans. Richard Howard (New York: Vanguard Press, 1975; Philadelphia: University of Pennsylvania Press, 2003), 21.

⁵⁰See his work on the notion of "salvation" for example: In his *City of God* he held that the source of salvation is God's eternal decree (XI, 21), which is unchangeable (XXII, 2). Also, predestination is in accord with God's foreknowledge of human free choice (V, 9). In his *On the Soul and Its Origin*, both those who are saved and those who are lost are so predestined (IV, 16). And he is clear in his *The Enchiridion* that salvation is wrought only through Christ's substitutionary death (33) and it is received by faith (31).

⁵¹One of the most commonly cited examples of this is Augustine's *City of God*, Book 18, Chapter 46. In this text, he attributes the "scattering of the Jews" in defeat by the Romans as part of a proof of prophecies fulfilled and as support for the Christian belief that Jesus is the Messiah. This is an apologetic work that followed in the line of numerous other early Christian texts that attempt to establish Christian identity and doctrine by using polemics. See prior examples in Tertullian, *Adversus Iudaeos*; Cyprian, *Testimonia ad Quirinum*; or Pseudo-Cyprian, *De Montibus Sina et Sion*. To place this text in perspective, see Bernhard Blumenkranz, *Die Judenpredigt Augustins* (Paris: Études Augustiniennes, 1973).

⁵²Fredrickson, *Racism: A Short History*, 19. See also Garvin I. Langmuir, *Toward a Definition of Antisemitism* (Berkeley: University of California Press, 1990), 63–133. Also see Robert Chazan, *Medieval Stereotypes and Modern Antisemitism* (Berkeley: University of California Press, 1997), 129–138.

⁵³See Garvin I. Langmuir, *History, Religion and Antisemitism* (Berkeley: University of California Press, 1990), 292. See also Norman Cohen, *The Pursuit of the Millennium: Revolutionary Millenarians and Mystical Anarchists of the Middle Ages* (New York: Oxford University Press, 1970). Also see Mark R. Cohen, *Under Crescent and Cross: The Jews in the Middle Ages* (Princeton, NJ: Princeton University Press, 1994), especially 77–88.

⁵⁴See Langmuir, *Toward a Definition of Antisemitism*, 100–133.

⁵⁵It is estimated that between 1347 and 1349 about 30 to 50 percent of Europe's populations was lost.

⁵⁶Fredrickson, *Racism: A Short History*, 22.

⁵⁷Hopkins, *Being Human*, 135–136. See also Byron, *Symbolic Blackness and Ethnic Difference in Early Christian Literature*.

⁵⁸Hopkins, *Being Human*, 135.

⁵⁹Ibid. 136. Slave trade began in England in 1555.

⁶⁰Robert Bartlett, *The Making of Europe: Conquest, Colonization and Cultural Change 910–1350* (Princeton, NJ: Princeton University Press, 1993), 239–240 and passim cited in Fredrickson, 23–24.

⁶¹Fredrickson, *A Short History*, 24–25, 28. See E. H. P Baudet, *Paradise on Earth: Some Thoughts on European Images of Non-European Man*, trans. Elizabeth Wentholt (New Haven, CT: Yale University Press, 1965). See also John Block Friedman, *The Monstrous Races in Medieval Art and Thought* (Cambridge, MA: Harvard University Press, 1981), 59–60; 64–65. Also see Snowdon, Jr., *Before Color and Prejudice*, 101–107. Also see Bernal, "Race in History," 81. George M. Fredrickson holds that only when the irretraceable difference is absolutized as residing in the blood of the "other" and organic and legally justified does he call the discrimination "racism." Indeed, such color-coded racism is a product of the Modern period. (Notably, this is not the definition of "racism" used by the Roman Catholic Magisterium. See the subsequent chapters of this volume.) Further, Fredrickson points out that while indeed there were monstrous images of the inhabitants of distant lands portrayed in black, there is also evidence of "Negrophilia" in parts of northern and Western Europe in the late Middle Ages. He holds up Henri Baudet's notion of "le bon Nègre" that stressed the reality that the first non-Jewish Christian convert was the Ethiopian eunuch (Acts 8) and which honored black converts and demonstrated the universality of the Christian faith. There is also the myth of "Prester John" that served to join Christians in the struggle against Islam. Prester John was a non-European wealthy Christian monarch who ruled over a paradisal realm where the peace of Christ prevailed. His realm was ultimately identified with the actual kingdom of Ethiopia. Additionally, throughout this period one of the Magi was always portrayed as black and was purported to be an ancestor of Prester John. There was also the cult of Saint Maurice (who was originally depicted as white) who now was suddenly pictured as black in the Germanic lands. Finally, there was the heroic Saint Gregory the Moor and knightly epic poem character Parzifal's mulatto half-brother Feirefiz. Fredrickson does admit that these were ultimately quite superficial in their effect on subsequent events concerning race and racism that transpired in Europe.

⁶²See James H. Sweet, "The Iberian Roots of American Racist Thought," *William and Mary Quarterly* 54 (1997): 143–166.

⁶³See Fredrickson, *A Short History*, 29. He cites Bernard Lewis and William McKee Evans.

⁶⁴See Bernard Lewis, *Race and Color in Islam* (New York: Harper and Row, 1971), 38; 64–65. Also see Sweet, "The Iberian Roots," 157–164.

⁶⁵See John Thornton, *Africa and Africans in the Marketing of the Atlantic World 1400–1800*, 2nd ed. (Cambridge, UK: Cambridge University Press, 1998), 72–97.

⁶⁶Fredrickson, *Racism: A Short History*, 32. See also B. Natenyahu, *The Origins of the Inquisition in Fifteenth Century Spain*, 2nd ed. (New York: New York Review of Books, 2001). Also see Henry Kamen, *The Spanish Inquisition: An Historical Revision* (London: Weidenfeld & Nicolson, 1997).

⁶⁷Fredrickson, *Racism: A Short History*, 33.

⁶⁸Léon Poliakov, *The History of Anti-Semitism* Vol. 2, *From Mohammed to the Marranos*, trans. Natalie Gerardi (New York: Vanguard Press, 1973), 181–182, cited in Fredrickson, 33.

⁶⁹Ronald Sanders, *The Lost Tribes and Promised Lands: The Origins of American Racism* (Boston: Little Brown Publishers, 1978), 92–102.

[70]Omi and Winant, *Racial Formation*, 182–183 n. 19.

[71]See Cinny Poppen, Michael McConnell, and Renny Golden, *Dangerous Memories: Invasion and Resistance Since 1492* (Chicago: Chicago Religious Task Force on Central America, 1991), 51–52: "The Governor could give ("commend") Indians to the colonists (*encomenderos*) to use as they chose, for tribute or forced labor; the masters would in return provide their servants with instructions on becoming good Christians."

[72]See Magnus Mörner, *Race Mixture in the History of Latin America* (Boston: Little Brown & Company, 1967). Also see Carl Degler, *Neither Black nor White: Slavery and Race Relations in Brazil and the United States* (New York: Macmillan, 1971).

[73]Fredrickson, *Racism: A Short History*, 40.

[74]Ibid. at 41: This was "a quasi-racialized religious nationalism and not a fully racialized secular nationalism" as in Nazi Germany.

[75]This point will be elaborated in the next chapter of this text.

[76]George M. Fredrickson, *White Supremacy: A Comparative Study in American and South African History* (New York: Oxford University Press, 1981), 73 cited in Fredrickson, *A Short History*, 42.

[77]Fredrickson, *A Short History*, 44. See also George M. Fredrickson, *The Black Image in the White Mind: The Debate on Afro-American Character and Destiny 1817–1914* (Middleton, CT: Wesleyan University Press, 1987).

[78]Fredrickson, *A Short History*, 45.

[79]The content, figures, and sources Hopkins uses are common and well known in this literature. His ordering and discussion of them in the categories of philosophy, anthropology, and missiology is particularly helpful. Thus, I follow Hopkins' discussion in *Being Human*, 138–159.

[80]The corollary notion is *color-coded racism*, which denotes the inferiority of the "other" that is claimed by the defining agent.

[81]Kant cited in Hopkins, *Being Human*, 139. See also Emmanuel Chukwudi Eze, *Race and the Enlightenment: A Reader* (Cambridge, MA: Blackwell, 1997).

[82]Hume cited in Hopkins, *Being Human*, 139–140.

[83]See Fredrickson, *Racism: A Short History*, 45. See also David Theo Goldberg, *Racist Culture: Philosophy and the Politics of Meaning* (Cambridge: MA: Blackwell, 1993).

[84]Montesquieu cited in Hopkins, *Being Human*, 140.

[85]Hopkins cites Thomas F. Gossett, *Race: The History of an Idea in America* (New York: Schocken, 1971), 44–45.

[86]Hopkins, *Being Human*, 140–141.

[87]Ibid. See also Martin Bernal, *Black Athena: The Afroasiatic Roots of Classical Civilization*, Vol. 1, *The Fabrication of Ancient Greece 1785–1985* (New Brunswick, NJ: Rutgers University Press, 1987), 201–204.

[88]Hopkins, *Being Human*, 143.

[89]Ibid.

[90]Ibid.

[91]Ibid. 144.

[92]Ibid. See also Winthrop D. Jordan, *White Over Black: American Attitudes Toward the Negro 1550–1812* (New York: Norton, 1995), especially 483.

[93]Hopkins, *Being Human*, 145.

[94]Ibid.

[95]Ibid.

⁹⁶Ibid.

⁹⁷Ibid. See also Kenan Malik, *The Meaning of Race: Race, History, and Culture in Western Society* (New York: New York University Press, 1996), 83–84.

⁹⁸Hopkins, *Being Human*, 145–146.

⁹⁹Ibid. 146.

¹⁰⁰Ibid. 146–147.

¹⁰¹Ibid. 147–148.

¹⁰²Livingston, cited in Hopkins, *Being Human*, 150.

¹⁰³Ibid., 149. See Gwinya H. Muzorewa, *The Origins and Development of African Theology* (Maryknoll, NY: Orbis Books, 1985), 24–26.

¹⁰⁴Hopkins, *Being Human*, 149. See also, Jesse N.K. Mugambi, *African Christian Theology: An Introduction* (Nairobi, Kenya: Heineman Kenya, 1989), especially 32.

¹⁰⁵Hopkins, *Being Human*, 150. See for example Ogbu U. Kalu, "Church Presence in Africa: A Historical Analysis of the Evangelization Process," in Kofi Appiah-Kubi and Sergio Torres, eds., *African Theologies en Route* (Maryknoll, NY: Orbis Books, 1979), 18. Also see Mercy Amba Oduyoye, *Hearing and Knowing: Theological Reflections on Christianity in Africa* (Maryknoll, NY: Orbis Books, 1986), 31.

¹⁰⁶Hopkins, *Being Human*, 151. See also Simon S. Miamela, *Proclaim Freedom to My People* (Johannesburg, South Africa: Skotaville, 1987). Also John W. de Gruchy, *The Struggle in South Africa* (Grand Rapids, MI: Eerdmans, 1979). See Charles Villa-Vicencio, *Trapped in Apartheid* (Cape Town, South Africa: David Philip, 1988). Also see Richard Elphick and Rodney Davenport, eds., *Christianity in South Africa: A Political, Social, and Cultural History* (Berkeley: University of California Press, 1987).

¹⁰⁷See Poppen, McConnell, and Golden, *Dangerous Memories*, especially 134–173.

¹⁰⁸Hopkins, *Being Human*, 152.

¹⁰⁹Maurio Batista, quoted by Hopkins, *Being Human*, 153.

¹¹⁰Cited by Hopkins, *Being Human*, 153. See her "Black Latin American Theology: A New Way to Sense, to Feel, to Speak of God," in Hopkins, ed., *Black Faith and Public Talk*, 191–192.

¹¹¹Hopkins, *Being Human*, 154. See Patrick "Pops" Hylton, *The Role of Religion in Caribbean History from Amerindian Shamanism to Rastafarianism* (Washington, DC: Billops, 2002). Also see Armando Lampe, *Christianity in the Caribbean: Essays in Church History* (Kingston: University of the West Indies Press, 2001).

¹¹²Hopkins, *Being Human*, 155–156. See also "Gumbo" Ted Thomas, "The Land is Sacred: Renewing the Dreaming in Modern Australia," in G.W. Trompf, ed., *The Gospel Is Not Western: Black Theologies from the Southwest Pacific* (Maryknoll, NY: Orbis, 1987). Also see Anne Pattel-Grey, *The Great White Flood: Racism in Australia* (Atlanta, GA: Scholars, 1998), especially 15–30. Also Anne Pattel-Grey *Through Aboriginal Eyes: The Cry From the Wilderness* (Geneva, Switzerland: World Council of Churches Publications, 1991).

¹¹³Hopkins, *Being Human*, 156.

¹¹⁴Ibid. 157. See also Suliana Siwtabau, "A Theology for Justice and Peace in the Pacific," in Trompf, ed., *The Gospel Is Not Western*, 192–197.

¹¹⁵See V. Davasahayam, "Pollution, Poverty, and Powerlessness: A Dalit Perspective," in Arvin Nirmal, ed., *A Reader in Dalit Theology* (Madras: The Gurukul Lutheran Theological College and Research Institute, n.d.), 1–22. Also see the entire collection of essays in this volume.

[116]John Francis Izzo, "'Dalit' Means Broken: Caste and Church in Southern India," in *America,* Vol. 192, no. 5, Whole no. 4680 (February 14, 2005): 11–14.

[117]See Frank Dikötter, ed., *The Construction of Racial Identities in China and Japan: Historical and Contemporary Perspectives* (London: C. Hurst and Company, Ltd., 1997). Since Dikötter's book is the best of only a few sources available in English that trace this history of ideas, this section closely follows his work.

[118]Ibid. 4.

[119]Ibid. 5.

[120]See Frank Dikötter, "Racial Discourse in China: Continuities and Permutations," in Dikötter, ed., *The Construction of Racial Identities in China and Japan,* 12.

[121]Ibid. 13.

[122]Ibid. 15.

[123]Ibid. 16.

[124]Ibid.

[125]Ibid. 18.

[126]Ibid. 18–19.

[127]Ibid. 21.

[128]Ibid. 27.

[129]Ibid.

[130]See Barry Sautman, "Myths of Descent, Racial Nationalism and Ethnic Minorities in the People's Republic of China," in Dikötter, ed., *The Construction of Racial Identities in China and Japan,* 75–95.

[131]Michael Weiner, "The Invention of Identity: Race and Nation in Pre-War Japan," in Dikötter, ed., *The Construction of Racial Identities in China and Japan,* 96. This section draws heavily from Weiner's work.

[132]Ibid. 98. The quote cited is from Suzuki Juro.

[133]Ibid. 100.

[134]Ibid. 101.

[135]Ibid. 101.

[136]Ibid. 102.

[137]Ibid. 103. There was a vocal minority of scholars who did not agree with his analysis, but they did not prevail, according to Weiner.

[138]Ibid. 106.

[139]Ibid.

[140]Ibid. 107.

[141]Ibid. 105.

[142]Ibid. 108.

[143]Ibid.

[144]Ibid. 110.

[145]Ibid. 109.

[146]Ibid. 111.

[147]Ibid. 111–112.

[148]Ibid. 112.

[149]Ibid. 113.

[150]Ibid.

[151]Ibid. 115.

[152]Ibid.

[153]Ibid. 99. Hozumi Nobushige is cited by Weiner.

[154]See John Dower, *War Without Mercy: Race and Power in the Pacific War* (New York: Pantheon, 1986), 267.

[155]Weiner, "The Invention of Identity," 99. Ihei Setsuzo is cited by Weiner.

[156]Ibid. 98.

[157]Ibid. His *The New Japanism and the Buddhist View on Nationality* is cited by Weiner.

[158]Ibid. 99. Kada Tetsuji, *Jinshu, minzoku, sensō* is cited by Weiner.

[159]See Anwar M. Barkat, "Director's Introduction," in *Racism in Asia: Race and Minority Issues*, PCR Information Reports and Background Papers 1986/22 (Geneva: Imprimerie Marc Picarat, 1986), 5.

[160]Richard Werly, "The Burakumin, Japan's Invisible Outcasts," *The UNESCO Courier* (September 2001): 29.

[161]Etienne Balibar, "Racism and Nationalism," in Etienne Balibar and Immanuel Walerstein, eds., *Race, Nation, Class: Ambiguous Identities* (London: Verso, 1992), 37–67.

[162]Etienne Balibar, *Masses, Classes, Ideas: Studies on Politics and Philosophy Before and After Marx* (New York: Routledge, 1994), 198.

[163]Hannah Arendt, *The Origins of Totalitarianism* (New York: Harcourt, Brace, and Jovanovich, 1966).

[164]Theodor W. Adorno and Max Horkheimer, *Dialectic of Enlightenment* (London: Verso, 1979).

[165]Alana Lentin, *Racism and Anti-Racism in Europe* (Ann Arbor, MI: Pluto Press, 2004), 67–68, quoting Etienne Balibar, *Masses, Classes, Ideas*.

[166]See Lentin, *Racism and Anti-Racism in Europe*, 73–85. The "culturalist" approach to anti-racism explains race the wide variety of differences between peoples. Culturalists pose the means to combat racism is education of all peoples about different cultures. They replace the notion of "race" with the concept of "cultural diversity" and stress the reality of difference while not asserting the superiority or inferiority of any over any others. Racism is understood primarily as individual prejudice consisting in personal likes and dislikes. The "statist" approach is rooted in anticolonial resistance movements of the 1960s and stresses the continuum of state involvement in sponsoring and tolerating racist policies. They stress that racism is alive and well in today's world and that it is in large part the result of state social, political, and economic policies. Racism is understood primarily as structural.

[167]Ibid. 75.

[168]Ibid. 89.

[169]Ibid. 311.

[170]See Gargi Bhattacharyya and John Gabriel, "Anti-Deportation Campaigning in the West Midlands," in Floya Anthias and Cathie Lloyd, eds., *Rethinking Anti-Racisms: From Theory to Practice* (New York: Routledge, 2002), 49.

[171]Barnor Hesse, "Diasporicity: Black Britain's Post Colonial Formations," in Barnor Hesse, ed., *Un/Settled Multiculturalisms: Diasporas, Entanglements, 'Transruptions'* (London: Zed Books, 2000), 145.

2. Foundations for a Diagnostic Dilemma

[1]See Albert Memmi, *Racism*, trans. Steve Martinot, (Minneapolis: University of Minnesota Press, 2000).

[2]Ibid. 100.

[3]Ibid. xvii.

[4]Ibid. xviii.

[5]Ibid. xix.

[6]Ibid. xviii.

[7]Robert J.C. Young, *Colonial Desire: Hybridity in Theory, Culture, and Race* (New York: Routledge, 1995), 1–36.

[8]Ibid. 35.

[9]Ibid. 39–40, 46–47, 64–67, 120, 134.

[10]Ibid. 30–36.

[11]John Francis Maxwell, *Slavery and the Catholic Church: The History of Teaching Concerning the Moral Legitimacy of the Institution of Slavery* (London: Barry Rose Publishers and the Anti-Slavery Society for the Protection of Human Rights, 1975). In recent years some challenges have been brought to some of Maxwell's claims. See for example Joel S. Panzer, *The Popes and Slavery* (New York: Alba House, 1996). Panzer contests primarily Maxwell's research on papal magisterial teaching documents, not his assertions concerning biblical or patristic materials.

[12]See Carolyn Osiek, "Slavery in the Second Testament World," *Biblical Theology Bulletin* 22 (Winter 1992): 174–79. As Osiek points out, the Church's understanding of "person" was not developed until the sixth-century Christological debates. So when it came to interpreting sources, this defining combined to result in an ambiguous understanding that could be widely interpreted.

[13]Maxwell, *Slavery and the Catholic Church*, 13–21. Maxwell erroneously claimed that the Church did not condemn slavery (in the modern understanding of slavery) until Vatican Council II and *Gaudium et Spes*, 27 and 29. As subsequent scholarship has demonstrated, actual magisterial teaching and what was carried out in practice by ordinary Christians was often contradictory for a complex variety of reasons. Also, the character and political and economic entanglements of popes and bishops in nepotism and politics, as well as the vast geographical distances between Rome and local settings of oppression, made enforcement of magisterial mandates difficult, at best.

[14]See Osiek, "Slavery in the Second Testament World," 174–175. It is important to note that the modern notion of "selling one's labor" did not exist in ancient times. Thus the master owned the slave and had absolute control over the person of the slave. Thus slaves were "an outsider to society in an essential way." The "slave economy as a mode of production" was an innovation of the Greco-Roman world. There were two major types of enslavement: "agricultural, industrial, and penal slavery; and urban household, business, and imperial slavery." Maxwell's discussion seems to be focused primarily on the agrarian type of slavery.

[15]See John T. Noonan, Jr., "Making One's Own Act Another's," *Proceedings of the Catholic Theology Society of America* (1973), 32–44. Also see Daniel C. Maguire, "A Response (II) to Dr. Noonan" in the same volume, 49–54.

[16]See Peter T. Nash, *Reading Race, Reading the Bible*, The Facets Series (Minneapolis: Fortress Press, 2003), especially 29–58.

[17]See Albrecht Alt, *Essays on Old Testament History and Religion*, the Biblical Seminar, trans. R. A. Wilson (Sheffield, UK: JSOT Press, 1989). Also see Albrecht Alt, *Kleine Schriften zur Geschichte des Volkes Israel*, 2nd ed. (Munich, Germany: Beck, 1959).

[18]See Osiek, "Slavery in the Second Testament World," 174–175.

[19]See Maxwell, *Slavery and the Catholic Church*, 26–27. He cites passages from the work of Florentinus, Ulpianus, and Tryphoninus. He also holds that the Greek tradition passed on by Aristotle from Alcidamas was followed by Roman stoic philosophers including Cicero and Seneca. See also Osiek, "Slavery in the Second Testament World," 174–179.

[20]See Osiek, "Slavery in the Second Testament World," 176. Osiek cites Hadrian's outlaw of castration of slaves. Maxwell cites the Roman jurists Florentinius, Ulpianus, and Typhoninus as defenders of freedom as a natural human right.

[21]See Denise Kimber Buell and Caroline Johnson Hodge, "The Politics of Interpretation: The Rhetoric of Race and Ethnicity in Paul," *Journal of Biblical Literature* 123/2 (2004): 235–251.

[22]Maxwell, *Slavery and the Catholic Church*, 27–30 uses the terms "dogmatic theology" and "moral theology" to distinguish the two approaches of Paul.

[23]Cain Felder, "Racial Ambiguities in the Biblical Narratives," in Gregory Baum and John Colman, eds., *The Church and Racism*, Concilium 151/1 (New York: The Seabury Press, 1982), 17–24. Quote is at 17. See also the author's revised version of this article in Cain Hope Felder, ed., *Stony the Road We Trod: African American Biblical Interpretation* (Minneapolis, MN: Fortress Press, 1991), 127–145.

[24]Ibid. 18.

[25]See Felder, ed., *Stony the Road We Trod*, 132.

[26]Felder cites Gene Rice, "The Curse that Never Was (Gen 9:18–27)," *Journal of Religious Thought*, 29 (1972) in which Rice refers to the exegesis found in *Midrash Bereshith Rabbah* (London: 1939).

[27]Felder, "Racial Ambiguities," 20.

[28]Ibid. 21. The quote is from Moore. See note no. 21. Buell and Hodge caution that this position can also work to disempower and devalue the richness of particular ethnicity. They offer an alternative way to read Paul through an ethnically conscious lens.

[29]Ibid. 21.

[30]Ibid. 23.

[31]See Frank Snowdon, *Before Color Prejudice: The Ancient View of Blacks* (Cambridge, MA: Harvard University Press, 1983), especially 14–17 and 43–46. Also see Nicholas F. Gier, "The Color of Sin/The Color of Skin: The Ancient Colorblindness and the Philosophical Origins of Modern Racism," *Journal of Religious Thought* 46/1 (Summer/Fall 1989): 42–52.

[32]See Rosemary Radford Ruether, "Sexism and God-language," in Judith Plaskow and Carol P. Christ, eds., *Weaving the Visions: New Patterns in Feminist Spirituality* (San Francisco: Harper & Row, 1989), 156, cited in Buell and Hodge, "The Politics of Interpretation," 235.

[33]See Buell and Hodge, "The Politics of Interpretation," 235–251.

[34]The authors quote Diana Hayes, "To Be the Bridge: Voices from the Margins," in Eleazar S. Fernandez and Fernando F. Segovia, eds., *A Dream Unfinished: Theological Reflections on America from the Margins* (Maryknoll, NY: Orbis Books, 2001), 60–64.

[35]Note that in contrast to this ideal, Memmi holds that racism is characterized by absoluteness and timelessness. See his *Racism*, 114.

[36]The authors cite Judith A. Nagata, "What Is a Maylay? Situational Selection of Ethnic Identity in a Plural Society," *American Ethnologist* 1 (1974): 331–359. See also Charles F. Keyes, "Toward a New Foundation of the Concept of Ethnic

Group," *Ethnicity* 3 (1976): 202–213. Also see Michael Moerman, "Ethnic Identification in a Complex Civilization: Who Are the Lue?" *American Anthropologist* 67 (1965): 1215–1230. In addition see Carter Bentley, "Ethnicity and Practice," *Journal for the Comparative Study of Society and History* 29 (1987): 24–55.

[37]Buell and Hodge, "The Politics of Interpretation," 249. Emphasis is in the original text. They point to Rom 11:17–24 and Rom 1:16; 2:9–10 as examples of this intention.

[38]The content in this section is well-known and commonly found in the literature on the Church's dealings and teaching on slavery. See Maxwell's helpful framing of the discussion in his *Slavery and the Catholic Church*. See also Kimberly Flint-Hamilton, "Images of Slavery in the Early Church: Hatred Disguised in Love?," *Journal of Hate Studies* 2/27 (2002/2003): 27–45.

[39]Flint-Hamilton, "Images of Slavery in the Early Church," 29–30.

[40]The Council of Gangra, a town in Paphlagonia, which took place between 325 and 381, although one can probably date it more precisely to between 362 and 370. http://www.aroundomaha.com/ecf/volume37/ECF37THE_COUNCIL_OF_GANGRA_HISTORICAL.htm, Accessed Septmber 27, 2006.

[41]Maxwell, *Slavery and the Catholic Church*, 36.

[42]See Maxwell 38. He cites *C.J.C. Decret. Grat.* II, CXXXVI, Q.1.c.3.

[43]Maxwell cites *Via Regia*, c. XXX.

[44]In fairness to Aquinas, see Joseph E. Capizzi, "The Children of God: Natural Slavery in the Thought of Aquinas and Vitoria," *Theological Studies* (63): 31–52. He argues that Aquinas did not have the theological resources available to him in his time to allow him to condemn slavery.

[45]In *Sent.* D.44,q.1, a.3; *Sent.* D.36, q.1, a.1, ad2. *Summa Theologiae* III, Suppl. Q.52, a.1, ad 2; *ST* 1, q.96, a.4.

[46]*Summa Theologiae* II–II, q.57a 3, ad 2, ST I–II, q.94, a.5, ad 3.

[47]IV *Sent.* D.36, q.1, a.1.

[48]*ST* III Suppl. Q 52, a.4.

[49]II *Sent.* D.44, a.3, q.1, conclusion.

[50]See Maria Elena Martinez, "Religion, Purity, and Race: The Spanish Concept of *'Limpieza de Sangre'* in Seventeenth Century Mexico and the Broader Atlantic World," *Harvard International Seminar on the History of the Atlantic World, 1500–1800* (April 2002), 2–3.

[51]See the previous chapter for the review of the history of ideas of racism.

[52]See Eamon Duffy, *Saints and Sinners: A History of the Popes* (New Haven, CT: Yale University Press, 1997), especially 87–194.

[53]New York: Alba House, 1996.

[54]For a discussion of adequate approaches to moral formation and the effects of teachers and mentors on those being formed see Timothy E. O'Connell, *Making Disciples: A handbook of Christian Moral Formation* (New York: Crossroad, 1998), especially chapters 12–14.

[55]Ibid. 4–5. Though today the forms of "just title" servitude for purposes of reliving debt or time-limited contracted servitude no longer are held as just, it is possible to uphold some form of servitude objectively and in a limited way. This would be similar to Catholic teaching on the death penalty, for example. See the *Catholic Catechism*, no. 2267. See also John Paul II, *Evangelium Vitae*, 27.

[56]See Panzer, *The Popes and Slavery*, 3–4. Several forms of servitude were deemed morally just. Such forms included its imposition as a penalty on criminals and pris-

oners of war. For economic reasons workers might freely choose servitude for a limited period of time in order to work off a debt. Children born to servile parents were considered to be in the same state as their parents. Masters in all cases were obliged to provide fair and humane treatment and to encourage their charges to seek freedom.

[57]See for example Cinny Poppen, Michael McConnell, and Renny Golden, *Dangerous Memories: Invasion and Resistance Since 1492* (Chicago: Chicago Religious Task Force on Central America, 1991), especially chapters 1 and 2.

[58]Panzer, *The Popes and Slavery*, 7.

[59]Ibid. 10. Panzer notes that Pope Pius II and Pope Sixtus IV issued bulls defending the residents of the Canary Islands who were still being enslaved by Christians.

[60]See Frances Gardner Davenport, *European Treaties Bearing on the History of the United States and Its Dependencies to 1648,* Vol. 1 (Washington, DC: 1917). Also see Steve Newcomb, "Five Hundred Years of Injustice," *Shaman's Drum* (Fall 1992): 18–20.

[61]See the English translation of "The Bull *Romanus Pontifex* (Nicholas V), January 8, 1455," http://www.nativeweb.org/pages/ingig-romanus-pontifex.html, Accessed July 28, 2006.

[62]The Treaty of Alcaçovas or the Peace of Alcaçovas-Toledo was signed between the kingdoms of Castile (Castillia, Spain) and Portugal on September 4, 1479. That put an end to the War of the Castilian Succession, a civil war begun in 1474 over the succession of the Kingdom of Castile. By this agreement, ownership of the Canary Islands was transferred from Portugal to Castile in exchange for claims in West Africa. The Treaty of Alcaçovas established the Castilian and Portuguese spheres in the Atlantic and temporarily settled a period of open hostility, but also created the basis for future claims and conflicts.

[63]Panzer, *The Popes and Slavery*, 11.

[64]Ibid. 13.

[65]Ibid. 13–14.

[66]Ibid. 15.

[67]Panzer cites Gustavo Gutierrez, trans. Robert R. Barr, *Las Casas: In Search of the Poor of Jesus Christ* (Maryknoll, NY: Orbis Books, 1993), 302: "The bull of Pope Paul III, *Sublimis Deus* (June 2, 1537) is regarded as the most important papal pronouncement on the human condition of the Indians."

[68]Panzer, *The Popes and Slavery*, 31.

[69]See the previous chapter for the history of ideas during this time.

[70]Panzer, *The Popes and Slavery*, 34.

[71]Ibid. 45.

[72]Ibid. 48. This was contrary to the misguided interpretation given this document by the U.S. bishop of Charleston, John England, who claimed it only condemned the slave trade. Also see James Hennesey, *American Catholics: A History of the Roman Catholic Community in the United States* (New York: Oxford University Press, 1981), 145.

[73]Panzer, *The Popes and Slavery*, 58.

[74]Ibid. 58–59. All humans are "… created in one origin, redeemed by the same price and called to the same eternal happiness."

[75]Ibid. 58.

[76]Ibid. 60.

[77]Pontifical Justice and Peace Commission, *The Church and Racism: Toward a More Fraternal Society*, no. 2, *Origins* 18/37 (February 23, 1989): 613–626.

[78]See Gargi Bhattacharyya, John Gabriel, and Stephen Small, *Race and Power: Global Racism in the Twenty-First Century* (London: Routledge, 2002).

[79]Memmi, *Racism*, 92.

[80]Ibid. 93.

[81]Ibid. 94.

[82]See Michael Omi and Howard Winant, *Racial Formation in the United States: From 1960s to 1990s*, 2nd ed. (New York: Routledge, 1994), especially 117–18. Also see Bhattacharyya, Gabriel, and Small, *Race and Power*, 125–126 and 28–59.

[83]Memmi, *Racism*, 43.

[84]Ibid. 45.

[85]Neil MacMaster, *Racism in Europe: 1870–2000* (New York: Palgrave, 2001), especially 193–208. See also Omi and Winant, *Racial Formation in the United States: From 1960s to 1990s*, 117.

[86]Memmi, *Racism*, 96.

[87]See Bryan N. Massingale, "James Cone and Recent Catholic Episcopal Teaching on Racism," *Theological Studies* 61/4 (December 2000): 700–730.

[88]Ibid. 704–707. Massingale refers to the Illinois bishop's "Moving beyond Racism (2000)" and Cardinal Bevilacqua's "Healing Racism through Faith and Truth (1998)."

3. Some Key Doctrinal, Theological, and Ethical Warrants for Racial Justice

[1]James H. Cone, interviewed by George M. Anderson, "Theology and White Supremacy: An Interview with James H. Cone," *America*, Vol. 195 no. 16, Whole no 4753 (November 20, 2006): 10–15, quote at 11.

[2]See "Police Fire 50 Rounds, Kill Groom on his Wedding Day," *CNN News.com*, http://www.cnn.com/2006/US/11/25/nyc.shooting.ap/index.html, Accessed December 3, 2006.

[3]Clarence Page, "'Racial Eruptions' Leave Readers With Many Questions," *Chicago Tribune* (December 3, 2006) Section 2, p. 7.

[4]See Rocco Parascandola, "New Black Panthers to Rally at Shooting Site," *Newsday.com* (December 2, 2006), http://www.newsday.com/news/local/newyork/ny-nyshot024999390dec02,0,3747173.story?coll=ny-nynews-print, Accessed December, 3, 2006.

[5]Cone, "Theology and White Supremacy," 11.

[6]See for example Aquiline Tarimo, SJ, "Ethnicity, Common Good and the Church in Contemporary Africa," www.sedos.org/english/Tarimo.html, see especially 5–6, Accessed November 10, 2006. Also see James C. Cavendish, "A Research Report Commemorating the 25th Anniversary of *Brothers and Sisters to Us*" (Washington, DC: United States Conference of Catholic Bishops, 2004).

[7]Joseph Berger, "Bishops Link Abortion Fight to Efforts Over Other Issues," *New York Times*, Late City Final Edition, November 15, 1985, section D, page 19, column 1.

[8]See Cardinal Joseph Bernardin, "The Consistent Ethic of Life and Its Public Policy Consequences," Consistent Ethic of Life Conference, Catholic Conference of Ohio, June 4, 1988, in Thomas A. Nairn, ed., *The Seamless Garment: Writings on the Consistent Ethic of Life* (Maryknoll, NY: Orbis Books, 2008), espe-

165–170. Also see Cardinal Joseph Bernardin, "Christ Lives in Me: A Pastoral Reflection on Jesus and His Meaning for Life (1985)," in Alphonse P. Spilly, ed., *Selected Works of Joseph Cardinal Bernardin*, Vol. 1 Homilies and Teaching Documents (Collegeville, MN: The Liturgical Press, 2000), 132. Also in that same volume, see his "Here and Now: Pastoral Statement on Youth (Autumn 1994)," 224.

⁹See Louis DeTomasis, *Doing Right in a Shrinking World: How Corporate America Can Balance Ethics and Profit in a Changing Economy* (Austin, TX: The Greenleaf Book Group Press, 2006).

¹⁰See for example Margaret Ann Fisken, "What Does it Mean to be British?," *Priests and People*, 16/5 (May 2002), 177–182.

¹¹See especially Antonina Kloskowska, "Nation, Race, and Ethnicity in Poland," in Peter Ratcliffe, ed., *"Race," Ethnicity and Nation: International Perspectives on Social Conflict* (London: University College of London, 1994), 199–221. In that same volume, see Vasile Ziatdinov and Sviatoslav Grigoriev, "Between East and West: Tartars in the Former USSR," 222–243. Also see Neil MacMaster, *Racism in Europe 1870–2000* (New York: Palgrave, 2001) 205–208.

¹²See Tarimo, "Ethnicity, Common Good and the Church in Contempory Africa."

¹³It is equally interesting that the index of the *Catechism of the Catholic Church* (Washington, DC: United States Catholic Conference, 1994) has not a single entry for any of these terms. In the *Catechism* we do find references to "man"—sv. "the equality of all men (sic.)," no. 1934–1938; "human dignity," no. 27, 306–308, 1700, 1706, and 1930; and separate references to "slavery, no. 2414, and "genocide," no. 2313. In the popular paperback edition of Walter M. Abbott, General Editor, *The Documents of Vatican II* (New York: America Press, 1966), the index lists only two references: "Race prejudice, discrimination rejected," 688; and "Race problems; modern conditions," 206. The former reference cites *Nostra Aetate*, no. 5 and the latter refers to *Gaudium et Spes:* where "Significant differences crop up too between races and between various kinds of social orders ... " One has to go to sv. "Man, reverence for" to find the classic statements *Gaudium et Spes,* nos. 27–29 that speak at length to the essential equality of human persons.

¹⁴But there are some glimmers of hope! Some illustrative examples: The Catholic Theology Society of America and the Society of Christian Ethics in the United States both have recently opened sections on "White Privilege" and, as Cone acknowledged, some theologians are making some efforts to turn the tide. Also, Racial Justice Sunday, September 10, 2006, cosponsored by the Catholic Association for Racial Justice, of the Conference of Bishops of England and Wales, had as its theme, James 2:26: "Faith without actions is dead." The wonderful irony was that in a country where traditionally that text was the immediate basis for a heady theological discussion between Protestants and Catholics over "works versus grace" and the means of salvation, this packet was cosponsored by the ecumenical group Churches Together in Britain and Ireland. As the literature of this campaign reasserts, there is no doubt that Christians are not only called to believe and know, but they are required to act, if they would not lose their very salvation. The Racial Justice Sunday packet of materials is available from CARJ Head Office, 9 Henry Road, Manor House, N4 2LH, Phone: 020 8802 8080, Fax: 020 8211 0808.

¹⁵See Timothy Radcliffe, *I Call You Friends* (New York: Continuum, 2001), 73 and 44.

[16]See David Tracy, *The Analogical Imagination: Christian Theology and the Culture of Pluralism* (New York: Crossroad, 1989), 248–338.

[17]See Daniel C. Maguire, *The Moral Core of Judaism and Christianity: Reclaiming the Revolution* (Minneapolis: Fortress Press, 1993), 59.

[18]Pontifical Commission for Justice and Peace, *The Church and Racism: Toward a More Fraternal Society*, no. 25.

[19]See the Pontifical Council for Justice and Peace, *Compendium of the Social Doctrine of the Catholic Church* (Washington, DC: United States Catholic Conference, 2004), 410. It is interesting to note that there is no reference in the index of this volume to "tribalism," "xenophobia," or "ethnicity." There are, however, three entries for "genocide" and 16 entries for "slave-slavery," though several refer to "slavery to sin."

[20]See ibid. 63.

[21]*Catechism of the Catholic Church,* at 469: no. 1934: "Created in the image of the one God and equally endowed with rational souls, all men have the same nature and the same origin. Redeemed by the sacrifice of Christ, all are called to participate in the same divine beatitude: all therefore enjoy equal dignity."

[22]The Pontifical Council for Justice and Peace, *Compendium of the Social Doctrine*, 62.

[23]*Catechism of the Catholic Church* no. 1911: "Human interdependence is increasing and gradually spreading throughout the world. The unity of the human family, embracing people who enjoy equal natural dignity, implies a *universal common good.* This good calls for an organization of the community of nations able to "provide for the different needs of men; this will involve the sphere of social life to which belong questions of food, hygiene, education ... and certain situations arising here and there, as for example ... alleviating the miseries of refugees dispersed throughout the world, and assisting migrants and their families." The final quote in this citation refers to *Gaudium et Spes*, no. 84.2.

[24]Those statements cited are *Nostra Aetate*, no. 5; *Pacem in Terris*, no. 55; *Populorum Progressio*, no. 63; *Octogesima Adveniens*, no. 16; and the Pontifical Council for Justice and Peace, *Church and Racism*.

[25]Here racial justice refers to the present-day understanding that includes considerations of "the new racism." Recall Albert Memmi's definition of racism: "a generalizing definition and valuation of differences, whether real or imaginary to the advantage of the one defining or deploying them [*accusateur*], and to the detriment of the one subjugated to the act of definition [*victime*], whose purpose is to justify (social or physical) hostility and assault [*aggression*]." The quote is from Albert Memmi, *Racism*, trans. Steve Martinot (Minneapolis: University of Minnesota Press, 2000), 100.

[26]For more on the historical and systematic theology of the Trinity see Leonardo Boff, *Trinity and Society*, trans. Paul Burns, Theology and Liberation Series, (Maryknoll, NY: Orbis Books, 1988). See Catherine Mowry LaCugna, *God for Us: The Trinity and Christian Life* (San Francisco: Harper San Francisco, 1991). See also, Elizabeth A. Johnson, *She Who Is: The Mystery of God in Feminist Theological Discourse* (New York: Crossroads, 1992). Also see Anne Hunt, *What Are They Saying about the Trinity?* (New York: Paulist Press, 1998).

[27]See my *The Franciscan View of the Human Person: Some Central Elements*, The Franciscan Heritage Series, Vol. 3 (St. Bonaventure, NY: The Franciscan Institute, 2005), especially 45–62.

[28]Mary Beth Ingham, *Scotus for Dunces: An Introduction to the Subtle Doctor* (St. Bonaventure, NY: The Franciscan Institute, 2003), 230: "A general name for a per se being which has its ultimate actuality. In the case of a rational or intellectual nature, such a being is called a person. This term is a translation of hypostasis, the Greek term used to refer to the persons of the Trinity." See also her example at 110.

[29]Mary Beth Ingham, "John Duns Scotus: An Integrated Vision," in Kenan B. Osborne, ed., *The History of Franciscan Theology* (St. Bonaventure, NY: The Franciscan Institute, 1994), 213. Ingham cites *Lectura* n.54.

[30]Ingham, "Integrated Vision," 214. Ingham cites *Quodlibet* 1.n.3. (Alluntis 1:5–6) trans. Alluntis/Wolter, 6–7. Scotus is most clear about how God's essence is also communion in his discussion of the topic in the fourth of the *Quodlibetal Questions*. See Ingham, "Integrated Vision," 217. Ingham cites *Quodlibet* 4.n.28 (Alluntis 4:61) trans. Alluntis/Wolter, 103–104.

[31]See my *Mutuality: A Formal Norm for Christian Social Ethics* (San Francisco: Catholic Scholars Press, 1998). Reprinted Eugene, OR: Wipf & Stock Publishers, 2005.

[32]Ingham, "Integrated Vision," 218.

[33]Martin Luther King, Jr., *Why We Can't Wait* (New York: The New American Library, 1964), 77. See also Keith D. Miller, *Voice of Deliverance: The Language of Martin Luther King, Jr.* (New York: Free Press, 1992), Chapter 8, especially 166.

[34]See Kelly Brown Douglas, *Sexuality and the Black Church: A Woman's Perspective* (Maryknoll, NY: Orbis Books, 1999), 25–29.

[35]See Jamie Phelps, "Racism and the Church," in Dwight N. Hopkins, ed., *Black Faith and Public Talk* (Maryknoll, NY: Orbis Books, 1999), 53–76.

[36]This listing is Richard M. Gula's summary of the criteria Louis Janssens drew out of the documents of Vatican Council II. See Richard M. Gula, *Reason Informed by Faith: Foundations for a Catholic Morality* (Mahwah, NJ: Paulist Press, 1989), 66–74. Also see Louis Janssens, "Personalist Morals," *Louvain Studies* 3 (Spring 1970): 5–16. In addition see Louis Janssens, "Artificial Insemination Ethical Considerations," *Louvain Studies* 8 (Spring 1980): 5–13.

[37]See also Thomas Aquinas, *Summa Theologia*, I–II, 112.1 and II–II, 25.1, 6, 8,12.

[38]Francis of Assisi, "The Undated Writings—The Admonitions," in Regis J. Armstrong, J. A. Wayne Hellmann, and William J. Short, eds., *Francis of Assisi: Early Documents*, Vol. 1, *The Saint* (New York: New City Press, 1999), 131.

[39]See Douglas, *Sexuality and the Black Church*, especially 11–86. See also Kelly Brown Douglas, *What's Faith Got to Do With It? Black Bodies and Christian Souls* (Maryknoll, NY: Orbis Books, 2005).

[40]Edward Schillebeeckx addresses this most eloquently in his *The Church and the Human Story of God* (New York: Crossroad, 1994), especially Chapters 1 and 3.

[41]National Conference of Catholic Bishops, *Brothers and Sisters to Us: Pastoral Letter on Racism in Our Day* (1979), Bilingual Edition, Washington, DC: United States Conference of Catholic Bishops, 2000) no. 10.

[42]See John Paul II, *Ecclesia in Africa*, Post-Synodal Apostolic Exhortation (Nairobi, Kenya: Paulines Publications Africa, 1995).

[43]See Aylward Shorter, ed., *Theology of the Church as Family of God*, Tangaza Occasional Papers, no. 3 (Nairobi, Kenya: Paulines Publications Africa, 1997).

[44]See Maurice Schepers, "The Ecclesiology of the Church as Family of God: A Systematic Approach," in *Theology of the Church as Family of God*, 19–29.

[45]Ibid. 22–23.

[46]Ibid. 25.

[47]See John Paul II, *Ecclesia in Africa*, no. 63: "[T]he new evangelization along these lines will thus aim at building up the Church as Family, avoiding all ethnocentrism and excessive particularism, trying instead to encourage reconciliation and true communion between different ethnic groups, favoring solidarity and sharing of personnel and resources among the particular Churches, without undue ethnic consideration."

[48]A familial model frequently cited in this regard is the turbulent relationships within and among the various family members, tribe and nation found in the Joseph stories of Gen 37–50.

[49]Schepers, "The Ecclesiology of the Church as Family of God: A Systematic Approach," cites I Cor 12:14f and 20f.

[50]Ibid. 26.

[51]See more discussion on the Holy Spirit below. Acts 2:22, where Peter states that Israelites are responsible for the death of Jesus, needs to be read in the perspective of the narrative and in light of the overwhelming evidence elsewhere throughout the canon of scripture, and the doctrinal teaching of the Church that it was the sin of *all humankind* that stands behind the suffering and death of Christ. There are *no* grounds in this text for anti-Semitism.

[52]See *Lumen Gentium*, no. 1.

[53]See for example, D.W. Waruta, "Tribalism as a Moral Problem in Contemporary Africa, in J. N. K. Mugambi and A. Nasimiyu-Wasike, eds., *Moral and Ethical Issues in African Christianity* (Nairobi, Kenya: Initiatives Publishers, 1992), 127. Also see Aylward Shorter, "The Curse of Ethnocentrism in the African Church," *Ethnicity: Blessing or Curse*, Tangaza Occasional Papers, no. 8 (Nairobi, Kenya: St. Paul Publications, 1999), 28–29. See also David Hollenbach, "Report From Rwanda: An Interview with Augustine Karckezi," *America* (December 7, 1986), 13–17.

[54]Ched Myers, "Tearing Down the Walls," *Priests and People* 16/5 (May 2002): 171–176. See especially 174–75.

[55]Ibid. 176.

[56]See my *Mutuality: A Formal Norm for Christian Social Ethics*, especially Chapter 4, "The Moral Status of Mutuality: A Formal Norm."

[57]Ibid. 227–28.

[58]See Daniel C. Maguire, "*Ratio Practica* and the Intellectual Fallacy," *Journal of Religious Ethics* 10 (1982): 22–39. Also his *The Moral Choice* (Minneapolis, MN: Winston Press, 1979). See also Daniel C. Maguire and A. Nicholas Fargnoli, *On Moral Grounds: The Art/Science of Ethics* (New York: Crossroad, 1991).

[59]See James A. Nash, "Erasing Racism: A Strategy Paper for the COCU's Quest for a Racially Just Unity," *Mid-stream* (March 1998): 357–72. Seven dimensions of ethical praxis are enumerated in this paper and they are incorporated here.

[60]See nos. 18 and 19, particularly.

[61]See Daniel C. Maguire, *New American Justice* (Minneapolis, MN: Winston Press, 1980), especially Chapters 7 and 8. Note that this book was reprinted as *A Case for Affirmative Action* (Dubuque, IA: Shepherd Press, 1992). Citations given here are from the 1980 edition.

[62]See the discussion of hegemony and common sense in Michael Omi and Howard Winant, *Racial Formation in the United States: From the 1960s to the 1990s*, 2nd ed. (New York: Routledge, 1994), 66–70.

[63]Cited in Maguire, *New American Justice*, 108.

[64]Ibid. Maguire cites Aristotle, *Nichomachean Ethics*, Book V, Chapter 10.

[65]Maguire, *New American Justice*, 129–130. He presents several illustrations how various groups meet these criteria. Though the examples are a bit dated, essentially the moral dimensions they illustrate are unchanged.

[66]Limits of this book prohibit a review of the entirety of Maguire's refutations. I mention only several examples here. See his discussion, ibid, especially 169–188.

[67]Ibid. 179.

[68]Pierre Bigo, *La Doctrine Sociale de l'Eglise* (Paris: Presses Universitaires de France) 1965), 378. Also see my *Mutuality: A Formal Norm*, 219–23. Note the mutually corrective dynamics of the formal norms of love, justice and mutuality. Justice ensures mutuality of love. Justice saves love from condescension. Love saves justice from legalism and arbitrariness. Love saves mutuality from unjust agreements. Mutuality brings participation by the party (ies) affected to justice. Mutuality also brings active choice making to love.

[69]See Frank Crüsemann, "'You Know the Heart of a Stranger' (Exodus 23:9): A Recollection of the Torah in the Face of New Nationalism and Xenophobia," in Dietmar Mieth and Lisa Sowle Cahill, eds., *Migrants and Refugees, Concilium* Vol. 4 (Maryknoll, NY: Orbis Books, 1993).

[70]See ibid. 99.

[71]Ibid. 109.

[72]Notably, only the author of Luke recounts two incidents in which Samaritans are the exemplars of goodness. In Luke 17:11–19, of the ten lepers Jesus healed, only a Samaritan returned to give thanks.

[73]See James H. Cone, interviewed by George M. Anderson, "Theology and White Supremacy," at 11–12. At 11, Cone asserts: "White theologians have not succeeded in making an empathetic bond with the pains and hurts of people of color."

[74]See Robin Scroggs, "Threat and Terror in the New Testament," in Victoria Lee Erickson and Michelle Lim Jones, eds., *Surviving Terror: Hope and Justice in a World of Violence* (Grand Rapids, MI: Brazos Press, 2002), 234–235.

[75]See Z. Husain and D. Rosenbaum, "Perceiving Islam: The Causes and Consequences of Islamophobia in the Western Media," in Santosh C. Sana, *Religious Fundamentalism in the Contemporary World: Critical Social and Political Issues* (Oxford, UK: Lexington Books, 2004), 171–206. Fearful reactions to Islam have been prevalent since 9/11 in various parts of the world, particularly in the United States and Europe. Some typical articles in response to this by Christian theologians are: Ted Peters and Muzaffar Iqbal, "From Anxiety to Fascism: Letters by Ted Peters and Muzaffar Iqbal," *Dialog: A Journal of Theology* 42/2 (Summer 2003): 173–174. Also see Ted Peters, "Bush's Blasphamy," *Dialog: A Journal of Theology* 44/2 (Summer 2005): 128–129. See also James M. Wall, "Port Paranoia," *Christian Century* (March 21, 2006): 45.

[76]See the following for examples of this discussion: Donald W. Shriver, Jr., "Forgiveness? Now?: A Christian Dilemma," *Christian Century* 118/29 (October 24–31, 2001): 6. Carlyle Murphy, "The War on Terrorism: Why It Will Really Be a Long One," *America* 188/15, Whole no. 4609 (April 28–May 5, 2003): 8–12. Trudy

Bush, "Terrorist Timing," *Christian Century* 118/29 (October 24–31, 2001): 7. Joseph G. Bock, "You Can't Fight Fire with Bullets: A Look at Counterterrorism," *America* 118/13, Whole no. 4607 (April 14, 2003): 6–8, 10.

[77]For an excellent exegesis of this text see Christopher Owczarek, *Sons of the Most High: Love of Enemies in Luke-Acts—Teaching and Practice* (Nairobi, Kenya: Pauline Publications Africa, 2002).

[78]See Kathleen A. Warren, *Daring to Cross the Threshold: Francis of Assisi Encounters Sultan Malek al Kamil* (Rochester, MN: Sisters of St. Francis, 2003). Also see J. Joeberichts, *Francis and Islam* (Quincy, IL: Franciscan Press, 1997). Also for information on Franciscan Pilgrimage Programs, "Franciscan Interreligious Pilgrimage, see http://www.franciscanpilgrimages.com/pil_07Inter.php. See also for example the Interfaith Network of the UK at www.interfaith.org.uk. See also testimony of Fr. Phil Sumner about his work, given at the Oldham Interfaith Forum, Oldham, England, http://www.ncpew.org.uk/documents/2004%20Community%20Cohesion.pdf

[79]See Laura Westra and Bill E. Lawson, eds., *Faces of Environmental Racism: Confronting Issues of Global Justice*, 2nd ed. (New York: Rowman & Littlefield Publishers, Inc., 2001).

[80]Cited in Timothy Radcliffe, *What Is the Point of Being a Christian?* (New York: Continuum, 2005) 131.

[81]Francis of Assisi, "A Letter to the Entire Order (1225–1226)," 27, in Regis J. Armstrong, J. A. Wayne Hellmann, William J. Short, eds., *Francis of Assisi: Early Documents*, Vol. 1, *The Saint*, 118. See also "The Undated Writings—The Admonitions," I: 8–9, in ibid. 128.

[82]This is a paraphrase of the Pentecost Sequence.

[83]See Clarence Earl Williams, Jr., *Recovering From Everyday Racisms* (Detroit, MI: Institute for Recovery From Racisms, 2002), 134–35. Williams uses addictions and family systems models for discussion of racisms. Recovery involves a two-stage process whereby a person first becomes aware of their racialized self and then establishes healthy attitudes and behavior patterns of social interaction. Racial sobriety comes at the end of the second stage.

[84]Ibid. 8.

[85]Martin Niemöller, *Congressional Record* (October 14, 1968): 31636. Also see *The Columbia Encyclopedia*, 6th ed. (New York: Columbia University Press, 2005). Excerpt from Bartleby.Com—Great Books on Line, http://www.bartleby.com/65/ni/Niemoell.html, Accessed December 9, 2006, "1892–1984, German Protestant churchman. Though at first a supporter of National Socialism, Niemöller (then a pastor at Berlin-Dahlem) preached courageously against the Hitler regime after it came into power in 1933. He attacked Hitler's creation of the German Evangelical Church and became the leader of the German pastors' emergency league and of the Confessing Church. Briefly arrested in 1937, he was imprisoned again from 1938 until his liberation (1945) by the Allies. After his release Niemöller became (1947) church president of the Evangelical Church in Hesse-Nassau, with his seat at Wiesbaden, and founded (1948) a cooperative council of all German Protestant churches, of which he became president. Among his writings are his autobiography, *Vom U-Boot zur Kanzel* [From U-boat to pulpit] (1934)."

[86]The plan can be accessed at the Web site of the Catholic Bishops' Conference of England and Wales, www.catholicchurch.org.uk/equality.

[87]See Catholic Bishops' Conference of England and Wales, *Diversity and Equality Guidelines*, 22. The texts of the canons cited by the bishops are: Can. 208 "Flowing

from their rebirth in Christ, there is a genuine equality of dignity and action among all of Christ's faithful. Because of this equality they all contribute, each according to his or her condition and office, to the building up of the Body of Christ." Can. 220 "No one may unlawfully harm the good reputation which a person enjoys, or violate the right of every person to protect his or her privacy." Can. 222 no. 2 "[Christ's faithful] are also obliged to promote social justice and, mindful of the Lord's precept, to help the poor from their own resources."

[88]John 17:17–23. Citation is from the *Christian Community Bible*, Catholic Pastoral Edition, co-published by Quezon City, Philippines: Claretian Publications; SAV, Makati: St. Paul Publications; and Manila, Philippines: Divine Word Publications, 1988.

4. Techniques of Dominance

[1]See Albert Memmi, *Racism*, trans. Steve Martinot (Minneapolis: University of Minnesota, 2000).

[2]See Sebastião Salgado, *Migrations: Humanity in Transition*, Paperback Edition (New York: Aperture, 2003). See also an interactive exhibition of his photographs and an explanation of his seven-year project at http://www.terra.com.br/sebastiaos-algado/e1/, Accessed January 6, 2007.

[3]Sebastião Salgado, "Migrations: The Story of Humanity on the Move," *Nieman Reports* 60/3 (Fall 2006): 5. Digital reprint at www.nieman.harvard.edu/reports/06-3NRfall/Fall2006/Migration.pdf.

[4]Pontifical Justice and Peace Commission's *The Church and Racism: Toward a More Fraternal Society*, no. 8. See *Origins* 18/37 (February 23, 1989): 613–626.

[5]Ibid. no. 9.

[6]Ibid. no. 10.

[7]Ibid. no. 11.

[8]See especially Part 3: "Tribalism" of Jonathan Glover, *Humanity: A Moral History of the Twentieth Century* (New Haven, CT: Yale University Press, 1999), 119–152.

[9]Pontifical Justice and Peace Commission, *The Church and Racism*, no. 12.

[10]See Carrie McCracken, "The Impacts of Banana Plantation Development in Central America," http://members.tripod.com/foro_emaus/BanPlantsCA.htm, Accessed January 17, 2007.

[11]See "Petroleum Mining and the U'wa Indian Community—Case Study" at http://www.american.edu/TED/colspill.htm, Accessed January 17, 2007.

[12]One of the most environmentally destructive coal mining techniques is "mountain top removal." See the Ohio Valley Environmental Coalition of Huntington, WV at http://www.ohvec.org/galleries/mountaintop_removal/007/index.html, Accessed December 20, 2006.

[13]Pontifical Justice and Peace Commission, *The Church and Racism*, no. 13.

[14]Ibid. no. 14.

[15]Ibid. no. 15.

[16]See the UNESCO *Declaration on Race and Racial Prejudice* at http://www.unhchr.ch/html/menu3/b/d_prejud.htm, Accessed on January 11, 2007. See also the1978 *International Convention on the Elimination of All Forms of Racial Discrimination*, http://www.unhchr.ch/tbs/doc.nsf/0/2c62514131085337c125716c003494c4/$FILE/G0641115.pdf, Accessed January 11, 2007.

[17]Pontifical Justice and Peace Commission, *The Church and Racism*, no. 16.

[18] For an explanation of the "One Child" policy see http://www.overpopulation .com/faq/Population_Control/one_child.html, Accessed January 11, 2007.

[19] The pastoral cites Myron Orfield, *Metro-Politics: A Regional Agenda for Community and Stability*, Revised Edition (Washington, DC: Brookings Institution Press, 1998).

[20] Cardinal Francis George, *Dwell in My Love* (Chicago: The Catholic New World, 2001), 13.

[21] See Richard Rodgers and Oscar Hammerstein II, *South Pacific: A Musical Play* (New York: Random House, 1949), 136–137. "You've Got to Be Carefully Taught" is from *South Pacific* by Richard Rodgers (music), and Oscar Hammerstein II (lyrics), published in 1949.

[22] See Debera Van Ausdale and Joe R. Feagin, *The First R: How Children Learn Race and Racism* (Lanham, MD: Rowman and Littlefield, 2002).

[23] The literature relevant to this discussion is massive. A helpful though dated framework for the discussion is given in Martin N. Marger, *Race and Ethnic Relations: American and Global Perspectives*, 2nd ed. (Belmont, CA: Wadsworth Publishing Company, 1991). My discussion draws on Marger's third chapter. See Philip Mason, *Patterns of Dominance* (New York: Oxford University Press, 1970), 52.

[24] See G.M. Gilbert, "Stereotype Presence and Change among College Students," *Journal of Abnormal and Social Psychology* 46 (1951): 245–254.

[25] See William Buchanan and Hadley Cantril, *How Nations See Each Other* (Urbana: University of Illinois Press, 1953).

[26] See Gordon W. Alport, *The Nature of Prejudice* (Garden City, NY: Doubleday, 1958), 184. Also see George Eaton Simpson and J. Milton Yinger, *Racial and Cultural Minorities: An Analysis of Prejudice and Discrimination*, 4th ed. (New York: Harper and Row, 1972), 155.

[27] For excellent resources on the effects of the media on racism and the portrayal of diverse peoples in the media, see The University of Iowa College of Liberal Arts, Department of Communication Studies Web site "Gender, Race and Ethnicity in Media African Americans in Media," http://www.uiowa.edu/~commstud/resources/ GenderMedia/african.html, accessed January 11, 2007. See also Alysia Tate, "Who Shapes the Image of a Race?" *Chicago Tribune*, September 1, 2002, pages 1 and 3. See Michael C. Kotzin, "Tolerance and Reality in Collision," *Chicago Tribune*, November 17, 2002, Perspective Section, 1 and 8. Also see John Cook, "White Faces Still Prominent Behind the Scenes: Ethnic Shows Oft Created by Non-minorities," *Chicago Tribune*, September 14, 2003, Arts & Entertainment, Section 7, 13.

[28] See Rose Golden, *The Show and Tell Machine: How Television Works and Works You Over* (New York: Dell Books, 1977). Also see Herbert I. Schiller, *The Mind Managers* (Boston: Beacon Press, 1973).

[29] See for example Randall Kennedy, "Interracial Intimacy," *The Atlantic Monthly* 290/5 (December 2002): 103–110.

[30] See the classic study by Richard T. LaPiere, "Attitudes vs. Actions," *Social Forces* 13 (1934): 230–37.

[31] See Joe R. Feagin and Clairece Booher Feagin, *Discrimination American Style: Institutional Racism and Sexism* (Englewood Hills, NJ: Prentice Hall, 1978), 21–22.

[32] Apartheid in South Africa and the Jim Crow Laws in the southern United States exemplify this.

³³The placement of industries in the suburban areas rather than in the central area of a city making it more difficult for people of color living primarily in central city neighborhoods to have access to employment exemplifies this.

³⁴See Feagin and Booher Feagin, *Discrimination American Style,* 32.

³⁵William Ryan, *Blaming the Victim,* Revised Edition (New York: Vintage, 1975).

³⁶See Alport, *The Nature of Prejudice.*

³⁷See Alice Miller, *For Your Own Good: The Roots of Violence in Child-rearing,* trans. Hildegard and Hunter Hannum, 4th ed. (New York: Farrar, Straus and Giroux, 2002), 65.

³⁸Frank P. Westie, "Race and Ethnic Relations," in Robert E.L. Faris, ed., *Handbook of Modern Sociology* (Chicago: Rand McNally, 1964), 583–584.

³⁹See Van Ausdale and Feagin, *The First R.* Also see Barbara Mathias and Mary Ann French, *Forty Ways to Raise a Non-Racist Kid* (New York: Harper Perennial, 1996).

⁴⁰See James W. Vander Zanden, *American Minority Relations*, 4th ed. (New York: Knopf, 1983), 104 and Leonard I. Pearlin, "Shifting Group Attachments and Attitudes Toward Negroes," *Social Forces* 33 (1954): 47–50.

⁴¹See Glover, *Humanity: A Moral History of the Twentieth Century,* 379–93. Glover details the moral formation of those who were resistant to Nazi threats against Christians and others who did not cooperate in their atrocities.

⁴²Robert K. Merton, "Discrimination and the American Creed," in R.H. Mac Iver, ed., *Discrimination and the National Welfare* (New York: Harper and Row, 1949), 99–126.

⁴³See Studs Terkel, "C.P. Ellis," in Gary Colombo, Robert Cullen, and Bonnie Lisle, *Rereading America: Cultural Contexts for Critical Thinking and Writing,* 5th Edition (New York: Bedford/St. Martins, 2001), 562–572.

⁴⁴See Michael Omi and Howard Winant, *Racial Formation in the United States: From the 1960s to the 1990s,* 2nd ed. (New York: Routledge, 1994): 24–35.

⁴⁵Ibid. 27. See also Wilson's *The Declining Significance of Race,* 2nd ed. (Chicago: University of Chicago, 1978), 17.

⁴⁶Omi and Winant, *Racial Formation,* 28.

⁴⁷Ibid. 29.

⁴⁸Reich is quoted in Omi and Winant, *Racial Formation,* 31.

⁴⁹Ibid. 34.

⁵⁰Bonacich is quoted by Omi and Winant, *Racial Formation,* 33.

⁵¹See Werner Bergmann, "Xenophobia and Anti-Semitism After the Unification of Germany," *Patterns of Prejudice,* 28/1 (1994/0031–322X), 67–80. See also Michael Marrus, "Antisemitism and Xenophobia in Historical Perspective," *Patterns of Prejudice* 28/2 (1994/0031–3222X): 77–81.

⁵²Omi and Winant, *Racial Formation,* 34.

⁵³See Robert Schreiter, *Reconciliation: Mission and Ministry in a Changing Social Order,* The Boston Theological Institute Series, Vol. 3 (Maryknoll, NY: Orbis Books, 2003). See also Clarence Earl Williams, Jr., *Recovery from Everyday Racisms* (Detroit, MI: The Institute for Recovery From Racisms, 1999). Also Jody Tobin Miller Shearer, *Enter the River: Healing Steps from White Privilege to Racial Reconciliation* (Scottsdale, PA: Herald, 1994). In addition see Doris Donnelly, *Seventy Times Seven: Forgiveness and Peacemaking* (Erie, PA: Pax Christi USA, 1993).

[54] Quoted by Leonardo Boff, trans. Philip Berryman, *Cry of the Earth, Cry of the Poor* (Maryknoll, NY: Orbis Books, 1997), 13.

[55] See this volume Chapter 3. Also see my *Mutuality: A Formal Norm for Christian Social Ethics* (San Francisco: Catholic Scholars Press, 1998; reprinted Eugene, OR: Wifp & Stock Publishers, 2005).

[56] The Foundational Moral Experience (FME) is a classic concept in Daniel C. Maguire's work. See Daniel C. Maguire and A. Nicholas Fargnoli, *On Moral Grounds: The Art/Science of Ethics* (New York: Crossroads, 1991), 19–25.

5. Racism, Tribalism, and Xenophobia

[1] Simone Campbell, SSS, "Beckoned by Grace," *Network Connection* (July/August, 2006): 3.

[2] Margo Monteith and Jeffery Winters, "Why We Hate," *Psychology Today* (May/June 2002): 48. They cite the study by Henri Tajfel of the University of Bristol and John Turner of the National Australian University that explains the psychology behind a range of prejudices and biases.

[3] Ibid. 49–50. The work cited is that of psychologists Anthony Greenwald of the University of Washington, Seattle, and Mahzarin Banaji of Harvard.

[4] Ibid. 50–51. The studies cited are by Leda Cosmides and John Tooby of the Center for Evolutionary Psychology at the University of California, Santa Barbara, and anthropologist Robert Kurzban of the University of California at Los Angeles. Also referenced is the study by Samuel Gaertner of the University of Delaware, Newark, and John Dovidio of Colgate University in Hamilton, New York.

[5] Ibid. 51. See the work of psychologist Margo Monteith of the University of Kentucky.

[6] See Judith Nagata, "What Is a Maylay? Situational Selections of Ethnic Identity in a Plural Society," *American Ethnologist*, 1 (1974): 331–350.

[7] This document is available from the Web site of the United States Conference of Catholic Bishops at http://www.usccb.org/saac/ExccutiveSummary-GrayScale Final.pdf, Accessed January 22, 2007.

[8] Ibid. 12.

[9] For the text of this essay see http://www.case.edu/president/aaction/UnpackingTheKnapsack.pdf, Accessed January 22, 2007.

[10] See Cathleen Crayton, "Anti-Racism and the Dominant Gaze," *Network Connection* (July/August, 2006): 4–6.

[11] See an excellent elaboration of this in Robert J. Schreiter, "Ministry for a Multicultural Church," *Origins* 29/1 (May 20, 1999): 1, 3–8.

[12] Ibid. 8.

[13] See D. Goldberg, *Racist Culture: Philosophy and the Politics of Meaning* (Oxford, UK: Blackwell Publishers, 1993).

[14] R. Lenten, *Gender and Catastrophe* (London: Zed Books, 1997), 2.

[15] See Gargi Bhattacharyya, John Gabriel and Stephen Small, *Race and Power: Global Racism in the Twenty-First Century* (London: Routledge, 2002), 107.

[16] See J. Dreze and A. Sen, *The Political Economy of Hunger*, Vol. I, Entitlement and Well-being (Oxford, UK: Clarendon, 1990).

[17] See Bhattacharyya, Gabriel and Small, *Race and Power*, 114.

[18] Ibid. 135.

Selected Bibliography

Alport, Gordon W. *The Nature of Prejudice.* Garden City, NY: Doubleday, 1958.

Balibar, Etienne. *Masses, Classes, Ideas: Studies on Politics and Philosophy Before and After Marx.* New York: Routledge, 1994.

———. "Racism and Nationalism." In *Race, Nation, Class: Ambiguous Identities*, edited by Etienne Balibar and Immanuel Walerstein, 37–67. London: Verso, 1992.

Bergmann, Werner. "Xenophobia and Anti-Semitism After the Unification of Germany." *Patterns of Prejudice* 28, no. 1 (1994): 67–80.

Bernal, Martin. *Black Athena: The Afroasiatic Roots of Classical Civilization.* Vol. 1, *The Fabrication of Ancient Greece 1785–1985.* New Brunswick, NJ: Rutgers University Press, 1987.

Bernardin, Cardinal Joseph. "Christ Lives in Me: A Pastoral Reflection on Jesus and His Meaning for Life (1985)." In *Selected Works of Joseph Cardinal Bernardin.* Vol. 1, *Homilies and Teaching Documents*, edited by Alphonse P. Spilly, 132 . Collegeville, MN: The Liturgical Press, 2000.

———. "The Consistent Ethic of Life and Its Public Policy Consequences." In *The Seamless Garment: Writings on the Consistent Ethic of Life*, edited by Thomas A. Nairn. Maryknoll, NY: Orbis Books, 2008.

———. "Here and Now: Pastoral Statement on Youth (Autumn 1994)." In *Selected Works of Joseph Cardinal Bernardin.* Vol. 1, *Homilies and Teaching Documents*, edited by Alphonse P. Spilly, 224. Collegeville, MN: The Liturgical Press, 2000.

Bhattacharyya, Gargi, and John Gabriel. "Anti-Deportation Campaigning in the West Midlands." In *Rethinking Anti-Racisms: From Theory to Practice*, edited by Floya Anthias and Cathie Lloyd. New York: Routledge, 2002.

Bhattacharyya, Gargi, John Gabriel, and Stephen Small. *Race and Power: Global Racism in the Twenty-First Century.* London: Routledge, 2002.

Buell, Denise Kimber, and Caroline Johnson Hodge. "The Politics of Interpretation: The Rhetoric of Race and Ethnicity in Paul." *Journal of Biblical Literature* 123, no. 2 (2004): 235–251.

Byron, Guy L. *Symbolic Blackness and Ethnic Differences in Early Christian Literature.* New York: Routledge, 2002.

Cabal, Hugo Latorre. *The Revolution of the Latin American Church.* Translated by Frances K. Hendrickson and Beatrice Berler. Norman: University of Oklahoma Press, 1978.

Cashmore, Ernest. "Xenophobia." In *Dictionary of Race and Ethnic Relations,* by Ernest Cashmore, NetLibrary, Inc., et al., 346. London: Routledge, 1994.

Castles, Stephen. *Ethnicity and Globalization.* London: Sage, 2000.

Cavendish, James C. "A Research Report Commemorating the 25th Anniversary of Brothers and Sisters to Us." Washington, DC: United States Conference of Catholic Bishops, 2004.

Cone, James H. "Theology and White Supremacy: An Interview With James H. Cone," Interview by George M. Anderson. *America* 195, issue 16, whole no. 4753 (November 20, 2006): 10–15.

Crüsemann, Frank. "'You Know the Heart of a Stranger' (Exodus 23:9): A Recollection of the Torah in the Face of New Nationalism and Xenophobia." In *Migrants and Refugees.* Vol. 4, *Concilium,* edited by Dietmar Mieth and Lisa Sowle Cahill, 95–109. Maryknoll, NY: Orbis Books, 1993.

Davies, Susan E., and Sr. Paul Therese Hennessee, eds. *Ending Racism in the Church.* Cleveland, OH: United Church Press, 1998.

Davis, David Brion. "Constructing Race: A Reflection." In *In God's Image: Religion, Moral Values and Our Heritage of Slavery,* edited by David Brion Davis, 307–342. New Haven, CT: Yale University Press, 2001.

De Lima Silva, Silvia Regina. "Black Latin American Theology: A New Way to Sense, to Feel, to Speak of God." In *Black Faith and Public Talk: Critical Essays on James H. Cone's Black Theology and Black Power,* edited by Dwight N. Hopkins, 190–204. Maryknoll, NY: Orbis Books, 1999.

Degler, Carl. *Neither Black nor White: Slavery and Race Relations in Brazil and the United States.* New York: Macmillan, 1971.

DeTomasis, Louis. *Doing Right in a Shrinking World: How Corporate America Can Balance Ethics and Profit in a Changing Economy.* Austin, TX: The Greenleaf Book Group Press, 2006.

Devasahayam, V. "Pollution, Poverty, and Powerlessness: A Dalit Perspective." In *A Reader in Dalit Theology,* edited by Arvin Nirmal, 1–22. Madras, India: The Gurukul Lutheran Theological College and Research Institute, n.d.

Dikötter, Frank, ed. *The Construction of Racial Identities in China and Japan: Historical and Contemporary Perspectives.* London: C. Hurst and Company, Ltd., 1997.

Douglas, Kelly Brown. *Sexuality and the Black Church: A Woman's Perspective.* Maryknoll, NY: Orbis Books, 1999.

———. *What's Faith Got to Do With It? Black Bodies and Christian Souls.* Maryknoll, NY: Orbis Books, 2005.

Duffy, Eamon. *Saints and Sinners: A History of the Popes.* New Haven, CT: Yale University Press, 1997.

Eze, Emmanuel Chukwudi. *Race and the Enlightenment: A Reader.* Cambridge, MA: Blackwell, 1997.

Feagin, Joe R., and Clairece Booher Feagin. *Discrimination American Style: Institutional Racism and Sexism.* Englewood Hills, NJ: Prentice Hall, 1978.

Felder, Cain Hope. "Racial Ambiguities in the Biblical Narratives." In *The Church and Racism* Vol. 151, no. 1, *Concilium,* edited by Gregory Baum and John Colman, 17–24. New York: The Seabury Press, 1982.

Felder, Cain Hope, ed. *Stony the Road We Trod: African American Biblical Interpretation.* Minneapolis, MN: Fortress Press, 1991.

Fisken, Margaret Ann. "What Does it Mean to be British?" *Priests and People* 16, no. 5 (May 2002): 177–182.

Francis of Assisi. "A Letter to the Entire Order (1225–1226)." In *Francis of Assisi: Early Documents.* Vol. 1, *The Saint*, edited by Regis J. Armstrong, J. A. Wayne Hellmann, and William J. Short. New York: New City Press, 1999.

———. "The Undated Writings—The Admonitions." In *Francis of Assisi: Early Documents.* Vol. 1, *The Saint*, edited by Regis J. Armstrong, J. A. Wayne Hellmann, and William J. Short. New York: New City Press, 1999.

Fredrickson, George M. *The Black Image in the White Mind: The Debate on Afro-American Character and Destiny 1817–1914.* Middleton, CT: Wesleyan University Press, 1987.

———. *Race: A Short History.* Princeton, NJ: Princeton University Press, 2002.

———. *White Supremacy: A Comparative Study in American and South African History.* New York: Oxford University Press, 1981.

Gier, Nicholas F. "The Color of Sin/The Color of Skin: The Ancient Colorblindness and the Philosophical Origins of Modern Racism." *Journal of Religious Thought* 46, no. 1 (Summer/Fall 1989): 42–52.

Gilbert, G. M. "Stereotype Presence and Change among College Students." *Journal of Abnormal and Social Psychology* 46 (1951): 245–254.

Greenleaf, Richard E., ed. *The Roman Catholic Church in Colonial Latin America.* New York: Alfred A. Knopf, 1971.

Hannaford, Ivan. *Race: The History of and Idea in the West.* Baltimore: The Johns Hopkins University Press, 1996.

Harding, Sandra, ed. *The "Racial" Economy of Science: Toward a Democratic Future.* Bloomington: University of Indiana Press, 1993.

Hinze, Bradford F. "Ethnic and Racial Diversity and the Catholicity of the Church" In *Theology: Expanding the Borders.* Vol. 43, The Annual Publication of the College Theology Society, edited by Maria Pilar Aquino and Roberto S. Goizueta, 162–199. Mystic, CT: Twenty-Third Publications, 1998.

Hollenbach, David. "Report From Rwanda: An Interview With Augustine Karekezi." *America* (December 7, 1986): 13–17.

Hood, Robert E. *Begrimed and Black: Christian Traditions on Blacks and Blackness.* Minneapolis, MN: Fortress Press, 1994.

Hopkins, Dwight N. *Being Human: Race, Culture and Religion.* Minneapolis, MN: Fortress Press, 2005.

Hurbon, Leannec. "The Church and Afro-American Slavery." In *The Church in Latin America 1492–1992*, edited by Enrique Dussel, 372–382. Maryknoll, NY: Orbis Books, 1992.

Husain, Mir Zohair, and D. Rosenbaum. "Perceiving Islam: The Causes and Consequences of Islamophobia in the Western Media." In *Religious Fundamentalism in the Contemporary World: Critical Social and Political Issues*, edited by Santash C. Sana, 171–206. Oxford, UK: Lexington Books, 2004.

Ingham, Mary Beth. "John Duns Scotus: An Integrated Vision." In *The History of Franciscan Theology*, edited by Kenan B. Osborne, 185–230. St. Bonaventure, NY: The Franciscan Institute, 1994.

———. *Scotus for Dunces: An Introduction to the Subtle Doctor.* St. Bonaventure, NY: The Franciscan Institute, 2003.

Izzo, John Francis. "'Dalit' Means Broken: Caste and Church in Southern India." *America* 192, issue 5, whole no. 4680 (February 14, 2005): 11–14.

Jordon, Winthrop D. *White Over Black: American Attitudes Toward the Negro 1550–1812.* New York: Norton, 1995.

Kalu, Ogbu U. "Church Presence in Africa: A Historical Analysis of the Evangelization Process." In *African Theologies en Route*, edited by Kofi Appiah-Kubi and Sergio Torres. Maryknoll, NY: Orbis Books, 1979.

Kamen, Henry. *The Spanish Inquisition: An Historical Revision.* London: Weidenfeld & Nicolson, 1997.

King, Martin Luther, Jr. *Why We Can't Wait.* New York: The New American Library, 1964.

Langmuir, Garvin I. *Toward a Definition of Antisemitism.* Berkeley: University of California Press, 1990.

Lewis, Bernard. *Race and Color in Islam.* New York: Harper and Row, 1971.

MacMaster, Neil. *Racism in Europe: 1870–2000.* New York: Palgrave, 2001.

Maguire, Daniel C. *The Moral Core of Judaism and Christianity: Reclaiming the Revolution.* Minneapolis, MN: Fortress Press, 1993.

———. *New American Justice.* Minneapolis, MN: Winston Press, 1980.

———. "*Ratio Practica* and the Intellectual Fallacy." *Journal of Religious Ethics* 10 (1982): 22–39.

Marrus, Michael. "Anti-Semitism and Xenophobia in Historical Perspective." *Patterns of Prejudice* 28, no. 2 (1994): 77–81.

Martinez, Maria Elena. "Religion, Purity, and Race: The Spanish Concept of 'Limpieza de Sangre' in Seventeenth Century Mexico and the Broader Atlantic World." *Harvard International Seminar on the History of the Atlantic World, 1500–1800* (April 2002): 2–3.

Massingale, Bryan N. "James Cone and Recent Catholic Episcopal Teaching on Racism." *Theological Studies* 61, no. 4 (December 2000): 700–730.

Maxwell, John Francis. *Slavery and the Catholic Church: The History of Teaching Concerning the Moral Legitimacy of the Institution of Slavery.* London: Barry Rose Publishers and the Anti-Slavery Society for the Protection of Human Rights, 1975.

McGreevey, John T. *Parish Boundaries: The Catholic Encounter with Race in the Twentieth-Century Urban North.* Chicago: University of Chicago, 1996.

Memmi, Albert. *Racism.* Translated by Steve Martinot. Minneapolis: University of Minnesota Press, 2000.

Miller, Alice. *For Your Own Good: The Roots of Violence in Child-Rearing.* Translated by Hildegard and Hunter Hannum. 4th ed. New York: Farrar, Straus and Giroux, 2002.

Moerman, Michael. "Ethnic Identification in a Complex Civilization: Who Are the Lue?" *American Anthropologist* 67 (1965): 1215–1230.

Monteith, Margo, and Jeffery Winters. "Why We Hate." *Psychology Today* (May/June 2002): 44–49, 87.

Mörner, Magnus. *Race Mixture in the History of Latin America.* Boston: Little Brown & Company, 1967.

Mugambi, Jesse N. K. *African Christian Theology: An Introduction.* Nairobi, Kenya: Heineman Kenya, 1989.

Muzorewa, Gwinya H. *The Origins and Development of African Theology.* Maryknoll, NY: Orbis Books, 1985.

Myers, Ched. "Tearing Down the Walls." *Priests and People* 16, no. 5 (May 2002): 171–176.

Nagata, Judith A. "What Is a Maylay? Situational Selection of Ethnic Identity in a Plural Society." *American Ethnologist* 1 (1974): 331–359.

Nash, Peter T. *Reading Race, Reading the Bible.* The Facets Series. Minneapolis, MN: Fortress Press, 2003.

Natenyahu, Benjamin. *The Origins of the Inquisition in Fifteenth Century Spain.* 2nd ed. New York: New York Review of Books, 2001.

Niemöller, Martin. *Congressional Record* (October 14, 1968): 31636.

Nording, John G. "*Onesimus Fugitives*: A Defense of the Runaway Slave Hypothesis in Philemon." *Journal of the Study of the New Testament* 41 (Fall 1991): 91–119.

Nothwehr, Dawn M. *The Franciscan View of the Human Person: Some Central Elements.* Vol. 3, *The Franciscan Heritage Series.* St. Bonaventure, NY: The Franciscan Institute, 2005.

———. *Mutuality: A Formal Norm for Christian Social Ethics.* Eugene, OR: Wipf & Stock Publishers, 2005. First published 1998 by Catholic Scholars Press.

O'Connell, Timothy E. *Making Disciples: A Handbook of Christian Moral Formation.* New York: Crossroad, 1998.

Oduyoye, Mercy Amba. *Hearing and Knowing: Theological Reflections on Christianity in Africa.* Maryknoll, NY: Orbis Books, 1986.

Omi, Michael, and Howard Winant. *Racial Formation in the United States: From the 1960s to the 1990s.* 2nd ed. New York: Routledge, 1994.

Osiek, Carolyn. "Slavery in the Second Testament World." *Biblical Theology Bulletin* 22 (Winter 1992): 174–179.

Owczarek, Christopher. *Sons of the Most High: Love of Enemies in Luke Acts—Teaching and Practice.* Nairobi, Kenya: Pauline Publications Africa, 2002.

Panzer, Joel S. *The Popes and Slavery.* New York: Alba House, 1996.

Pattel-Grey, Anne. *The Great White Flood: Racism in Australia.* Atlanta, GA: Scholars, 1998.

———. *Through Aboriginal Eyes: The Cry From the Wilderness.* Geneva, Switzerland: World Council of Churches Publications, 1991.

Phelps, Jamie T. "Racism and the Church: An Inquiry Into the Contradictions Between Experience, Doctrine and Theological Theory." In *Black Faith and Public Talk*, edited by Dwight N. Hopkins, 53–76. Maryknoll, NY: Orbis Books, 1999.

Poliakov, Léon. *The History of Anti-Semitism.* Vol. 1, *From the Time of Christ to the Court Jews*, translated by Richard Howard. Philadelphia: University of Pennsylvania Press, 2003. First published 1975 by Vanguard Press.

———. *The History of Anti-Semitism.* Vol. 2, *From Mohammed to the Marranos*, translated by Natalie Gerardi. New York: Vanguard Press, 1973.

Poppen, Cinny, Michael McConnell, and Renny Golden. *Dangerous Memories: Invasion and Resistance Since 1492.* Chicago: Chicago Religious Task Force on Central America, 1991.

Ratcliffe, Peter. "Conceptualizing 'Race,' Ethnicity, and Nation: Toward a Comparative Perspective." In *"Race," Ethnicity and Nation: International Perspectives on Social Conflict*, edited by Peter Ratcliffe, 2–25. London: UCL Press, Ltd., 1994.

Salgado, Sebastião. *Migrations: Humanity in Transition.* New York: Aperture, 2003.

————. "Migrations: The Story of Humanity on the Move." *Nieman Reports* 60, no. 3 (Fall 2006): 5.

Sautman, Barry. "Myths of Descent, Racial Nationalism and Ethnic Minorities in the People's Republic of China." In *The Construction of Racial Identities in China and Japan: Historical and Contemporary Perspectives*, edited by Frank Dikötter, 75–95. London: C. Hurst and Company, Ltd., 1997.

Schepers, Maurice. "The Ecclesiology of the Church as Family of God: A Systematic Approach." In *Theology of the Church as Family of God*, Tangaza Occasional Papers, no. 3, edited by Aylward Shorter, 19–29. Nairobi, Kenya: Paulines Publications Africa, 1997.

Schreiter, Robert J. *Reconciliation: Mission and Ministry in a Changing Social Order.* Vol. 3, *The Boston Theological Institute Series.* Maryknoll, NY: Orbis Books, 2003.

Shorter, Aylward. "The Curse of Ethnocentrism in the African Church." In *Ethnicity: Blessing or Curse*, Tangaza Occasional Papers, no. 8, edited by Albert de Jong, 28–29. Nairobi, Kenya: St. Paul Publications, 1999.

————. *Theology of the Church as Family of God.* Tangaza Occasional Papers, no. 3. Nairobi, Kenya: Paulines Publications Africa, 1997.

Siwtabau, Suliana. "A Theology for Justice and Peace in the Pacific." In *The Gospel is Not Western*, edited by G. W. Trompf, 92–97. Maryknoll, NY: Orbis Books, 1997.

Snowden, Frank M., Jr. *Before Color and Prejudice: The Ancient View of Blacks.* Cambridge, MA: Harvard University Press, 1983.

————. *Blacks in Antiquity: Ethiopians in the Greco-Roman Experience.* Cambridge, MA: Harvard University Press, 1970.

————. "The Negro in Ancient Greece." *American Anthropologist* 50 (1948): 31–44.

Sweet, James H. "The Iberian Roots of American Racist Thought." *William and Mary Quarterly* 54 (1997): 143–166.

Tappen, Mark B. "Narrative, Authorship, and the Development of Moral Authority." In *Narrative and Storytelling: Implications for Understanding Moral Development*, Vol. 54, *New Directions in Child Development*, edited by Mark B. Tappen and Martin J. Packer. San Francisco: Jossey-Bass, 1991.

Tarimo, Aquiline S. J. "Ethnicity, Common Good and the Church in Contemporary Africa." http://www.sedos.org/english/Tarimo.html (accessed November 10, 2006).

Terkel, Studs. "C. P. Ellis." In *Rereading America: Cultural Contexts for Critical Thinking and Writing*, 5th ed., edited by Gary Colombo, Robert Cullen, and Bonnie Lisle, 562–572. New York: Bedford/St. Martins, 2001.

Thompson, Lloyd A. *Romans and Blacks.* Norman: University of Oklahoma Press, 1989.

Thornton, John. *Africa and Africans in the Marketing of the Atlantic World 1400–1800.* 2nd ed. Cambridge, UK: Cambridge University Press, 1998.

United Nations. *International Convention on the Elimination of All Forms of Racial Discrimination.* http://www.unhchr.ch/tbs/doc.nsf/0/2c62514131085337c125716c003494c4/$FILE/G0641115.pdf (accessed January 11, 2007).

United Nations Educational, Scientific, and Cultural Organization. *1950 Statement on Race.* http://portal.unesco.org/es/ev.php-URL_ID=17993&URL_DO=DO_TOPIC&URL_SECTION=201.html (accessed January 13, 2007).

———. *1951 Statement on the Nature of Race and Race Differences.* http://www
.unhchr.ch/html/menu3/b/d_prejud.htm (accessed on January 11, 2007).

———. *1964 Statement on the Biological Aspects of Race.* http://www.unhchr
.ch/html/menu3/b/d_prejud.htm (accessed on January 11, 2007).

———. *1967 Statement on Race and Racial Prejudice.* http://www.unhchr
.ch/html/menu3/b/d_prejud.htm (accessed on January 11, 2007).

———. *1978 Declaration on Race and Racial Prejudice.* http://www.unhchr.ch/
html/menu3/b/d_prejud.htm (accessed on January 11, 2007).

Venkatesh, Sudhir Alladi. *Off the Books: The Underground Economy of the Urban Poor.* Boston: Harvard University Press, 2006.

Villa-Vicencio, Charles. *Trapped in Apartheid.* Cape Town, South Africa: David Philip, 1988.

Vitz, Paul. "The Use of Stories in Moral Development." *American Psychologist* 45 (June 1990): 709–720.

Voster, John M. "Racism, Xenophobia and Human Rights." *The Ecumenical Review* 54, no. 3 (July 2002), 7.

Warren, Kathleen A. *Daring to Cross the Threshold: Francis of Assisi Encounters Sultan Malek al Kamil.* Rochester, MN: Sisters of St. Francis, 2003.

Waruta, D. W. "Tribalism as a Moral Problem in Contemporary Africa." In *Moral and Ethical Issues in African Christianity*, edited by Jesse N. K. Mugambi and Anne Nasimiyu-Wasike, 119–135. Nairobi, Kenya: Initiatives Publishers, 1992.

Weiner, Michael. "The Invention of Identity: Race and Nation in Pre-War Japan." In *The Construction of Racial Identities in China and Japan: Historical and Contemporary Perspectives*, edited by Frank Dikötter, 96–117. London: C. Hurst and Company, Ltd., 1997.

Werly, Richard. "The Burakumin, Japan's Invisible Outcasts." *The UNESCO Courier* (September 2001): 29.

Westra, Laura, and Bill E. Lawson, eds. *Faces of Environmental Racism: Confronting Issues of Global Justice.* 2nd ed. New York: Rowman & Littlefield Publishers, Inc., 2001.

Young, Robert J. C. *Colonial Desire: Hybridity in Theory, Culture, and Race.* New York: Routledge, 1995.

Index

Note: Page numbers in *italics* refer to the church documents reproduced in Part II of the book.

247